ADAM NICOLSON is the author of many books on history, travel and the environment. He is the winner of the Somerset Maugham Award, the British Topography Prize and the W. H. Heinemann Award. His other works for HarperCollins are *Sissinghurst, Sea Room, Seamanship, Men of Honour* and *Arcadia*.

'This fascinating story is told with brilliance by Adam Nicolson.'
Glasgow Herald

'An engaging and moving account … marvellous.' - *Economist*

'Pays that Bible eloquent tribute, not least in its passionate homage to the power of language as, and in, history. His own words give us not only the rich history but a moving commemoration of the Bible that has so much shaped our utterances and lives.'
Independent

'Nicolson's portraits of Jacobean intellectuals, theologians, politicians and princes overlay the lasting achievement that underpins this book. His approach to personalities humanises the beauty and ceremony of the biblical prose that still transcends its makers.'
The Times

'Conversational, witty and engaging. It is extraordinarily readable … Adam Nicolson gives us a swashbuckling and fast-moving account of the accession of King James I of England and VI of Scotland in 1603 … he catches the spirit of the age in his own literary style … There is power and glory here in spadefuls, and a great deal of kingdom too.'
Tablet

WINCHESTER SCHOOL OF MISSION

03817

'It is a popular book as popular books used to be, a breeze rather than a scholarly sweat, but humanely erudite, elegantly written, passionately felt … Nicolson's excitement is contagious.'

New Yorker

'Nicolson shows us in captivating detail how the diverse translators of the King James Bible captured compelling debates that remain relevant to this day.'

Newsweek

'A readable, immaculately researched book … The author has a clear understanding of the time, the issues involved and, above all, of the people who made the King James Bible. He could not have told his story more compellingly.'

Country Life

'Adam Nicolson's stunning history of the Authorised Version is really a prosopography, a study of the dynamic group of scholars who put together what some call the best book in the English language. Nicolson's focus on the words these men left behind enables him to combine scholarship with a greater emotional sensitivity.'

Observer

'Adam Nicolson's book is unobtrusively learned, rich in curious and purposeful detail, an ideal balance between fervent enthusiasm and elegantly witty detachment. The story of the translation's origins and production is a subject which, one always felt, would be nice to hear from a really sparkling and sharp guide. This volume strikes me as exactly that, a brilliantly entertaining, passionate, funny and instructive telling of an important and gripping story.'

PHILIP HENSHER, *Spectator*

'Adam Nicolson has a nose for quirks, follies and ironies … Nicolson fascinatingly demonstrates how these translators took the plain, sinewy prose of the fugitive martyr William Tyndale – written 80 years previously – and polished it to gem-like brightness, looking for words which would resonate with passion and ring sonorously amid the solemnity of worship ... He has written a marvellous book: there are few more stylish or sensitive introductions than this to the personalities, the sights and the smells, as well as to the words, of Jacobean England.'

Sunday Telegraph

'Nicolson really deserves at least an 18-gun salute. This is a fine piece of history, ecclesiology and literature all rolled into one and, what's more, like the Authorised Version itself, it sings.'

Guardian

'This is an easygoing, companionable exploration of Elizabethan and Jacobean England ... will delight the general reader, for whom it was written ... Nicolson takes one back to the Bible with a fresh eye and ear, which is not easily done these days.'

New Statesman

'The story of the seven years between commissioning and printing fascinates from start to finish. It is told in a way which combines scholarship and entertainment.' *Independent on Sunday*

'Vivid,exhilarating, consistently intelligent, you can almost taste the air breathed by these Jacobean heroes, who gave English its most famous book. History at its best.' SIMON JENKINS

'Nicolson vividly evokes many aspects of Jacobean England: the secret police, religious passions, a profligate court, an atmosphere of emotional extravagance, splendid architecture, stained glass ... Adam Nicolson has deepened my understanding of the greatest work of English prose, for which I am grateful.' *Literary Review*

BY THE SAME AUTHOR:

Sissinghurst: An Unfinished History
Wetland: Life in the Somerset Levels
Restoration: The Rebuilding of Windsor Castle
Smell of Summer Grass: Pursuing Happiness – Perch Hill 1944–2011
Sea Room
Atlantic Britain
Men of Honour: Trafalgar and the Making of the English Hero
Arcadia: The Dream of Perfection in Renaissance England

IACOBVS, REX.

Blessed be they that blesse you.
And cursed be they that curse you.

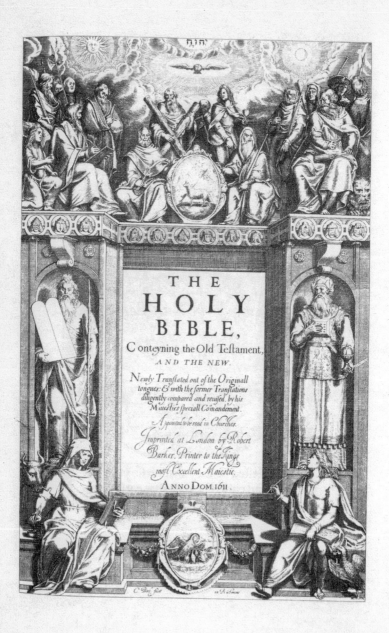

THE HOLY BIBLE,

Conteyning the Old Testament,

AND THE NEW.

Newly Translated out of the Originall
tongues: & with the former Translations
diligently compared and reuised, by his
Maiesties speciall Cõmandement.

Appointed to be read in Churches.

Imprinted at London by Robert
Barker, Printer to the Kings
most Excellent Maiestie.

ANNO DOM. 1611.

WHEN GOD
SPOKE ENGLISH

The Making of the King James Bible

ADAM NICOLSON

Harper
Press

Harper*Press*
An imprint of HarperCollins*Publishers*
77–85 Fulham Palace Road,
Hammersmith, London W6 8JB

This Harper*Press* paperback edition published 2011

Previously published in paperback as *Power and Glory:
Jacobean England and the Making of the King James Bible*

I

First published by HarperCollins*Publishers* 2003

First published in paperback by Harper*Press* 2004

Copyright © Adam Nicolson 2003

Portrait/Literature by Committee © Sam Leith 2004

Adam Nicolson asserts the moral right to
be identified as the author of this work

A catalogue record for this book
is available from the British Library

ISBN 978-0-00-743100-7

Printed and bound in Great Britain by
Clays Ltd, St Ives plc

Mixed Sources
Product group from well-managed
forests and other controlled sources
www.fsc.org Cert no. SW-COC-001806
© 1996 Forest Stewardship Council

FSC is a non-profit international organisation established to promote the
responsible management of the world's forests. Products carrying the FSC
label are independently certified to assure consumers that they come
from forests that are managed to meet the social, economic and
ecological needs of present or future generations.

Find out more about HarperCollins and the environment at
www.harpercollins.co.uk/green

All rights reserved. No part of this publication may be
reproduced, stored in a retrieval system, or transmitted,
in any form or by any means, electronic, mechanical,
photocopying, recording or otherwise, without the
prior permission of the publishers.

This book is sold subject to the condition that it shall not, by
way of trade or otherwise, be lent, re-sold, hired out or otherwise
circulated without the publisher's prior consent in any form of
binding or cover other than that in which it is published and
without a similar condition including this condition being
imposed on the subsequent purchaser.

CONTENTS

APPENDICES

LIST OF ILLUSTRATIONS

James I and VI attributed to Adrian Vanson. © Scottish National
Portrait Gallery.

Robert Cecil, 1st Earl of Salisbury, by John de Critz the elder.
© National Portrait Gallery.

Panorama of London and the Thames, 1616, (detail) by Claes van
Visscher. © Guildhall Library, Corporation of London/
Bridgeman Art Library.

Hampton Court Palace (detail) by Anthonis van den Wyngaerde,
c. 1544. © Ashmolean Museum Oxford/Bridgeman Art Library.

Richard Bancroft, Archbishop of Canterbury, unknown artist.
© National Portrait Gallery.

Lancelot Andrewes, Bishop of Winchester. © Bodleian Library,
University of Oxford.

Sir Henry Savile, Warden of Merton College, Oxford, 1594, by
Hieronimo Custodis. © Weiss Gallery, London.

John Overall, Bishop of Norwich, engraving by Wenceslaus
Hollar. © National Portrait Gallery.

James Montagu, Bishop of Bath and Wells. © Sidney Sussex
College, Cambridge.

Miles Smith, Bishop of Gloucester. © Christ Church College,
Oxford.

George Abbot, Archbishop of Canterbury. © National Portrait
Gallery.

Costume design for 'The Masque of Blacknesse'. © The
Devonshire Collection, Chatsworth. By permission of the Duke
of Devonshire and the Chatsworth Settlement Trustees.

Contemporary handbill of the Gunpowder conspirators, 1605.
© National Portrait Gallery.

Frances Howard, Countess of Somerset, attributed to William
Larkin. © National Portrait Gallery.

Christian IV of Denmark. © National Historical Museum,
Frederiksborg.

William Sancroft, Master of Emmanuel College, Cambridge.
© The Master and Fellowes of Emmanuel College, Cambridge.

Loughwood Meeting House c. 1653. © National Trust
Photographic Library.

Integrated Illustrations

James I and VI – 'Blessed is that Blesse you . . .' © The
Huntingdon Library, San Marino, California.

Title page of the King James Bible. © The British Library.

Dedication page of the King James Bible. © Bridgeman Art
Library.

Opening recto and verso pages of the Book of Genesis, King
James Bible. © Bodleian Library, University of Oxford.

Portrait of James I and Anne of Denmark. © The Stapleton
Collection/Bridgeman Art Library.

TO THE MOST
HIGH AND MIGHTIE
Prince, IAMES by the grace of God
King of Great Britaine, France and Ireland,
Defender of the Faith, &c.

THE TRANSLATORS OF *THE BIBLE,*
wish Grace, Mercie, and Peace, through IESVS
CHRIST *our* LORD.

Reat and manifold were the blessings (most dread
Soueraigne) which Almighty GOD, the Father
of all Mercies, bestowed vpon vs the people of
ENGLAND, when first he sent your Maiesties
Royall person to rule and raigne ouer vs. For
whereas it was the expectation of many, who
wished not well vnto our SION, that vpon the
setting of that bright *Occidentall Starre* Queene
ELIZABETH of most happy memory, some
thicke and palpable cloudes of darkenesse would so haue ouershadowed
this land, that men should haue bene in doubt which way they were to
walke, and that it should hardly be knowen, who was to direct the vnsetled
State: the appearance of your MAIESTIE, as of the *Sunne* in his strength,
instantly dispelled those supposed and surmised mists, and gaue vnto all
that were well affected, exceeding cause of comfort; especially when we be-
held the gouernment established in your HIGHNESSE, and your hope-
full Seed, by an vndoubted Title, and this also accompanied with Peace
and tranquillitie, at home and abroad.

But amongst all our Ioyes, there was no one that more filled our hearts,
then the blessed continuance of the Preaching of GODS sacred word a-
mongst vs, which is that inestimable treasure, which excelleth all the riches
of the earth, because the fruit thereof extendeth it selfe, not onely to the time
spent in this transitory world, but directeth and disposeth men vr to that
Eternall happinesse which is aboue in Heauen.

Then, not to suffer this to fall to the ground, but rather to take it vp, and
to continue it in that state, wherein the famous predecessour of your HIGH-
NESSE did leaue it; Nay, to goe forward with the confidence and reso-
A 2   lution

PREFACE

The making of the King James Bible, in the seven years between its commissioning by James VI & I in 1604 and its publication by Robert Barker, 'Printer to the King's Most Excellent Majestie', in 1611, remains something of a mystery. The men who did it, who pored over the Greek and Hebrew texts, comparing the accuracy and felicity of previous translations, arguing with each other over the finest details of chapter and verse, were many of them obscure at the time and are generally forgotten now, a gaggle of fifty or so black-gowned divines whose names are almost unknown but whose words continue to resonate with us. They have a ghost presence in our lives, invisible but constantly heard, enriching the language with the 'civility, learning and eloquence' of their translation, but nowadays only whispering the sentences into our ears.

Beyond that private communication, they have left few clues. Surviving in one or two English libraries and archives are the instructions produced at the beginning of the work, a couple of drafts of short sections sketched out in the course of it, some fragments of correspondence between one or two of them and a few pages of notes taken at a meeting near the end. Otherwise nothing.

But that virtual anonymity is the power of the book. The translation these men made together can lay claim to be the greatest work in prose ever written in English. That it should be the creation of a committee of people no one has ever heard of – and who were generally unacknowledged at the time – is the key to its grandeur. It is not the poetry of a single mind, nor the effusion of a singular vision, nor even the product of a single moment, but the child of an entire culture stretching back to the great Jewish poets and storytellers of the Near Eastern Bronze Age. That sense of an entirely embraced and reimagined past is what fuels this book.

The divines of the first decade of seventeenth-century England were alert to the glamour of antiquity, in many ways consciously archaic in phraseology and grammar, meticulous in their scholarship and always looking to the primitive and the essential as the guarantee of truth. Their translation was driven by that idea of a constant present, the feeling that the riches, beauties, failings and sufferings of Jacobean England were part of the same world as the one in which Job, David or the Evangelists walked. Just as Rembrandt, a few years later, without any sense of absurdity or presumption, could portray himself as the Apostle Paul, the turban wrapped tightly around his greying curls, the eyes intense and inquiring, the King James Translators could write their English words as if the passage of 1,600 or 3,000 years made no difference. Their subject was neither ancient nor modern, but both or either. It was the universal text.

The book they created was consciously poised in its rhetoric between vigour and elegance, plainness and power. It is not framed in the language, as one Puritan preacher described it, of 'fat and strutting bishops, pomp-fed prelates', nor of Puritan controversy or intellectual display. It aimed to step beyond those categories to embrace the universality of its subject. As a result, it does not suffer from one of the defining faults of the age: a form of anxious and egotistical self-promotion. It exudes, rather, a shared confidence and authority and in that is one of the greatest of all monuments to the suppression of ego.

It is often said that the King James Translators (a word that was capitalised at the time), particularly in the New Testament, did little more than copy out the work of William Tyndale, done over eighty years before in the dawn of the Reformation. The truth of their relationship to Tyndale, as will emerge, is complex but the point is surely this: they would have been pleased to acknowledge that they were winnowing the best from the past. They would not have wanted the status of originators or 'authors' – a word at which one of their Directors, Lancelot Andrewes, would visibly shudder. They took from Tyndale because Tyndale had done well, not perfectly and not always with an ear for the richness of the language, but with a passion for clarity which the Jacobean scholars shared. What virtue was there in newness when the old was so good?

Of course, the King James Bible did not spring from the soil of Jacobean England as quietly and miraculously as a lily. There were arguments and struggles, exclusions and competitiveness. It is the product of its time and bears the marks of its making. It is a deeply political book. The period was held in the grip of an immense struggle: between the demands for freedom of the individual conscience and the need for order and an imposed inheritance; between monarchy and democracy; between extremism and toleration. Early Jacobean England is suffused with this drama of authority and legitimacy and of the place of the state within that relationship. 'The reformers', it has often been said, 'dethroned the Pope and enthroned the Bible.' That might have been the case in parts of Protestant Europe, but in England the process was longer, slower, less one-directional and more complex. The authority of the English, Protestant monarch, as head of the Church of England, had taken on wholesale many of the powers which had previously belonged to the pope. The condition of England was defined by those ambiguities. In the years that the translation was being prepared, *Othello*, *Volpone*, *King Lear* and *The Tempest* – all centred on the ambivalences of power, the rights of the individual will, the claims of authority and the question of liberty of conscience – were written and staged for the first time. The questions that would erupt in the Civil War three decades later were already circling around each other here.

But it is easy to let that historical perspective distort the picture. To see the early seventeenth century through the gauze of the Civil War is to regard it only as a set of origins for the conflict. That is not the quality of the time, nor is the King James Bible any kind of propaganda for an absolutist king. Its subject is majesty, not tyranny, and its political purpose was unifying and enfolding, to elide the kingliness of God with the godliness of kings, to make royal power and divine glory into one indivisible garment which could be wrapped around the nation as a whole. Its grandeur of phrasing and the deep slow music of its rhythms – far more evident here than in any Bible the sixteenth century had produced – were conscious embodiments of regal glory. It is a book written for what James, the self-styled *Rex Pacificus*, and his councillors hoped – a vain hope, soon shipwrecked on vanity, self-indulgence and incompetence – might be an ideal world.

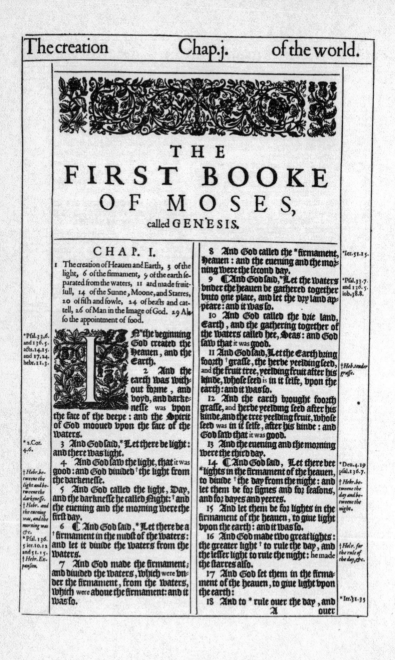

THE
FIRST BOOKE
OF MOSES,
called GENESIS.

CHAP. I.

1 The creation of Heauen and Earth, 3 of the light, 6 of the firmament, 9 of the earth separated from the waters, 11 and made fruitiull, 14 of the Sunne, Moone, and Starres, 20 of fish and fowle, 24 of beasts and cattell, 26 of Man in the Image of God. 29 Also the appointment of food.

*Psal.33.6. and 136.5. acts.14.15. and 17.24. hebr.11.3.

IN the beginning God created the Heauen, and the Earth.

2 And the earth was without forme, and voyd, and darkenesse was vpon the face of the deepe : and the Spirit of God mooued vpon the face of the waters.

*2.Cor. 4.6.

3 And God said,* Let there be light: and there was light.

†Hebr. betweene the light and betweene the darkenesse.
†Hebr. and the euening was, and the morning was &c.
*Psal.136. 5.ier.10.12 and 51.15. †Hebr. Expansion.

4 And God saw the light, that it was good : and God diuided † the light from the darkenesse.

5 And God called the light, Day, and the darkenesse he called Night: † and the euening and the morning were the first day.

6 ¶ And God said, * Let there be a † firmament in the midst of the waters: and let it diuide the waters from the waters.

7 And God made the firmament; and diuided the waters, which were vnder the firmament, from the waters, which were aboue the firmament: and it was so.

8 And God called the *firmament, Heauen : and the euening and the morning were the second day.

9 ¶ And God said, Let the waters vnder the heauen be gathered together vnto one place, and let the dry land appeare: and it was so.

10 And God called the drie land, Earth, and the gathering together of the waters called hee, Seas : and God saw that it was good.

11 And God said, Let the Earth bring foorth † grasse, the herbe yeelding seed, and the fruit tree, yeelding fruit after his kinde, whose seed is in it selfe, vpon the earth: and it was so.

12 And the earth brought foorth grasse, and herbe yeelding seed after his kinde, and the tree yeelding fruit, whose seed was in it selfe, after his kinde : and God saw that it was good.

13 And the euening and the morning were the third day.

14 ¶ And God said, Let there bee *lights in the firmament of the heauen, to diuide † the day from the night : and let them be for signes and for seasons, and for dayes and yeeres.

15 And let them be for lights in the firmament of the heauen, to giue light vpon the earth : and it was so.

16 And God made two great lights: the greater light † to rule the day, and the lesser light to rule the night: he made the starres also.

17 And God set them in the firmament of the heauen, to giue light vpon the earth:

18 And to * rule ouer the day, and
A   ouer

*Ier.51.15.

*Psal.33.7. and 136.5. iob.38.8.

†Heb.tender grasse.

*Deu.4.19 psal.136.7.
†Heb. betweene the day and betweene the night.

†Hebr. for the rule of the day, &c.

*Ier.31.35

ouer the night, and to diuide the light from the darkenesse: and God saw that it was good.

19 And the euening and the morning were the fourth day.

20 And God said, *Let the waters bring foorth aboundantly the ‖ mouing creature that hath † life, and foule that may flie aboue the earth in the † open firmament of heauen.

21 And God created great whales, and euery liuing creature that moueth, which the waters brought foorth aboundantly after their kinde, and euery winged foule after his kinde: and God saw that it was good.

22 And God blessed them, saying,*Be fruitfull, and multiply, and fill the waters in the Seas, and let foule multiply in the earth.

23 And the euening and the morning were the fift day.

24 ¶And God said, Let the earth bring forth the liuing creature after his kinde, cattell, and creeping thing, and beast of the earth after his kinde: and it was so.

25 And God made the beast of the earth after his kinde, and cattell after their kinde, and euery thing that creepeth vpon the earth, after his kinde: and God saw that it was good.

26 ¶And God said, *Let vs make man in our Image, after our likenesse: and let them haue dominion ouer the fish of the sea, and ouer the foule of the aire, and ouer the cattell, and ouer all the earth, and ouer euery creeping thing that creepeth vpon the earth.

27 So God created man in his owne Image, in the Image of God created hee him; * male and female created hee them.

28 And God blessed them, and God said vnto them, *Be fruitfull, and multiply, and replenish the earth, and subdue it, and haue dominion ouer the fish of the sea, and ouer the foule of the aire, and ouer euery liuing thing that † mooueth vpon the earth.

29 ¶And God said, Behold, I haue giuen you euery herbe † bearing seede, which is vpon the face of all the earth, and euery tree, in the which is the fruit of a tree yeelding seed, *to you it shall be for meat:

30 And to euery beast of the earth, and to euery foule of the aire, and to euery thing that creepeth vpon the earth,

wherein there is † life, I haue giuen euery greene herbe for meat: and it was so.

31 And * God saw euery thing that hee had made: and behold, it was very good. And the euening and the morning were the sixth day.

CHAP. II.

1 The first Sabbath. 4 The maner of the creation. 8 The planting of the garden of Eden, 10 and the riuer thereof. 17 The tree of knowledge onely forbidden. 19, 20 The naming of the creatures. 21 The making of woman, and institution of Mariage.

Thus the heauens and the earth were finished, and all the hoste of them.

2 * And on the seuenth day God ended his worke, which hee had made: And he rested on the seuenth day from all his worke, which he had made.

3 And God blessed the seuenth day, and sanctified it: because that in it he had rested from all his worke, which God † created and made.

4 ¶These are the generations of the heauens, & of the earth, when they were created; in the day that the LORD God made the earth, and the heauens,

5 And euery plant of the field, before it was in the earth, and euery herbe of the field, before it grew: for the LORD God had not caused it to raine vpon the earth, and there was not a man to till the ground.

6 ‖But there went vp a mist from the earth, and watered the whole face of the ground.

7 And the LORD God formed man †* of the dust of the ground, & breathed into his nostrils the breath of life; and * man became a liuing soule.

8 ¶And the LORD God planted a garden Eastward in Eden; and there he put the man whom he had formed.

9 And out of the ground made the LORD God to grow euery tree that is pleasant to the sight, and good for food: the tree of life also in the midst of the garden, and the tree of knowledge of good and euill.

10 And a riuer went out of Eden to water the garden, and from thence it was parted, and became into foure heads.

11 The name of the first is * Pison: that is it which compasseth the whole land of Hauilah, where there is gold.

12 And

Marginal notes (left column):
*4. Esdr. 6. 47.
‖Or, creeping.
†Heb. soule.
†Heb. face of the firmament of heauen.

*Chap.8. 17. and 9.1.

*Chap.5.1. and 9.6. 1. corin. 11. 7. ephef. 4. 14. col. 3. 10.

*Math.19 4. wisd.2. 23.

*Chap.9.1.

†Heb. creepeth.

†Hebr. seeding seed.

*Chap.9.3.

Marginal notes (right column):
†Hebr. a li-uing soule.
*Ecclus.39 16.

*Exod. 20. 11. and 31. 17. deut.5. 14. hebr. 4. 4.

†Heb. created to make.

‖Or, a mist which went vp from &c.

†Hebr. dust of the ground. *1.Cor.15 47. *1.Corin 15.45.

*Ecclus.24. 29.

ONE

A poore man now arrived at the *Land of Promise*

And the LORD magnified Solomon exceedingly in the sight of all Israel, and bestowed vpon him *such* royal maiestie as had not bene on any king before him in Israel.

1 Chronicles 29:25

ew moments in English history have been more hungry for the future, its mercurial possibilities and its hope of richness, than the spring of 1603. At last the old, hesitant, querulous and increasingly unapproachable Queen Elizabeth was dying. Nowadays, her courtiers and advisers spent their lives tiptoeing around her moods and her unpredictability. Lurching from one unaddressed financial crisis to the next, selling monopolies to favourites, she had begun to lose the affection of the country she had nurtured for so long. Elizabeth should have died years before. Most of her great men – Burleigh, Leicester, Walsingham, even the beautiful Earl of Essex, executed after a futile and chaotic rebellion in 1601 – had gone already. She had become a relict of a previous age and her wrinkled, pasteboard virginity now looked more like fruitlessness than purity. Her niggardliness had starved the fountain of patronage on which the workings of the country relied and those mechanisms, unoiled by the necessary largesse, were creaking. Her exhausted impatience made the process of government itself a labyrinth of tact and indirection.

The country felt younger and more vital than its queen. Cultural conservatives might have bemoaned the death of old values and the corruption of modern morals (largely from Italy, conceived of as a louche and violent place), but these were not the symptoms of decline. England was full of newness and potential: its population burgeoning, its merchant fleets combing the world, London growing like a hothouse plum, the sons of gentlemen crowding as never before into the colleges of Oxford and Cambridge, plants and fruits from all over the world arriving in its gardens and on its tables – but the rigid carapace of the Elizabethan court lay like a cast-iron lid above it. The queen's motto was still what it always had been: *Semper eadem*, Always the same. She hadn't moved with the times. So parsimonious had she been in elevating men to the peerage that by the end of her reign there were no more than sixty peers in the nobility of England. Scarcely a gentleman had been knighted by the queen for years.

That drought of honours was a symptom of a kind of paralysis, an indecisive rigidity. None of the great issues of the country had been resolved. Inflation had transformed the economy but the Crown was still drawing rents from its properties that had been set in the 1560s. The relationship between the House of Commons and the queen, for all her wooing and flattery, had become angry, tetchy, full of recrimination. The old war against Spain, which had achieved its great triumph of defeating the Armada in 1588, had dragged on for decades, haemorrhaging money and enjoying little support from the Englishmen whose taxes were paying for it. The London and Bristol merchants wanted only one outcome: an end to war, so that trade could be resumed. Religious differences had been buried by the Elizabethan regime: both Roman Catholics, who wanted England to return to the fold of the Roman Church, and the more extreme, 'hotter' Protestants, the Puritans, who felt that the Reformation in England had never been properly achieved, had been persecuted by the queen and her church, fined, imprisoned and executed. Any questions of change, tolerance or acceptance had not been addressed. Elizabeth had survived by ignoring problems or suppressing them and as a result England was a cauldron which had not been allowed to boil. Later history – even in the seventeenth century itself – portrayed Elizabeth's death as a dimming of the brilliance, the moment at which England swopped a heroic, gallant, Renaissance freshness for something more degenerate, less clean-cut, less noble, more self-serving, less dignified. But that is almost precisely the opposite of what England felt at the time. Elizabeth was passé, decayed. A new king, with wife, children (Anne was pregnant with their sixth child) an heir for goodness' sake, a passionate huntsman, full of vigour, a poet, an intellectual of European standing, a new king, a new reign and a new way of looking at the world; of course the country longed for that. Elizabeth's death held out the prospect of peace with Spain, a new openness to religious toleration, and a resolution of the differences between the established church and both Catholics and Puritans. More than we can perhaps realise now, a change of monarch in an age of personal rule meant not only a change of government and policy, but a change of culture, attitude and belief. A new king meant a new world.

James Stuart was an unlikely hero: ugly, restless, red-haired, pale-skinned, his tongue, it was said, too big for his mouth, impatient, vulgar, clever, nervous. But his virtues, learned in the brutal world of Scottish politics, were equal to the slurs of his contemporaries. More than anything else he wanted and believed in the possibilities of an encompassing peace. He adopted as his motto the words from the Sermon on the Mount, *Beati Pacifici*, Blessed are the Peacemakers, a phrase which, in the aftermath of a European century in which the continent had torn itself apart in religious war, would appear over and over again on Jacobean chimneypieces and carved into oak testers and over-mantels, crammed in alongside the dreamed of, wish-fulfilment figures of Peace and Plenty, Ceres with her overbrimming harvests and luscious breasts, Pax embracing Concordia. The Bible that is named after James, and whose translation was authorised by him, was central to his claim on that ideal.

James was in bed, but not yet asleep, when he learned that he had become King of England. He had been King of Scotland since he was one year old, when his mother Mary, Queen of Scots had been deposed thirty-five years before. He had spent his life in the wings and now, at last, his great scene was about to begin. A rather handsome and deeply indebted English gentleman, Sir Robert Carey, who at different times had been a commander against the Spanish Armada and a court dandy – just the sort of glamorous and rather sexy man to whom James was instinctively drawn – had ridden night and day on his own behalf to bring the news of Elizabeth's death to Scotland. For decades, Carey had been living beyond his means and was desperate for advancement. This was his main chance too. Having fallen off his horse and been kicked in the face en route, he finally reached the palace of Holyroodhouse in Edinburgh on the evening of 26 March 1603, some seventy hours after Queen Elizabeth had died in her palace at Richmond on the Thames. His head was bleeding from his fall.

Several weeks before, as Elizabeth had entered what was clearly her terminal illness, long, moping, energyless silences absorbing her, Carey had arranged for a string of horses to be waiting at inns all along the Great North Road and now he was well ahead of the game. Not until the following day were the proclamations made in Shrewsbury or York, and in Bristol only the day after that. But the English Privy Council already had their own spies in place at the Scottish court, and were curious to know how James had taken the news. 'Even, my Lords,' their reporter, Sir Roger Aston, told them later that week, 'like a poore man wandering about 40 years in a wildernesse and barren soyle, and now arrived at the *Land of Promise*.'

It was the most perfect moment of James's life. He received Carey in his bedroom. The Englishman knelt before the king and 'saluted him by his title of *England, Scotland, France* and *Ireland*. Hee gave me his hand to kisse, and bade me welcome.' James wanted to know what letters Carey brought with him from the English Council, but Carey had to confess he had none. This was private enterprise, against the wishes of the English Secretary of State, Robert Cecil, and the only sign that Carey had brought from the south was a sapphire ring, which James had once sent to Carey's sister, Philadelphia, Lady Scroope, with the express purpose that she would return it as soon as she knew that Elizabeth had died.

It was enough. James had come into his own. He rewarded Carey with a place as one of the Grooms of the Bedchamber. Or so he promised; within a few weeks Carey was squeezed out of the position, probably by Cecil, who objected to the vulgarity of Carey's dash north, perhaps by jealous and ambitious Scots. For them, as much as for James, the kingdom of England, increasingly rich, populous, powerful, well governed and civilised, lay to the south glittering like a jewel, or at least a money pump, a promise of riches after years of making do.

The Scottish crown was one of the weakest in Europe. It had no money and could command no armed strength of its own. England, France and Spain wooed and threatened it in turn. The Scottish magnates plotted and brawled with each other. The culture was murderous and James had no natural allies. The Presbyterian Church, taking its cue from the words of the Apostle Peter ('We ought to obey God rather than men') and of Calvin ('Earthly princes deprive themselves of all authority when they rise up against God ... We ought rather to spit in their faces than to obey them') considered the king and the monarchy inferior both to the word of God and to those who preached it. In 1596, the firebrand Presbyterian Andrew Melville had told James exactly where he stood: 'I mon tell yow, thair is twa Kings and twa Kingdomes in Scotland. Thair is Chryst Jesus the King, and his Kingdome the Kirk, whase subject King James the Saxt is, and of whase kingdome nocht a king nor a lord nor a heid, bot a member.'

To survive in this net of hostility, James had been forced to compromise and dissemble, to become cunning and to lie. His favourite tag was from Tacitus: 'Those who know not how to dissimulate, know not how to rule.' His face had become sly, his red, tufty moustache hanging down over his lips, his eyes somehow loose in their sockets. He regards his portrait painters with an inward, wary, intellectual look. Out of his mouth he would occasionally shoot harsh, witty, testing jokes. The sight of a drawn sword could make him faint and on his body the glorious gold-threaded doublets and ermine capes looked like fancy-dress; a private, isolated, cunning man disguised as a king. Elizabeth had been painted holding a rainbow, standing astride the map of England, bedecked with the symbols of purity. James in his portraits (he hated being painted) never reached for any mythological significance: he sat or stood red-faced, bad-tempered, irredeemably a man of this world, no distant image of a king but a king whose task, as God's lieutenant, was to resolve and unify the tensions and fractures of his kingdom.

His upbringing had been deeply disturbed. David Rizzio, secretary and lover of Mary, Queen of Scots, was brutally murdered in an adjoining room as she listened to his screams. James was in her womb at the time. His father, the charming Henry Darnley, was murdered by his mother's next lover, the Earl of Bothwell, blown up when lying ill in his Edinburgh house. James never saw his mother after he was one year old and, although baptised, like her, a Catholic, was then put in the care of a string of terrifying Presbyterian governors, in particular George Buchanan, a towering European intellectual, the tutor of Montaigne, friend of Tycho Brahe, who considered the deposing of wicked kings perfectly legitimate, and whose memory continued to haunt James in adult life. As a boy king, he had been a trophy in the hands of rival noble factions in Scotland, kidnapped, held, threatened and imprisoned. 'I was alane,' he wrote later, 'without fader or moder, brither or sister, king of this realme, and heir apperand of England.'

James retreated from the brutality and anarchy. He became chronically vulnerable to the allure of beautiful, elegant, rather Frenchified men. He loved hunting, excessively, an escape from the realities, at one point killing every deer in the royal park at Falkland in Fife, which had to be restocked from England. It has been calculated that he spent about half his waking life on the hunting field. And he became immensely intellectual, speaking 'Greek before breakfast, Latin before Scots', composing stiff Renaissance poetry, full of a clotted and frustrated emotionality, translating the Psalms, capable on sight of turning any passage of the Bible from Latin to French and then from French to English.

In 1584, when James was eighteen, the French agent Fontenoy sent home a report on this strange, spiky-edged, intellectualised, awkward and oddly idealistic king:

> He is wonderfully clever, and for the rest he is full of honourable ambition, and has an excellent opinion of himself. Owing to the terrorism under which he has been brought up, he is timid with the great lords, and seldom ventures to contradict them; yet his special concern is to be thought hardy and a man of courage . . . He speaks, eats, dresses, dances and plays like a boor, and he is no better in the company of women. He is never still for a moment, but walks perpetually up and

down the room, and his gait is sprawling and awkward, his voice is loud and his body is feeble, yet he is not delicate; in a word he is an old young man.

Fontenoy had asked him about the time he spent hunting: 'He told me that, whatever he seemed, he was aware of everything of consequence that was going on. He could afford to spend time in hunting, because when he attended to business he could do more in an hour than others could do in a day.'

Behind the bravado lay weakness. Scotland was no place to be a king. The English throne, infinitely more powerful in relation to the nobility than his own; supported by the structures and doctrines of the church, rather than eroded and undermined by them; rich, potent and admired – all this awaited him like a harbour tantalisingly visible from far out to sea, but, until Elizabeth's death, only to be longed for and lusted after.

Elizabeth taunted him. James had often sent his spies to Whitehall or to Richmond to see how near to death the ageing queen was coming. But the English Council was aware of this too and whenever a curious Scotsman seemed to be watching and attending on the queen more carefully than usual, it was arranged for him to stand waiting in a lobby from where he could see, 'through the hangings, to the queen dancing to a little fiddle'. Over and over again, James would hear reports of her fitness and her vigour.

Meanwhile, she dandled her kingdom and her money in front of his eyes. There were other claimants to the English throne, but none so strong. Both his mother and father carried Tudor genes but Elizabeth would make nothing sure. In 1586, all too vaguely, she had promised to do nothing that would take away from 'any greatness that might be due to him, unless provoked on his part by manifest ingratitude'. She began to send him money, and in the letters that accompanied the cash, Elizabeth allowed herself to speak to James from the enormous and magnificent height of an imperial throne. As she wrote to him in June 1586:

Considering that God hath endewed ws with a crown that yeildeth more yerly profeit to us, than we understand yours doth to youe, by reason of the dissipation and evill governement thereof of long tyme before your birth, we have latelie sent to youe a portion meete for your awin privat use.

The English carefully varied the amount from year to year, sometimes £3,000, sometimes £5,000, so that James would never quite know where he stood. The Scots always called the grant an 'annuity' – a payment due every year – and the English 'a gratuity', made out of the kindness of their hearts. The English policy had its effect. Although James's mother was a Catholic, and although he had flirted with the Catholic states in Europe and had made vague, lying promises to English Roman Catholics that he would introduce something like toleration when he acceded to the English throne, he had never done anything to put his chances of succession in jeopardy. He had been bought. By the time of Elizabeth's death – she died, in the end, 'mildly like a lamb, easily like a ripe apple from the tree', so quietly that no one was quite sure of the precise time of her death – James's mouth was dry with years of panting.

It was a difficult role to play. Although there is no evidence of his affection for a mother he hadn't seen since he was an infant, James had been forced to acquiesce in her execution in 1587. The unstated but implicit assumption was that he had bargained that acceptance for a recognition of his title to the English throne. The conventional modern view of such an upbringing would be negative: such abuse would be bound to destroy the person. James, for all his strange, unaccommodated behaviour, went precisely the other way. The outcome of his violent, threatened youth was not someone filled with vitriol and vengeance, although James could be foul-mouthed, but what might be called exaggeratedly social behaviour, a longing for acceptance and a desire for a life and a society in which all conflicting demands were reconciled and where all factions felt at home. At his twenty-first birthday, he had invited all the warring magnates and grandees of Scotland to walk hand in hand through the streets of Edinburgh. It was a ritual, a pantomime of the good society which lasted scarcely longer than the birthday itself; Scotland was not suited to amity. But England was different and for James it must have seemed that at last, that dream of coherence would become a reality.

The reign began with a month-long fiesta during which James was introduced to England and England to James. In London, the Secretary of State, little shrunken Robert Cecil, his back humped like a lute, his wry neck holding his head to one side, his twisted foot giving him an awkward stance, read out the proclamation of the new king at four in the morning in the Tudor palace at Richmond, at 10 a.m. at the ramshackle royal palace in Whitehall, then in great state at various places in the City of London. Cecil, subtle, secretive, immensely courteous and prodigiously hard-working, was at the heart of English government, as his father, Lord Burghley, had been before him. Both were royal servants intent on continuity and on the coherence of the state. They were merciless in the destruction of their enemies, against whom they deployed an array of spies, charm and money. Only when Robert Cecil died did the world discover the reality. He had sunk himself into almost irretrievable debt. He had plotted and misinformed against everyone. Through the impartiality of his courtesy and the ubiquity of his deceit, he had maintained his unrivalled position of influence. As his father had done with Elizabeth before her accession, Cecil had been in secret correspondence with James, via an intermediary, for two years.

In letter after letter, Cecil flattered and cajoled him, portrayed England as a place of civility and charm, a featherbed into which James could at last relax after all the stony travails of his Scottish youth. The warm and civilised care which Cecil lavished on the future king represented to James everything he hoped of England. And, of course, the letters portrayed Cecil himself as the indispensable gatekeeper who could usher James into the promised land. The Earl of Essex, before his disastrous rebellion and death in 1601, had been playing the same role. Once Essex was out of the way, Cecil had slid smoothly into position and now at last, with the queen dead, he could bring the secret arrangements to conclusion: he dispatched the English Privy Council's envoys to Scotland. They invited James 'to repair into England with all speed'.

'Good news makes good horsemen', and before James began his long progress south, a stream of interested Englishmen made their way to Holyrood, anxious to mould and influence the reign from its very beginning. Lewis Pickering, a Puritan gentleman from Northamptonshire, soon to be involved in the widespread manoeuvrings for the reform of the English Church, was one of the first to be admitted to James's presence. Would the king look more kindly than Elizabeth on the need to banish all papist practices from the English Church? Would the Reformation in England at last be made complete by the Calvinist king? Political to his core, James would not dream of giving more than a gracious answer. Dr Thomas Neville, envoy from the Archbishop of Canterbury, followed him. Neville was one of the most passionate opponents of extreme Puritanism, and of everything Pickering represented. Would the king stand firm for the House of Bishops against all the demands of the Presbyterian clergy in England? Would he support the status quo? Surely the last thing he wanted was to turn the English Church into anything resembling the church of John Knox and George Buchanan? Again, no answer. Others clustered in their sycophancy. Sir Oliver Cromwell, uncle of the regicide, came to pay his respects. 'One saith hee will serve him by daie,' the world-weary wit and courtier Sir John Harington wrote to a friend, 'another by night. The women are for servynge him both day and nighte.'

James requested cash from the Privy Council and it arrived by the coachload. They sent £5,000 in gold and £1,000 in silver. Jewellery for his Danish Queen Anne arrived from London (although not the Crown Jewels which were not allowed out of the country) as well as a selection of Elizabeth's hundreds of garnet- and pearl-encrusted dresses. Six geldings and a coach with four horses were dispatched to bring the king into England. On 5 April 1603, leaving his wife and children to follow him, James left Edinburgh for a journey through his new kingdom. It lasted over a month, spreading on through the beautiful spring weather into May. Nobility, gentlemen and chancers from north and south of the border accompanied him. It was a cavalcade. Most rode on horses. The wife of the French Ambassador was carried to London in 'a chair with slings', eight porters hired for the task, four to carry, four to relieve them.

The English turned out in their thousands to see the spectacle. James may have been unaware that the Privy Council had instructed them to do so and 'if any shall be found disobedient, negligent or remisse therein, these are to let them know, that they are to sustaine such condigne punishment as their offense in that behalfe deserveth'. The gaiety had a whip at its back and the glittering pageant was an instrument of authority.

In Berwick-on-Tweed, all the guns of the border fortress town were fired at once. It was to be for the last time. The newly unified country needed no internal border fortresses and money could be saved if the garrison was dispersed. James was invited to fire one cannon himself. In Newcastle all prisoners were released except those in prison for 'treason, murther and papistrie'. All those gaoled for debt had those debts paid off. James was hosing the money around him. In York a conduit ran all day with white wine and claret. At Worksop, the king was entertained to 'excellent, soule-ravishing musique' by the Earl of Shrewsbury, who had hurried from Whitehall to meet him there.

James was nothing but bonhomie. The previously violent and lawless Scottish borders were to become, he announced, the 'very heart of the Country' in the new united empire of Great Britain, a phrase in use since the 1540s when Henry VIII and Edward VI had been anxious to unite England and Scotland, but now given a whole new Jacobean impetus. James had ordered new signets in which the rose and the thistle were to be intertwined. Unity and togetherness was his dream. An ensign for shipping was to be designed in which the Scottish saltire of St Andrew and the English cross of St George were to float side by side so that neither should have precedence over the other. There was to be a single currency in which the 20-shilling gold piece was to be called 'The Unite', with 'Our picture' on one side and 'Our Armes Crowned' on the other, emblazoned with the Latin motto *Faciam eos in gentem unam*, I shall make them into one nation. Here, in a practical and symbolic programme, the dream of authority and wholeness was, in James's vision at least, to become reality.

The new king would soon discover, however, that seventeenth-century Englishmen had about as much love for union, whether fiscal or political, as their modern descendants. The dream of unity – an abstract, intellectualised, Scottish and hence European ideal of political togetherness – would within a year fall foul of an English conservatism which valued its own hard-won freedoms far above any high-falutin' ideas of political unity. England was England, the *rosbifs* dominated parliament, civilisation stopped at the Cheviots and the English Channel and ever, alas, would it remain so.

For the time being, life was a holiday. Largesse had been pouring in an unending fountain from James's hand. He had, in places, literally showered the streets with gold coins. Teams of the gentry were queueing up to be knighted, 237 of them in the first six weeks of the reign, 906 in the first four months, a sudden gush from the Fount of Honour, which under Elizabeth's last years had run virtually dry.

Then, on 21 April, as the pageant arrived at Newark in Lincolnshire, James made his first mistake. It was a bad one.

> In this Towne, and in the Court, was taken a cut-purse doing the deed; and being a base pilfering theefe, yet was a Gentle-man-like in the outside. This fellow had good store of coyne found about him; and upon examination confessed that he had from Barwick to that place plaied the cut-purse in the Court ... His Majestie hearing of this nimming gallant directed a warrant presently to the Recorder of New-warke, to have him hanged, which was accordingly executed.

What can have possessed James? Perhaps he was rattled by the presence of a thief in the midst of all this springtime hope and optimism? Maybe he assumed that the English king, so much more powerful than the Scottish, could from time to time behave with autocratic authority? Maybe, in a complex and troubled personality, it was simply a blip, an aberration? He could cer-tainly behave very oddly at times. (Later in his reign, travelling back to Scotland, he dismounted at the border between the two countries and lay down across it to demonstrate to his courtiers how two kingdoms could exist in one person.) Whatever the cause, here in Newark he made the wrong decision.

Summary execution was not done in England, nor had it been for centuries. The government habitually tortured and executed people and displayed their heads (hard-boiled, so that the skin went black and had some resistance to the weather) on spikes at the south end of London Bridge, but none of this was done without going through the proper procedures. The Privy Coun-cil alone could authorise torture and execution. James's summary justice made all the talk of peacemaking and constitutional king-ship look hollow. The courtiers were appalled. 'I heare our new Kinge hath hanged one man before he was tryed,' Sir John

Harington wrote. 'Tis strangely done; now if the wynde bloweth thus, why not a man be tryed before he hath offended?' A doubt was sown that James did not really comprehend the promised land in which he had arrived. Was the Scottish king suddenly out of his depth in the more evolved world of English politics? Was he likely to override or ignore the long established rule of the common law, of which the English were deeply proud? Harington would play it carefully. 'I wyll keepe companie with my oves and boves, and go to Bathe and drinke sacke.' Or so he told his friends; in fact, he had sent James an elaborate and expensive astrological lantern by which the king could tell his fortune, and composed elegant, supplicatory letters to his new sovereign. Nothing was entirely as it seemed.

The thief dead, the show went on. James appeared one day as Robin Hood, 'his clothes as green as the grass he trod on'. At Exton in Rutland he hunted 'live hares in baskets'. Outside Stamford, visible from miles away, 'an hundred high men, that seemed like the *Patagones*, huge long fellows of twelve and four-teene feet high, that are reported to live on the Mayne of Brasil, neere to the Streights of Megallane' turned out to be 'a company of poore honest suitors, all going upon high stilts'. Outside Huntingdon, a crowd on their knees begged James to reopen some common land which had been enclosed and denied to them. The king ignored the request. Another crowd from God-manchester greeted him with seventy ploughs, drawn by seventy plough-teams, but that too was just a show, another means, however oblique, of asking for money.

This was not the serious business, not the power-playing which would become more intense and more real once the caval-cade reached London. For now it was play-acting. For a few days, the king and the itinerant court stayed at Hinchinbrooke Abbey outside Huntingdon. It was the house of Sir Oliver Cromwell, MP, himself a loyal monarchist, drainer of the Fens, and subscriber to the planting and cultivating of Virginia.

Cromwell put on a spectacular show for the new king and for the crowds, providing 'bread and beefe for the poorest', meat and wine 'and those not riffe-ruffe, but ever the best of the kinde' for the gentry. Cromwell gave the king a gold cup, 'some goodly horses', a pack of 'flete and deep-mouthed houndes' as well as 'divers hawkes of excellent winge'. Everything was calculated to make England look like an Arcadia of riches, and James appeared to believe the propaganda.

England was salivating over James, submissive and obsequious in turns, in a way that is so unabashed that it strikes us as odd. But this too requires an act of the imagination. Submissiveness and obsequiousness were signals of the social order at work. Social differences between men were not an unfortunate result of economics or power politics, nor a distortion of how things ought to be but a sign that society was well ordered. Life, happily, was arranged on a slope as steeply pitched as a church spire. What looks to us now like the most unctuous kind of self-abasement was symbolic of civilisation. A man making a request to his superior happily knelt before him, as a straight-forward sign of submission. Plaintiffs knelt in court, children to their fathers, MPs and bishops when addressing the king. When John Donne hoped he might become Dean of St Paul's Cathedral in London, a position in the gift of George Villiers, Duke of Buckingham, the king's favourite, Donne wrote to him:

> All that I mean in usinge thys boldnes, of puttinge myselfe into your Lordship's presence by thys ragge of paper, ys to tell your Lordship that I ly in a corner, as a clodd of clay, attendinge what kinde of vessell yt shall please you to make of Your Lordship's humblest and thankfullest and devotedst servant.

The 'poore worme' who wrote this letter was no pitiable youth; Donne was almost fifty and probably accompanied the letter with a bribe.

There was biblical sanction for all of this. Paul in his Epistle to the Romans, a favourite text for Jacobean England, says quite straightforwardly: 'Let euery soule bee subject vnto the higher powers: For there is no power but of God. The powers that be are ordeined of God. Whosoeuer therefore resisteth the power, resisteth the ordinance of God: and they that resist, shall receiue to themselues damnation.'

The condition in Eden had been one of obedience; a steeply raked social structure was ordained by God; and so crawling to the great could be holy in England too.

The climax of James's journey into his new kingdom came on 3 May when he arrived at the enormous, multi-winged, many-towered palace of Theobalds in Hertfordshire. This was no royal residence, although Elizabeth had often treated the house as if she owned it. Theobalds in fact belonged to Robert Cecil. James, who had scarcely before been outside Scotland, was overwhelmed by the riches of England and the welcome of its people. Cushioned by the grande luxe of Theobalds – the nearest comparison is a great nineteenth-century hotel, or a liner: the *Titanic* had several public rooms decorated in a wildly overblown Jacobean style – all the gratitude he had felt to Cecil during their secret correspondence, he now poured out to the nation as a whole: 'a people so loving, so dutifull, and so deere unto us, may know and feele that we are as desirous to make them happy by our Justice and grace towards them in all reasonable things, as they have been redy to increase our comfort and contentment in yeelding their loyalty and obedience'. Monopolists were to be obliged to give up their monopolies, creditors to pay their debts, lawyers to reduce their fees. Heaven was about to descend on England.

This proclamation was made from Theobalds, where Cecil had not stinted. The building, which was confiscated by parliament after the Civil War, sold off for its raw materials and demolished in about 1650, was everything the king could have dreamed of. It was enormous, an English Chambord, with five courtyards, three storeys high, stretched along a front a quarter of a mile long. The walls seemed to consist almost entirely of vast glazed surfaces. Golden lions holding golden vanes stood on the peak of one tower after another. James had been exposed to modern architecture – the palace at Falkland was a Renaissance building – but he would never have seen richness on such a scale.

Little, crumpled Robert Cecil, 'my elf, my beagle, my pygmy', as James would part affectionately, part humiliatingly call him (Elizabeth had used the same tease-taunts), with his pale, almond-shaped face, his stooped figure, his evaluating eyes, guided the king around the stupendous palace: the hall decorated with the signs of the Zodiac, where the stars shone at night and which a mechanical sun traversed by day; another hall containing a painted map of England showing all the cities, towns and villages, as well as 'the armorial bearings and domains of every esquire, lord, knight and noble who possess lands and retainers to whatever extent'. There was an open loggia in which the whole history of England was painted on the walls. In the Long Gallery were portraits of all the great men there had ever been. There were pleasure gardens. There were pictures of all the cities of Christendom. Life can never have seemed so rich. Cecil loved toys and rarities of all kinds, from tortoise-shaped clocks to the 'nests of little boxes of China' and the 'cabinet of china gilt all over' which were among his possessions at his death. He paid for lion cubs to be trained up in the Tower of London as pets for the king. He had a tame parrot which drank red wine from Bordeaux and walked up and down his dinner table making 'his choice of meat'. After taking its fill, the bird used to sit 'in a gentlewoman's ruff all day'.

The troubled and difficult soul of James Stuart, for so long exposed to parsimony, betrayal and violence in his native Scotland, had arrived in a world of marvels, as if England was a cabinet of rarities to which he had at last been given the key. He immediately elevated Robert Cecil to the peerage (and the following year made him Earl of Salisbury) the first of the fifty-six baronies, nineteen viscountcies, thirty-two earldoms, one marquisate and three dukedoms which James scattered like sequins across the country. The bridegroom was in the full and expansive flush of his honeymoon (James's own comparison) and England, the heiress he had married, was happy for the moment to walk alongside him, glowing with the riches she had brought him.

TWO

The multitudes of people covered the beautie of the fields

> And the mixt multitude that was among them fell a lusting: and the children of Israel also wept againe, and said, Who shall giue vs flesh to eate?
>
> We remember the fish, which wee did eate in Egypt freely: the cucumbers and the melons, and the leekes, and the onions, and the garlicke. [. . .]
>
> And while the flesh was yet betweene their teeth, yer [ere] it was chewed, the wrath of the LORD was kindled against the people, and the LORD smote the people with a very great plague.
>
> And he called the name of that place Kibroth-hattaavah*: because there they buried the people that lusted.
>
> **That is, The graues of lust*
>
> Numbers 11:4–5, 33–34

ames finally moved on from the enveloping luxuries of Theobalds and arrived at London on 7 May. He found a city full of flowers. James Nasmyth, who was to become chief surgeon to the king, had at last persuaded one of his Persian black fritillaries to bloom. He had seen a printed illustration, he had the bulbs from what he considered a good source, and now at last its dark plum-coloured pagoda of hanging heads was up and mysteriously beautiful in his Long Acre garden. Robert Cecil himself had a garden he treasured next to his house on the Strand, shaded with lime trees and where tulips from Crete and Turkey, globe flowers from the Peloponnese and American yuccas all grew. In the

ferocious outbreak of the plague throws the nature of Jacobean England into sudden highlight. People felt they understood the plague. It was a moral affliction which attacked cities because cities were wicked and disgusting. London was a sucking sink of iniquity, with something murderous and dissolving at its core. Disintegrating medieval palaces and abandoned monastic houses lay about the city like scavenged animals. Next to these half-rotting corpses, there was a strange and disturbing intensity, the product of a new and bewildering urge to cluster at the commercial centre of England. London was stretching, groaning, falling apart with its own growth. The open spaces which had brought air into the medieval city were filled with new buildings. All its sustenance was dragged in from the surrounding countryside, which for miles around had become one vast market garden. Fewer than half the houses in London had their own kitchen and almost none their own oven. It was a fast-food city, mutton pasties and fruit pies available at street stands; early asparagus would be there in season, swathed in butter. Tavern-keepers provided free 'thincut slices of roast-beef on the bar', heavily dosed with salt to increase customers' thirst. Everything was for sale: the title of Thomas Middleton's *A Chaste Maid in Cheapside*, which was first performed in 1613, was a joke. There was no such thing.

The city seemed to be rising and falling at the same time. Ministers were climbing into trees and preaching seditious novelties to the chance crowds in the graveyards below them. Crowds cluttered the narrow medieval thoroughfares. Outside the theatres, as the city corporation complained, 'there is such a resort of people and such multitudes of coaches ... that sometimes all our streets cannot contain them'.

At the urging of radical Puritan ministers, maypoles, stored from one Maytime to the next under the eaves of city houses, were being cut up and used as firewood, each house allotted its length for an evening's blaze. There were plans to pave the Strand but for now every winter it was ooze.

London was more of an agglutination than any kind of classical construction, buildings stuck together and clotted as a mass of swallows' or bats' nests. The many official attempts in the first decade of the century to clarify and cleanse the city, to impose order and uniformity on its bubbling and anomalous being, repeatedly failed. This animal aspect of London was always too powerful. When William Harvey, the physician, anatomist of the human heart and friend of several of the Bible Translators, wanted to describe the different parts of the gut, the comparison that naturally came to mind was the streets of his own city: the alimentary canal, he wrote in 1613, was like the long wandering thoroughfare that ran 'from Powles to Ledenhale, one way but many names, as Cheape, Powtry, &c.'.

If the city was a body, in the summer of 1603 that body was diseased, or at least parts of it were, particularly those occupied by the poor. They suffered from plague more than the rich because they were wicked. The London parishes in which they lived were the disgusting ones, filled with reprobates: near the docks, in the suburbs outside the old walls where building had been haphazard and unregulated, at Houndsditch where dead dogs were indeed thrown into the rubbish-filled ditch. The word 'suburb' still carried some of its Latin effect. If *urbs* was the city itself, *sub-urbs* were the under-city, the lower part. Should any of the poor wander into the richer parishes, particularly if they were visibly sick or weak, the churchwardens would have them taken back to the slums with which London was ringed. Those who were dying in the back alleys of St Bartholomew Exchange or St Saviour's Southwark were to be kept there. Eight hundred plague deaths occurred in a single building in 1603, an enormous, abandoned town palace, so subdivided that it could house 8,000 people. In the suburbs outside Cripplegate and Bishopsgate, growth had been so rapid that the parish officials trying to trace the boundaries on the annual beating of the bounds had to break their way through people's gardens and backyards. Markets at

Queenhithe, Billingsgate, Bridewell and Smithfield – as well as the city's main granary across the river in Southwark – were the breeding grounds of rats, but also magnets for human vagrants, the corrupt and ragged fringes of unintegrated society. These were the places where the poor lived and where child mortality in an ordinary year ran higher than anywhere else in England. Approaching a quarter of all children born in England would die before they were ten (a rate higher than in any country in the modern world); in these slums, the proportion of child deaths could triple. Plague simply exaggerated the savage social distinctions of everyday life.

But there was something strange about the plague: it seemed to pick and choose among its victims. Why? Nicholas Bound, a Puritan Sabbatarian, had the answer. His pamphlet, *Medicines for the Plague*, published in 1604, is alive with both the appalled anxiety of the time and a terrifying certainty over God's role:

> For what is the cause that this pestilence is so greatly in one part of the land, and not another? and in the same citie and towne why is it in one part, or in one house, and not in another? and in the same house, why is it vpon one, and not vpon all the rest, when they all liue together, and draw in the same breath, and eate and drinke together, and lodge in the same chamber, yea sometimes in the same bed? what is the cause of this, but that it pleaseth the Lord in wisdom, for some cause to defend some for a time, and not the rest? Therefore let vs beleeue, that in these dangerous times God must bee our onely defence.

As another preacher, Thomas Pullein, said in *Ieremiah's Teares*, published in 1608, the plague is nothing but 'the will of God rightfullie punishing wicked men'.

Henoch Clapham, a wild and cantankerous Puritan controversialist, claimed in one 1603 pamphlet that people who saw anything in the plague but a working of the divine will were 'atheistes, mere naturians and other ignorant persones'. Clapham had seen men and women, walking the streets, suddenly stumble and collapse, clearly knocked down by one of God's avenging angels. One only had to inspect them afterwards to see 'the plaine print of a blue hand left behind vpon the flesshe'. And what had medicine got to do with that? (The modern use of the word 'stroke' to mean an apoplectic seizure is a faint memory of that angelic blow.)

By midsummer, London under plague now looked, sounded and smelled like a city at war. It was by far the worst outbreak England had known. Here now, grippingly, and shockingly, the first and greatest of the Bible Translators appears on the scene. It is not a dignified sight. Lancelot Andrewes was a man deeply embedded in the Jacobean establishment. He was forty-nine or fifty, Master of Pembroke College, Cambridge. He was also Dean of Westminster Abbey, a prebendary of St Paul's Cathedral, drawing the income from one of the cathedral's manors, and of Southwell Minster, one of the chaplains at the Chapel Royal in Whitehall, who under Elizabeth had twice turned down a bishopric not because he felt unworthy of the honour but because he did not consider the income of the sees he was offered satisfactory. Elizabeth had done much to diminish the standing of bishops; she had banished them from court and had effectively suspended Edmund Grindal, the Archbishop of Canterbury whose severe and Calvinist views were not to her liking. Andrewes, one of the most astute and brilliant men of his age, an ecclesiastical politician who in the Roman Church would have become a cardinal, perhaps even pope, was not going to diminish his prospects simply to carry an elevated title.

Andrewes plays a central role in the story of the King James Bible, and the complexities of his character will emerge as it unfolds – he is in many ways its hero; as broad as the great Bible itself, scholarly, political, passionate, agonised, in love with the English language, endlessly investigating its possibilities, worldly, saintly, serene, sensuous, courageous, craven, if not corrupt then at least compromised, deeply engaged in pastoral care, generous, loving, in public bewitched by ceremony, in private troubled by persistent guilt and self-abasement – but in the grim realities of plague-stricken London in the summer of 1603, he appears in the worst possible light. Among his many positions in the church, he was the vicar of St Giles Cripplegate, just outside the old walls to the north of the city.

The church was magnificent, beautifully repaired after a fire in 1545, full of the tombs of knights and aldermen, goldsmiths, physicians, rich men and their wives. The church was surrounded by elegant houses and the Jews' Garden, where Jews had been buried before the medieval pogroms, was now filled with 'fair garden plots and summer-houses for pleasure . . . some of them like Midsummer pageants, with towers, turrets and chimney-tops'.

But there was another side to Cripplegate. This was the London that was overflowing its own bounds, 'replenished with many tenements of poor people', many of the streets filled with bowling alleys and dicing houses, the part of London where, as one royal proclamation said, there was 'a surcharge of people, specially of the worse sort, as can hardly be either fed and sustained, or preserved in health or governed from the dearth of victuals, infection of plague and manifold disorders'. There were too many Irish people here, and, as all Jacobeans knew, the Irish meant plague. There was a playhouse, the Fortune, modelled on the Globe, and the air was thick with stench from the seventy breweries in the parish. This was the London of Grub Street, not yet filled with scribblers for the press, but with the diseased poor. No part of London suffered more horrifyingly in the plague of 1603. 'Open graves where sundry are buried together' were dug in the parish, 'an hundred hungry graves each to be filled with 60 bodies'. The graves, Thomas Dekker, the sardonic, sententious, gossiping newsmonger of plague London, wrote, were 'like little cellars, piling up forty or fifty in a Pit'. At the beginning of the year, there were about 4,000 people in Lancelot

Andrewes's parish. By December 1603, 2,878 of them had been killed by the disease.

Andrewes wasn't there. He had previously attended to the business of the parish, insisting that the altar rails should be retained in the church (which a strict Puritan would have removed), doubling the amount of communion wine that was consumed (for him, Christianity was more than a religion of the word) and composing a *Manual for the Sick*, a set of religious reassurances, beginning with a quotation from Kings: 'Set thy house in order, for thou shalt die.' And he certainly preached at St Giles's from time to time. But throughout the long months of the plague in 1603, he never once visited his parish.

It was generally understood that by far the best way to avoid catching the plague was to leave the city. Contemporary medical theory was confused between the idea of a disease spreading by contagion and by people breathing foul air, but the lack of certainty didn't matter: the solution was the same. Go to the country; fewer people, cleaner air. From late May onwards, James and his followers had been circling London, staying at Hampton Court and Windsor, hunting at Woodstock in Oxfordshire or at Royston in Hertfordshire, staying at Farnham, Basing, Wilton and Winchester. It was, as Cecil described it, 'a camp volant, which every week dislodgeth'. For the king to absent himself (even though the crowds accompanying his travels took the plague with them, infecting one unfortunate town after another) was only politic. But for the vicar of a parish to do so was another question.

The mortality had spread to Westminster. In the parish of St Margaret, in which the Abbey and Westminster School both lie, dogs were killed in the street and their bodies burnt, month after month, a total of 502 for the summer. The outbreak was nothing like as bad as in Cripplegate, but Andrewes, who as dean was responsible for both Abbey and school, with its 160 pupils, was not to be found there either. He had ordered the college closed for the duration and had gone down himself to its 'pleasant retreat at Chiswick, where the elms afforded grateful shade in summer and "a retiring place" from infection'. He might well have walked down there, as he often did, along the breezy Thameside path through Chelsea and Fulham 'with a brace of young fry, and in that wayfaring leisure had a singular dexterity to fill those narrow vessels with a funnel'. He was lovely to the boys. 'I never heard him utter so much as a word of austerity among us,' one of his ex-pupils remembered. The Abbey papers still record the dean's request in July 1603 for 'a butler, a cooke, a carrier, a skull and royer' – these last two oarsmen for the Abbey boat – to be sent down to Chiswick with the boys. Richard Hakluyt, historian of the great Elizabethan mariners, and Hadrian à Saravia, another of the Translators, signed these orders as prebendaries of the Abbey. Here, the smallness of the Jacobean establishment comes suddenly into focus. Among the Westminster boys this summer, just eleven years old, was the future poet and divine George Herbert, the brilliant son of a great aristocratic family, his mother an intimate of John Donne's. From these first meetings in a brutal year, Herbert would revere and love Andrewes for the rest of his life. Meanwhile, in Cripplegate, the slum houses were boarded up, the poor died and in the streets the fires burned. Every new case of the disease was to be marked by the ringing of a passing bell down the street. Each death and burial was rung out too so that 'the doleful and almost universal and continual ringing and tolling of bells' marked the infected parishes. From far out in the fields, you could hear London mourning its dead. In the week of 16 September, the outbreak would peak at 3,037 dead. Proportionately, it was a scale of destruction far worse than anything during the Blitz.

Was Andrewes's departure for Chiswick acceptable behaviour? Not entirely. There was the example of the near-saintly Thomas Morton, one of John Donne's friends and the rector of Long Marston outside York, later a distinguished bishop, who, in the first flush of this plague epidemic as it attacked York in the summer of 1602, had sent all his servants away, to save their lives, and attended himself to the sick and dying in the city pesthouse. Morton slept on a straw bed with the victims, rose at four every morning, was never in bed before ten at night, and travelled to and from the countryside, bringing in the food for the dying on the crupper of his saddle.

Alongside this, Andrewes's elm-shaded neglect of the Cripple-gate disaster looks shameful. While he was at Chiswick, he preached a sermon on 21 August that compounded the crime. 'The Rasor is hired for us,' he told his congregation, Hakluyt and Herbert perhaps among them, 'that sweeps away a great number of haires at once.' Plague was a sign of God's wrath provoked by men's 'own inventions', the taste for novelty, for specious newness, which was so widespread in the world. The very word 'plague' – and there is something unsettling about this pedantic scholarship in the face of catastrophe – came from the Latin *plaga* meaning 'a stroke'. It was 'the very handy-worke of GOD'. He admitted that there was a natural cause involved in the disease but it was *also* the work of a destroying angel. 'There is no evill but it is a sparke of God's wrath.' Religion, he said, was filled by Puritan preachers with 'new tricks, opinions and fashions, fresh and newly taken up, which their fathers never knew of'. The people of England now 'think it a goodly matter to be *wittie*, and to find out things our selves to *make to our selves*, to be Authors, and inventors of somewhat, that so we may seem to be as wise as GOD, if not wiser'. What could be more wicked than the idea of being an Author? Let alone *wittie*? New-ness was the sin and novelty was damnable. 'That Sinn may cease, we must be out of love with our own inventions and not goe awhoring after them . . . otherwise, his anger will not be turned away, but his hand stretched out still.'

The educated, privileged and powerful churchman preaches his own virtue and ignores his pastoral duties, congratulating himself on his own salvation. The self-serving crudity of this stance did not escape the attentions of the Puritans. If Andrewes sincerely believed that the plague was a punishment for sin and 'novelty', and if he was guiltless on that score, then why had he run away to Chiswick? Surely someone of his purity would have been immune in the city? And if his pastoral duties led him to the stinking death pits of Cripplegate, as they surely did, why was he not there? Did Andrewes, in other words, really believe what he was saying about the omnipotent wrath of the Almighty?

In a way he didn't; and his hovering between a vision of overwhelming divine authority and a more practical understanding of worldly realities, in some ways fudging the boundaries between those two attitudes, reveals the man. Henoch Clapham, the angry pamphleteer, lambasted Andrewes in his *Epistle Discoursing upon the Present Pestilence*. All Londoners, Andrewes included, should behave as though plague was not contagious. Everybody should attend all the funerals. There was no need to run away. It was a moral disease. If you were innocent you were safe. And not to believe that was itself a sin. How innocent was Andrewes in running to save his own skin? Did the innocent require an elm-tree shade? Clapham was slapped into prison for asking these questions. To suggest that the Dean of Westminster was a self-serving cheat was insubordinate and unacceptable. Andrewes interrogated him there in a tirade of anger and attempted to impose on him a retraction. Clapham had to agree (in the words written by Andrewes):

> That howsoever there is no mortality, but by and from a supernatural cause, so yet it is not without concurrence of natural causes also . . . That a faithful Christian man, whether magistrate or minister, may in such times hide or withdraw himself, as well corporeally as spiritually, and use local flight to a more healthful place (taking sufficient order for the discharge of his function).

Clapham refused to sign this and stayed in prison for eighteen months until he finally came up with a compromise he could accept: there were two sorts of plague running alongside each other. One, infectious, was a worldly contagion, against which you could take precautions. The other, not infectious, was the stroke of the Angel's hand. A pre-modern understanding of a world in which God and his angels interfered daily, in chaotic and unpredictable ways, was made to sit alongside something else: the modern, scientific idea of an intelligible nature. The boundary between the two, and all the questions of authority, understanding and belief which hang around it, is precisely the line which Andrewes had wanted to fudge.

If this looks like the casuistry of a trimming and worldly churchman, there were of course other sides to him. Down at Chiswick, as throughout his life, the time he spent in private, about five hours every morning, was devoted almost entirely to prayer. He once said that anyone who visited him before noon clearly did not believe in God. The prayers he wrote for himself, first published after his death in 1648 as *Preces Privatae*, have for High Church Anglicans long been a classic of devotional literature. Andrewes gave the original manuscript to his friend Archbishop Laud. It was 'slubbered with his pious hands and watered with his penitential tears'. This was no rhetorical exaggeration: those who knew him often witnessed his 'abundant tears' as he prayed for himself and others. In his portraits he holds, gripped in one hand, a large and absorbent handkerchief. It was a daily habit of self-mortification and ritualised unworthiness in front of an all-powerful God, a frame of mind which nowadays might be thought almost mad, or certainly in need of counselling or therapy. But that was indeed the habit of the chief and guiding Translator of the King James Bible: 'For me, O Lord, sinning and not repenting, and so utterly unworthy, it were more becoming to lie prostrate before Thee and with weeping and groaning to ask pardon for my sins, than with polluted mouth to praise Thee.'

This was the man who was acknowledged as the greatest

preacher of the age, who tended in great detail to the school-children in his care, who, endlessly busy as he was, would never-theless wait in the transepts of Old St Paul's for any Londoner in need of solace or advice, who was the most brilliant man in the English Church, destined for all but the highest office. There were few Englishmen more powerful. Everybody reported on his serenity, the sense of grace that hovered around him. But alone every day he acknowledged little but his wicked-ness and his weakness. The man was a library, the repository of sixteen centuries of Christian culture, he could speak fifteen modern languages and six ancient, but the heart and bulk of his existence was his sense of himself as a worm. Against an all-knowing, all-powerful and irresistible God, all he saw was an ignorant, weak and irresolute self:

A Deprecation

O Lord, Thou knowest, and canst, and willest
the good of my soul.
Miserable man am I;
I neither know, nor can, nor, as I ought
will it.

How does such humility sit alongside such grandeur? It is a yoking together of opposites which seems nearly impossible to the modern mind. People like Lancelot Andrewes no longer exist. But the presence in one man of what seem to be such divergent qualities is precisely the key to the age. It is because people like Lancelot Andrewes flourished in the first decade of the seventeenth century – and do not now – that the greatest translation of the Bible could be made then, and cannot now. The age's lifeblood was the bridging of contradictory qualities. Andrewes embodies it and so does the King James Bible.

By the late summer of 1603, the Privy Council was cancelling Bartholomew Fair, ordering the demolition of slums and starting to clear out 'the great confluence and accesse of excessive numbers of idle, indigent, dissolute and dangerous persons'. Meanwhile, other movements were afoot which would shape the birth of the King James Bible. Outside the central religious and political establishment, plans were being laid to steer that establishment in a direction which neither Elizabeth nor those around her had ever contemplated nor would ever have allowed.

The Puritan reformists within the Church of England saw the new reign as a chance for a new start. One of their secular leaders, Lewis Pickering, had already buttonholed the king in Edinburgh, and on James's way south a petition had been presented to him, signed it was said by a thousand ministers, asking for a reformation of the English Church, to rid it of the last vestiges of Roman Catholicism and to bring to a conclusion the long rumbling agony of the English Reformation. 'Renaissance' was not a word that was known or used in seventeenth-century England, but 'Reformation' was and it was clear to the reformists that a full Reformation had never occurred in England. Now, perhaps, at last, with a Scottish king, well versed in the ways of Presbyterianism, brought up under the ferocious eye of George Buchanan, there was an opportunity to turn the Church of England into a bona fide Protestant organisation, as purified of Roman practices as those on the continent of Europe. This Millenary Petition, named after its thousand signatures, was the seed from which the new translation of the Bible would grow.

The king, filled with delight at his reception in England, the wonderful hunting that was laid on, the fat and eminently shootable stags that were provided (his habit was to ride hard and fast and to end the hunt with an embarrassing tendency to miss), had agreed to a conference at which all the outstanding church issues could be discussed with the Puritans and with their opponents, the defenders of the status quo, the bishops and deans, the leading intellectuals and ecclesiastical politicians of the church. The conference had been a Puritan idea and was cannily calculated to appeal to James's idea of himself as the new Solomon, judiciously sowing peace where there had been discord, a notion of himself as the great doctor, the therapeutic king who would usher in an age of sacred and beneficent peace.

Throughout that exciting summer of 1603, as it felt for a moment that England was going to change, the Puritans were busy raising the stakes. Word was sent around the counties that the old complaints could be given new life. Thomas Cranmer's Book of Common Prayer, as revised in 1552, embodying the English compromise between Protestant language and Catholic ceremonies, had always been for the Puritans 'an unperfect booke, culled and picked out of the popishe dunghill, the Masse boke full of all abhominations'. Now they could say so. Bishops, they claimed, were nowhere endorsed by the word of Christ. Trumped up, fat 'pomp-fed prelates' could not 'clayme any other authorities than is geeven them by the statute of the 25 of Kynge Henry the 8'. They were royal placeholders, parasitical government officials, nothing to do with God or his church. A sudden electric current ran through the English shires. The Puritans arranged public debates on the question of the wearing of the surplice, and on the use of the cross, on the bishops' laying on of hands at confirmation, and on the all-important question of whether ministers should be learned or not. In a Catholic or sub-Catholic church, where the visual and the ceremonial dominated the verbal and intellectual, it scarcely mattered if the priest was well qualified; he was simply the conduit for divine meaning. But in a proper, pure reformed church, the minister needed to be, more than anything else, an effective preacher of the word, not a mere 'dumme dogge', as the phrase went at the time – it came from Isaiah – who would go through the motions and convey nothing of the intellectual spirit of reformed Christianity.

The suggestion of a conference appalled the bishops. All these old issues which had riven the church in the 1570s and '80s, and which had been effectively shut down since then by rigid suppression, were now to be given new life. James's all-too-Scottish and intellectual readiness to talk through difficult questions was going to release a log-jam. Everything in the new Jacobean England suddenly felt more fluid than before and a conference with the Puritans on the future governance and doctrines of the English Church was going too far.

One needs reminding, perhaps, of just how passionate was the loathing among Puritans of that symbolic strain in the English Church. Few modern Christians, however severe, would be quite as brave as Richard Parker, the author of *A Scholasticall Discourse against Symbolizing with AntiChrist in Ceremonies: especially in the Signe of the Crosse*, published in London in 1607, who was keen to point out to the ignorant, at some length, 'the idolatrie of the Crosse, the Superstition of the Crosse, the Hipocrisie of the Crosse, the impietie of the Crosse, the injustice of the Crosse and the soule murther of the Crosse'. The cross was 'a part of deuill worship . . . The vsing of the Crosse is but an idle apishe toye, and lighter than the surplice, which is also too light.'

Why did these things matter so much? Why did people care about the wearing of a surplice, or the emblem of the cross, or the use of a ring in the wedding service? Why was so much agony expended on the relative weight of symbol and word, of text and ceremony, on the precise bodily movements of Englishmen at prayer? There is a straightforward answer: two entirely different and opposing worldviews, and two views of the nature of human beings, are bound up in this debate. For the strict reformers, only the naked intellectual engagement with the complexities of a rational God would do. All else was confusion and obfuscation. The word was the route to understanding. Everything else was mud in the water. Men were essentially thinking and spiritual creatures. Bodily observance was an irrelevance. A Calvinist religion, as Milton later said, was 'winnow'd, and sifted, from the chaffe of overdated Ceremonies'. It was free of irrelevance. The only desire of ceremonialists like Lancelot Andrewes and his disciple William Laud was to distort this precious purified religion of the word. 'They hallow'd it, they fum'd it, they sprincl'd it, they be deck't it,' Milton raged, 'not in robes of pure innocency, but of pure Linnen, with other deformed, and fantastik dresses in Palls, and Miters, gold, and guegaws fetcht from Arons old wardrobe.'

For those like Andrewes who held on to the place of symbol in the life of religion (and they were a small if powerful minority even among the bishops of the Jacobean church), and who saw God not as an intellectual system but as a mystery, the stripping of the altars was an unpardonable arrogance. The church had always used ritual and ceremony to approach the divine. It was the conduit through which grace could reach the believer. Only big-headed modern 'novelists' could assume that, without any guidance from the wisdom of the church fathers, ordinary people could approach God direct, as no one had done since the Apostles. Mystery for Andrewes required ceremony and a respect for the inherited past.

Bowing to the name of Jesus was the hinge and fulcrum of this debate. The later pamphleteer William Prynne (whose cheeks were to be branded on the orders of William Laud with the letters SL standing for 'Seditious Libeller' – Prynne called them 'Stigmata Laudiana') considered the habit of bowing 'a meere Popish Inuention of *punie* times'. And, anyway, bowing at the name of Jesus 'disturbes and interupts men in their deuotions, by auocating their bodies and minds from those serious duties about which they are imployed and to which they should be wholy intent'. Prayer was as serious and technical as a law lecture; and what did bobbing and dipping have to do with that? A habit of mind further from the passionate emotionalism of

Andrewes's private prayers it would be difficult to imagine. These were the polarities across which the King James Bible was to have its life and being.

The organisers of the petitioning campaign were canny, or at least thought they were. The line they had to follow was precise. Even if the bishops felt alarmed at any kind of change to the status quo, they knew James himself would be quite open to an examination of the theological basis of the Church of England. It was one of his areas of expertise and he was relaxed and even intrigued by the idea of discussing doctrine and the form of church ceremonial. He had been brawling with the Scottish Presbyterians on these subjects for years.

What he would not tolerate, however, was any suggestion of his own royal authority being questioned. The royal supremacy over church and state was the foundation of his position as King of England, the very reason he felt so at home in this marvellous new country he had inherited. That melding of secular and religious authority had been the secret at the heart of the immensely successful Tudor monarchy. In Scotland, and in other fully reformed countries in Europe, the new churches had established themselves as powers quite distinct from and independent of the state. In Catholic countries all the potency of the Protestant idea, the great revolutionary engine of sixteenth-century Europe, had been put to ends directly in conflict with the state. Uniquely in England, an increasingly powerful state had made itself synonymous with a – more or less – Protestant Church. This state Protestantism was the great and accidental discovery of the English Reformation. It bridged the divisions which in the rest of Europe had given rise to decades of civil war.

But now in the summer and autumn of 1603, the existence of a Protestant state church made the Puritans' task extremely tender. Precisely because the head of the church was also the head of state, it was critical for their cause to separate theological questions from political. They had to establish themselves as politically loyal even while asking for changes to the state religion and the form of the state church. And it was equally critical for the bishops to conflate them. Throughout the summer the bishops maintained that any questioning of the doctrine and articles of the Church of England was politically subversive, dangerous and to be expunged. Anti-Puritan propaganda flooded the country. The Puritans were teetering along a narrow rock ledge and they wrapped their suggestions in swathes of submiss-ive cotton wool. They addressed James, they said, 'neither as factious men affecting a popular parity in the Church [no hint of getting rid of the bishops], nor as schismatics aiming at the dissolution of the state ecclesiastical [they wanted to distinguish themselves from the true extremists, who took from the New Testament that each congregation should be independent and free of all worldly authority] but as faithful servants of Christ and loyal subjects'. Describing themselves as 'Ministers of the Gospell, that desier not a disorderly innovation [nothing was more loathsome to the seventeenth-century mind than the idea of innovation; 'novelist' was a term of abuse, 'primitivist' of the highest praise] but a due and godlie reformation', they laid on the supplicatory language:

> Thus with all dutifull submission, referring our selues to your Maiesties pleasure for your gracious aunswere, as God shall direct you, wee most humblie recommend your Highness to the Devine maiestie, whom wee beseech for Christ, his sake to dispose your royall harte to doe herein what shalbee to his glorie, the good of his Churche, and your endles Comforte.

Things weren't quite so unctuous in private. Both Lewis Pickering and Patrick Galloway, a Presbyterian minister who had come south with James, were making sure that the campaign didn't look like a conspiracy. Galloway wanted 'a resident Moyses in euerye parishe' but there were to be many different petitions each with slightly different wording, and not too many ministers on one petition. Nothing should be done to make it look like a set-up. No one was to ask for the removal of bishops outright. In all the parishes across the country, ministers were to stir up the people to ask for a reformation. They were to pray 'against the superstitious ceremonies, and tirannie of Prelates'. Lawyers were instructed to prepare some draft bills for parliament to bring about the changes they wanted. Scholars were hired to write learned treatises. It was precisely like a modern, single-issue campaign, dragooning the media, whipping up local excitement, lobbying in private, agitating in public.

Petitions and representations streamed into the court. The two sides were gathering for the climax: bishops and the conservative establishment on one side; radical reformists on the other; with the king in between, sympathetic to some of the radical demands but also to the idea of no disturbance, no disruption to good order. Majesty was attentive; a good king was a listening king. The conference between the two sides had been set for 1 November. It was assumed, on past form, that the plague would have ebbed by then, but because the outbreak had been so devastating, the conference was delayed until after Christmas. It would be held in early January.

Meanwhile, at the end of October, and under pressure from the bishops, James issued a proclamation. He faced both ways. An episcopal church was 'agreeable to God's word, and near to the condition of the primitive church'. Nevertheless, there were 'some things used in this church [which] were scandalous'. The king, who felt that he had in himself 'some sparkles of the Divinity', would resolve the agony. He would not countenance 'tumult, sedition and violence', he didn't want 'open invectives or indecent speeches', but his conference would consider 'corruptions which may deserve a review and amendment'. The parties were to meet in the Tudor brick palace of Hampton Court on 12 January. There the idea for a new translation of the Bible would be born.

THREE

He sate among graue, learned and reuerend men

Now I beseech you brethren by the name of our Lord Iesus Christ, that yee all speake the same thing, and that there be no diuisions among you: but that ye be perfectly ioyned together in the same minde, and in the same iudgement.

1 Corinthians 1:10

hristmas at Hampton Court had been draining. Late in December 1603 an already exhausted and clearly distracted Cecil wrote to his friend Lord Shrewsbury: 'We are nowe to feast seven ambassadors; Spayne, France, Poland, Florence and Savoy, besydes maskes and mvch more; during all wch time, I wold with all my hearte I were with that noble Ladie of yours, by her turfe fire.'

By mid-January, the partying and the politicking were over and the king and Council could turn their minds to the conference which would discuss the future of the church. The letters issuing the invitations had gone out from the Privy Council and on the appointed day at nine o'clock in the morning, the great men of the Church of England, a clutch of future Translators (a word that was capitalised at the time) among them, gathered at the palace. It was freezing. The banks of the Thames were encrusted with ice and enormous fires burned in the Renaissance fireplaces which Cardinal Wolsey and Henry VIII had installed here seventy years before. Old John Whitgift, the Archbishop of Canterbury, was surrounded by the men whose appointments by the Crown he had sponsored and argued for. The bishops around him were all, in some way or other, reliant on him for their status and their well-being. He had been the great manager of the Elizabethan church, the queen's 'husbandman', who had pursued with equal ruthlessness the papists who wished to return England to the dominion of the pope; Presbyterians, who would be rid of all bishops and archbishops, replacing their authority with local committees; and those Puritan Separatists who believed in no overarching structure for the church beyond their own, naturally fissive local gatherings. Now, with the ecclesiastical magnates of England gathered around his frail and shrinking presence, he was facing the last challenge from a new king, son of a Catholic queen, brought up by Presbyterian divines: an uncertain quantity.

The Lord Bishops of London, Durham, Winchester and Worcester, of St David's in the far west of Wales, of Chichester, Carlisle and Peterborough were fully robed in the uniform the church required and which the Puritans loathed: the tippet (a long rich silk scarf draped around the shoulders); the big-sleeved rochet or episcopal surplice, much loved by the bishops, an ocean of ceremonial cambric; a chimere, a loose over-mantle, which, throughout the Middle Ages and until the early years of Elizabeth, had been of a dazzling scarlet silk, but which, under Calvinist influence was thought 'too light and gay for the episcopal gravity', now had become strict and elegant black satin – it was Whitgift's black chimere that led Elizabeth to call him 'my little black husband'; and on their heads as they came in, but then removed, the three- or four-cornered caps which were the mark of a divine or of a member of the universities. The mitre, which had been worn before the Reformation, and would return later in the seventeenth century to Milton's disgust, was for now banished as a sign of popish ceremony. With the bishops came the next generation of ecclesiastical power-brokers, the

Deans of the Chapel Royal, of St Paul's, of Chester, Windsor and, silent, his famous public serenity intact, Lancelot Andrewes, Dean of Westminster. All, in a year or two, would be bishops themselves.

This Tudor Hampton Court, before Christopher Wren transformed it in the 1690s into a massive red-brick slab of power and grandeur, an attempt at an English Versailles, was a fairy palace, full of little towers and toy battlements, weathervanes that caught the light, as romantic and play-chivalric as an illumination in a Book of Hours. Here and there, the Italian craftsmen imported by the cardinal and king had contributed a terracotta medallion or a frieze of satyrs. Plaster ceilings, in which large pendant bosses hung down over the heads of the churchmen, and whose panels were filled with papier mâché roses and sculpted ostrich feathers, were painted light blue and gold. Braziers stood glowing in the rooms.

The delegates were ushered by the Gentlemen of the Royal Household into the Presence Chamber, just before eleven. A large cloth of state, emblazoned with the royal arms, hung on the far wall. A velvet-covered chair – the king's – stood empty a few feet, 'a prettie distance', in front of it. It was perhaps the chair that survives at Knole, given by the king to the Earl of Dorset in 1606, its back and seat, under the velvet, formed from a thick canvas bag stuffed with feathers, and its egg-shaped finials studded with gilt nails. Beside it, the Lords of the Privy Council were standing in groups, and, lined up, sitting on a plain wooden bench or form, the Puritans with whom the bishops and the deans were to dispute. One of the gentlemen there, writing to a friend in the country, said that the four of them looked as if they were wearing their 'clokes and Nitecaps'.

This seems at first like a cartoon of Jacobean England: the grand theatre of the royal Presence Chamber, derisive courtiers, satin-lined prelates, a self-indulgent king, and a pitiable line-up of put-upon and ascetic Puritans, sitting on their bench more

like the accused at a trial than the equal partners in a negotiation
for the future of the church. But it wasn't quite as simple as that.
The four representatives of the Puritan party were in fact old
friends of many of the bishops and deans. John Reynolds or
Rainolds, one of the Puritans, was not only Master of Corpus
Christi Oxford but had been Dean of Lincoln Cathedral, a position in the gift of the archbishop himself. So happy was Reynolds
at Lincoln and then at Corpus Christi, that he had had actually
refused a bishopric offered him by Queen Elizabeth. Here in
the Presence Chamber he found himself face to face with his
oldest friend, Henry Robinson, now Bishop of Carlisle. They
had known each other since they were boys, they had been at
Oxford together; as Jacobean England was an expressive culture
(strait-laced continentals remarked on how often and warmly
the English kissed), the two men would certainly have embraced.
Robinson had taken a different path from Reynolds, but in many
ways was indistinguishable from his friend. An evangelical
Calvinist, an assiduous preacher, scarcely bothering to enforce
the strict anti-Puritan requirements (ministers in his diocese did
not have to kneel for communion nor always wear a surplice), a
ferocious pursuer of Catholics in the Protestant north: there was
more uniting these men than dividing them.

Two of the other Puritans, John Knewstubs and the charming, mild-mannered Laurence Chaderton, had been at Cambridge with Lancelot Andrewes and used to have 'constant
meetings' with him there. Their lives had certainly diverged –
Chaderton and Knewstubs both had a radical Presbyterian past
behind them, of which Andrewes would certainly have disapproved – but even so there was a great deal uniting them.
They had all studied the ancient languages together, read the
Bible together and teased out the details of 'Grammatical
Interpretation' together, 'till at last they went out, like Apollos,
eloquent men, and mighty in the Scriptures'.

This was not an encounter of parties at each other's throats.

Chaderton, who was now the Master of Emmanuel College, Cambridge, and one of the most loved of all men in that university, had also as an undergraduate been the greatest friend of Richard Bancroft, another man who now stood opposite him, as his chief opponent and Bishop of London, scourge of Puritans and Whitgift's chosen successor for the see of Canterbury. When they were students together at Cambridge, during one of the often-repeated clashes between town and gown, Chaderton had actually saved Bancroft from a mob of enraged citizens.

Bancroft had become a severe, ruthless sleuth after Puritan error. As Whitgift's right-hand man in the 1580s and '90s he had hunted out and destroyed the Elizabethan Presbyterian movement (of which Chaderton and Knewstubs had been a part). It was a bruising process, which according to Thomas Fuller, the seventeenth-century church historian, 'hardened the hands of his soul, which was no more than needed for him who was to meddle with nettles and briars'. That is certainly what Bancroft looks like in his portraits: a weather-tested man, as rough as a hill-farmer, ruthless with any opposition. But he and Chaderton remained friends. Both were from Lancashire where wrestling is a traditional sport and the two men, Master of Emmanuel and Bishop of London, liked to wrestle when they met.

The establishment of Jacobean England was as small as a village. It was intimate with itself, engaged in endless conversation. The currency of this world was talk between people who had known each other all their lives, and the intimacy of those relationships was crucial to the nature of the conference and its outcome, and to the qualities of the Bible that would eventually emerge from it. As usual, in what is billed as a critical public meeting, a great deal had been squared off in private beforehand. There had been manoeuvrings for months, a little ballet at the heart of seventeenth-century England, in which bishops, both Calvinist and anti-Calvinist, moderate reformists, politically radical Puritans, an episcopally-minded but reformist-sympathetic king and a wary Council, had danced around each other, if not with swords out, at least with hands on hilts. And this was the result.

The true extremists, those who wanted to dismantle the Church of England and replace it either with a confetti of independent and Separatist congregations or with a true Presbyterian system from which bishops were to be abolished, had been excluded. Many of them were meeting in London at this very moment, frustrated and outplayed. James had said quite explicitly that he didn't want the 'brainsick and heady preachers' but 'the learned and grave men of both sides'. That is what he had got. The so-called Puritan party had probably been chosen by the Privy Council, perhaps by Cecil. Various preparatory lists and suggestions survive; those eventually chosen were the most moderate, bishop- and king-friendly. Dressed up as a meeting of opposites, this conference was in fact the bringing together of a near-consensus.

Not all the people gathered in this room were well born, and hypersensitivity to class origins coloured all relationships, but that is far from the whole story. The Cecils themselves had been little more than Welsh farmers only sixty years before (and remained crushingly aware of the meanness of their origins). Lancelot Andrewes's father had been a master mariner in London, Bancroft's a minor member of the northern gentry, Whitgift's a Grimsby merchant, Chaderton's a rich squire who taught him to hunt and little else. But brilliance and education had lifted them all into the intimacy of this elite. These were the people in whose hands the future of the Church of England lay and they all knew each other. They were deeply opposed on important issues but a single envelope, what would nowadays be called a single discourse, contained them, and much of the peaceableness of England can be explained by that. One governing culture was accessible to the gifted sons of great and relatively humble families. It is not difficult to imagine the murmured conversations between them as they stood waiting in groups as the winter sunshine made its way through the thick grey-green panes of the Tudor windows.

The only outsider, ironically enough, was the king. He had scarcely known bishops, and never seen the surplice or the cross before coming to England. He spoke with an acutely Scottish accent, and pronounced his Latin and Greek in ways the English could scarcely understand. And as the incident at Newark had shown, his touch was not always sure. It was in many ways James's sheer oddness which steered the conference into its rather dark and confused channels.

First he sent word that the reformists should retire. He wanted to speak to the bishops and deans alone; they were to sit on one side of the room. The Privy Council was to sit and listen on the other. The four Puritans left and the Lord Chamberlain shut the door behind them. After a while, as the lords and bishops waited there in silence, the king came in. He was charm itself, 'passed a few pleasant gratulations with some of the Lords', and then sat down in the chair that stood in front of the cloth of state. He kept his hat on as he surveyed the great Englishmen around him.

He was of course practised in the role. He had been king of a bitterly divided nation for as long, quite literally, as he could remember and now he wooed his audience. 'Salomon *speaketh*', the unctuous William Barlow, Dean of Chester, reported, in the ever-repeated cliché of the reign. James's words, falling on the ears of his amazed and delighted hearers, Barlow said, were 'like Apples of gold, with pictures of siluer'.

Barlow's account makes it seem as if king and bishops had shown little but love and harmony to each other, but they hadn't. Barlow (a Translator – he would chair the key committee in charge of the New Testament epistles) was lying. The king had fiercely attacked the bishops and openly slapped them down. The dean was the official propagandist for the bishops' cause, and his pamphlet was a carefully slanted version of events. When he tried to dedicate it to Robert Cecil, Cecil refused. Anyone whose method of survival was distance and non-commitment would certainly not have wanted to be identified so thoroughly with a single party. Barlow was acting on Bancroft's instructions. Bancroft wanted to make it appear that the king was on the bishops' side. But there were others, more objective (their identity has never been established), taking notes at the same time and it is clear from what they wrote that things on this first day were far from harmonious.

James did begin smoothly and graciously.

> It pleased him both to enter into a gratulation to Almightie God (at which wordes he put off his hat) for bringing him into the promised land, where Religion was purely professed; where he sate among graue, learned and reuerend men; not, before, elsewhere, a King without state, without honour, without order; where beardless boys would braue him to his face.

It was charming, crafty, complicit, flattering, collusive, the speech of a politician three decades on a throne. A smile hangs about the words, his doffing of his hat to God surely a witticism, the description of England as the promised land surely an act of flattery to the Englishmen around him.

The bishops, too, began emolliently. Poor old John Whitgift addressed the king on his knees as they discussed technical points about baptism, confirmation, the too frequent use of excommunication. Whitgift and Bancroft quoted both the Bible and 'Mr Calvin'. James congratulated himself on his own moderation. It was only a matter of months ago, he told them, that he was berating a Scots minister on not paying enough attention to the rite of baptism; now he had to instruct these English bishops on revering it too highly. Again, there is that Jamesian note of seriousness and jokiness lying unresolved together.

The kneeling bishops insisted that the Church of England

as it had stood these last forty years was as near the perfect state of the primitive church as any in the world. And if the church had persisted well enough for forty years, then why the need to change anything? Suddenly this was too much, and James could be patient and politic no longer: 'It was no reason that because a man had been sicke of the poxe 40 years, therefore he shoold not be cured at length.'

It was a coarse interjection: had anyone previously compared the Church of England to a man with the clap? James, clearly, was not entirely reliable, unwilling to be boxed into the conservative, anti-Puritan compartment the bishops would have liked. History may have confined James to a proto-absolutist, Divine Right of Kings advocate, but the reality, inevitably, was more complicated. To the bishops' horror, James began to lecture them, 'playing the puritan' as Andrewes later described it. They were not to pursue Nonconformists with the violence they were accustomed to (this was aimed at both Whitgift and Bancroft for their stamping out the English Presbyterians under Elizabeth) but were to treat them 'more gently than euer they had don before'. These statements were politically canny – the bishops were still unsure where James stood – and were a means of establishing him as the holder of the ring, the Solomon-like judge and arbiter who belonged to no one side. Anyway, the questions implied, why did these bishops think that their church, unlike any other human institution, was not corrupt and in need of repair? What arrogance was that? Wasn't everything in this world subject to decay and decline? Where did they think they were? In some kind of perfected heaven? The atmosphere of the conference had suddenly sharpened.

In the discussion on baptism, the Bishop of Peterborough then made a fool of himself. Apropos of nothing much, he said that he knew of one case in which an ancient father had baptised with sand instead of water. 'Whereto his Majesty answered pleasantly, "A turd for the Argument. He might as well have pissed

on them, for that had been more liker to water than sand."'
The bishop's reputation never recovered. Bancroft, who in his
organisational ability could exercise a cold rationality but who
could also turn intemperate and angry, 'now spake with too ruf
boldness'. He had been goaded by the figure before him of James
Mountagu, Dean of the Chapel Royal.

Mountagu embodies all the unclassifiability of Jacobean attitudes to state and religion, to holiness and power. He would in
time become both a Translator and a bishop. He edited, with a
lake full of obsequiousness, the king's own collected works. He
was a beautifully mannered aristocrat, with one brother an earl,
the other a baron. He sounds like a Cavalier in the making.
Surely a figure such as Mountagu should have been repulsed by
Calvinist severity and strictness, by the whole notion of Puritanism? He wasn't. He was deeply sympathetic to the reformist
camp, having been Master of the Puritan Sidney Sussex College
in Cambridge. At this period, at the head of each of his letters,
he used to put the word 'Emmanuel', meaning 'God be with us',
a signal among the stricter sort of the supremacy of scripture
over the worldly structures of the church. He did his best to
promote the hotter Protestants within the church and would not
accept any kind of lush ceremonial, nor any hint of a drift back
to Rome.

Bancroft loathed him. For Bancroft, bishops and the accustomed hierarchy were agents of the divine. The true church
couldn't hope to rely on the Bible alone. Almost no one understood what it meant and so people like Mountagu represented
a most alarming subversion of the order on which civilised life
relied. Now their simmering hostility boiled over. At one point
early that afternoon, when the dean leaned over and whispered
in the king's ear – he was giving him some details on ancient
baptism – Bancroft could contain himself no longer. 'Speake
out, Mr Doctor, and do not crosse us, underhand,' he shouted
violently across the room. Barlow would report none of this.

They had been talking for three hours. It was not a good atmosphere. This was a court that knew everything about duplicity and politicking, constantly aware of the unreliability of language and men, of whisperings in ears and comments muttered behind the hand, but which nevertheless valued a courteous surface, the smooth and upholstered working of the demands of power. Robert Cecil, a well-honed liar, sitting with the Council to one side, said nothing. Sitting among the deans, Lancelot Andrewes, who had often preached against the very offences of pluralism and nepotism which he and all the others practised, remained silent. And Bancroft's faux pas allowed James to resume his unique combination of Solomon-like distance and joky vulgarity. Religion, he told them, was the soul of a kingdom, and unity the life of religion. He would clear up some doubts, he would have a few passages changed in the prayer book, in the rubrics rather than the body of the text, 'to be inserted by waie rather of some some explanation than of any alteration at all'. He would see the Puritan party on Monday morning. He was not looking forward to it: 'howsoeuer he lived among *Puritans*, and was kept for the most part, as a Ward under them, yet, since hee was the age of his Sonne, 10. years old, he euer disliked their opinions; as the Sauiour of the world said, *Though he liued among them, he was not of them.*'

With that breathtaking comparison between his own position and Christ's walking among the heathen, James dismissed the bishops and deans. It was a confession that, in effect, he had been playing with them. He may have appeared to be taunting them with the very charges the Puritans were laying against them, but, when it came to the point, James wanted to buttress the established church. Nevertheless, Solomon-like to the end, he was anxious that the established church itself should be cleansed of impurities. It is the classic Jamesian position: self-congratulatory, vain, and perhaps, in the end, surprisingly, and against the odds, rather wise.

On Monday, the tactics were exactly and intelligently handled by James to put the burden of proof on the Puritans. Unless they could show that there was something in scripture explicitly condemning the bishops' administration of confirmation, or the use of the cross in baptism, or of the ring in a wedding service, or kneeling to receive communion, or the wearing of the surplice, or about the institution of episcopacy itself, he would not interfere with the accustomed ceremony or government of the church. That church, for all its abuses, was a comfortable bed in which to set a monarchy. Any radicalisation of it, diminishing the power and status of the bishops, or replacing them with presbyteries, inherently argumentative and overweening groups of know-all elders or presbyters, would, in essence, be too Scottish. The last thing he wanted was a return to the horrors north of the border. Presbyteries represented everything he most loathed and despised.

James may have been rude, challenging and clever with the bishops. Now, he was even worse with the Puritans. The four 'plaintiffs', as Barlow called them, were ushered into the Presence Chamber, where little ten-year-old Prince Henry was sitting beside his father on a stool. With them were Thomas Bilson, Bishop of Winchester, the most political of all courtier bishops, a member of the Privy Council, who scarcely ever visited his diocese except to administer oppressive justice and who with Miles Smith would play a critical role in the final stages of the translation, and Bancroft. No Henry Robinsons or James Mountagus, nor any other sympathetic bishops here: just the two hard-core royal apologists.

It must have been alarming. James told them: 'he was now ready to heare, at large, what they could obiect or say; and so willed them to beginne: whereupon, they 4 kneeling downe, *D. Reynolds* the *Foreman* began'. They were on the spot. James was famous across Europe as a theological disputant. Seventeenth-century hunting often involved the enclosing of semi-tame animals within the pales of a park and then slaughtering them at one's leisure, sometimes from a stand in front of which the animals would be driven. And now this too felt a little like another day at that strange, enclosed kind of chase.

It lasted five hours and the Puritans were humiliated. James sniped at them and pursued them into awkward corners, occasionally calling in Bilson and Bancroft, 'and then for variety sake, rather then for necessity'. The four Puritans tried to parry the blows. John Reynolds was 'the principall mouthe and speaker', Chaderton 'mute as any fishe', Knewstubs spoke a little about his loathing of the cross (for which Lancelot Andrewes, at least in one account, took him to task) and the fourth, an obscure and moderate preacher called Thomas Sparke or Sparkes (who within a year or two would share with Bancroft the idea that bishops like kings were appointed by God), said hardly anything at all. But James was freewheeling through their points as though dancing in a kind of theological party. 'We have kept suche a revell with the puritanis heir these two days,' he wrote afterwards to the violent anti-Puritan and duplicitous crypto-Catholic, Henry Howard, Earl of Northampton.

> I have pepperid thaime as soundlie, as ye have done the papists ... They fledde me so from argument to argument, without ever ansouring me directlie, ut est eorum moris [as is their way], as I was forcid at last to saye unto thaime, that if any of thaime hadde bene in a colledge disputing with thair skollairs, if any of thaire disciples hadde ansourid thaim in that sorte, thay wolde have fetchid him up in place of a replye & so shoulde the rodde have plyed upon the poore boyes buttokis.

Poor, dignified, generous Reynolds and Chaderton stood as if in the stocks, the royal squibs falling around them. Reynolds named the familiar abuses: the ceremony of confirmation, which had no basis in scripture, where adult baptism was the only recognised form of induction into the church; the use of the cross as a kind of magic symbol; the surplice – a papist joke, which clearly had nothing whatsoever to do with Christ, the apostles, or anything discoverable in scripture; kneeling at communion – another piece of superstitious symbolism, as though the bread and wine were indeed the blood and body of Christ, when it was an essential aspect of all Protestant thought that they were merely reminders of what had happened on the cross, not a magical re-enactment of it, and not to be bowed to. To Lancelot Andrewes, always insistent on the value of ceremony, this was absurd. Did Protestants pretend, he asked, that God 'will have us worship him like elephants, as if we had no joints in our knees?'

James dismissed all the Puritan objections. He was familiar with them all. They were the points which any Scots Presbyterian would have made and which strict English Protestants, dissatisfied with the compromise of the English Church, had been making since the 1550s. Everyone knew the territory; there were no surprises, but the atmosphere was nasty. These were moderate and distinguished men, suggesting moderate changes. But James – and Bancroft who seems to have been in an excitable state at the theatre unfolding around him – was treating them like extreme schismatics from the outer reaches of Anabaptist lunacy. Nothing like this had ever happened under Elizabeth, simply because Elizabeth, a more distant and less engaged monarch, basing her authority on the aura of that very distance, would not have countenanced it. James enjoyed the roughness of theological argument and Bancroft's eyes must have been wide with delight.

Reynolds, who had never married, said he didn't like the phrase 'with my body I thee worship', which formed part of the marriage service. James couldn't resist a vulgarity: 'Many a man speaks of Robin Hood', he said, 'who never shot his bow; if you had a good wife yourself, you would think that all the honour and worship you could do her were well bestowed.' It was said with a leery grin, the paterfamilias taunting the celibate.

Reynolds said he didn't like the sign of the cross. James told him that by making such an objection he was playing into the hands of the papists.

Bancroft, after addressing the king on his knees, was then allowed to abuse the Puritans, calling them 'schismatic scholars, breakers of your laws; you may know them by their Turkey grograins', a concentrated insult from the beautifully and correctly dressed bishop. A 'grograin' was a gown in grogram, a coarse cloth, part wool, part silk, often worn by merchants. These moderate Puritans, Bancroft was telling the king in his frenzy, were breaking the dress code. What else might they want to break? Was the body of the church safe in their hands? His remarks might be taken as a joke until it is remembered that Bancroft had been closely involved in the pursuit, arrest, interrogation and execution of all those Puritans and Separatists in the past whom he and Whitgift considered a threat to the English Church. It is the kind of joke that is made in totalitarian show-courts.

Reynolds then raised the question of church government. Should the bishop alone be judge and administrator in his diocese? Or could there be a kind of committee of other ministers to help him? That was Reynolds's reasonable meaning. But he used the wrong word. He must have cursed himself as it slipped out. Why shouldn't the bishops govern, Reynolds suggested, 'ioyntly with a Presbyterie of their brethren the pastors and Ministers of the Churche'. The word presbytery released a torrent in the king. A presbytery? 'If you aim at a Scots Presbytery, it agreeth as well with monarchie as God and the devil!': 'He would haue the Presbitery buried in silence for these 7 yeares, and yf then he grewe idle, lasie, fatt, and pursie [short of breath], I will set vp a Presbitery (saith he) to exercise my body and my patience.'

This was the crux. James's experience of angry and threatening Presbyterians in Scotland, who endlessly and loudly promoted the theory that kings were subject to God's and so to the church's judgement, was never going to return to that. It was too challenging and too uncomfortable. The beauty of the Church of England, with its full panoply of bishops and archbishops, was its explicit acceptance of the king as its head. Bishops without a king, an episcopal republic, was perhaps a possibility. But a king without bishops, subject to a presbytery, was always in danger of being removed; it was a revolution waiting to happen. Bishops were the *sine qua non* of the kind of monarchy and church James needed, wanted and believed in. 'No bishops,' he told Reynolds furiously, 'no king.' That, of course, was precisely the elision of the political and the religious points which the moderate Puritans had been anxious to avoid, and which the bishops, for months now, had been working to achieve. It meant one thing: the bishops' party had won.

Into this fierce, overheated atmosphere, where the mild divisions in the Church of England were being whipped into extremity by the quick, intellectual, joky, combative, slightly unsocialised banter, argument and bullying of the king, egged on by the excited Bancroft, the first suggestion, the seed of the King James Bible, dropped. It came from John Reynolds, at the end of a long list of suggestions. The petitioning ministers he represented would like 'one only translation of ye byble to be authenticall and read in ye churche'.

In another jotted-down account of the scene, Reynolds is more courteous: 'May your Majesty be pleased that the Bible be new translated?' Bancroft immediately slammed back at the idea: 'If every man's humour might be followed, there would be no end of translating.' That is the voice of the instinctive authoritarian, happier with the status quo than with any possible revision of it, the voice of the bishop who at the Earl of Essex's futile rebellion in 1601 had personally gathered a gang of pikemen around him, holding a pike himself, and had repulsed the slightly pathetic and misguided rebels at Ludgate, as they tried to enter the City of London.

James, though, was a more complex character than the fierce anti-Puritan bishop, and craftier. Without hesitation – or at least in Barlow's crawling account, where the words read as if they have been tidied up after the event – the king turns Reynolds's suggestion on its head. Implicit in the Puritan divine's request was a criticism of the official Elizabethan Bible, known as the Bishops' Bible after the bishops who had translated it in 1568. It was a royalist and anti-Puritan document, larded with a frontispiece showing Queen Elizabeth and her ministers presiding over a bishop-dominated church. It was a Bible of the hierarchy, not of the people, and no Puritan liked it. Puritans preferred the translation of the Bible made by Calvinist Englishmen in the 1550s in Geneva, the headquarters of Calvinism. The Geneva Bible came interleaved with a large number of explanatory notes, many of them explicitly anti-royalist. The word 'tyrant', for example, which is not to be found in the King James Bible, occurs over 400 times in the Geneva text.

Reynolds was without doubt asking for a revision to the Bishops' Bible, probably in favour of the Geneva Bible which he would have used himself. That is the meaning of his phrase 'one only translation', which also makes a subtle appeal to James's dream of unity. But James – and if Barlow's account can be trusted, this is a witness to his quickness and sharpness – caught the suggestion and reversed it, 'professing that he could neuer, yet, see a Bible well translated in English; but the worst of all, his Maiestie thought the *Geneua* to be'. Barlow explains why: 'Withal he gave this caveat (upon a word cast out by my Lord of London) that *no marginal notes* should be added – having found in them which are annexed to the *Geneva* translation ... some notes very partial, untrue, seditious, and savoring too much of dangerous and traitorous conceits.'

James was particularly exercised by the Geneva note at Exodus 1:19. It was an all-important passage, in his view, for understanding the nature of royal authority and the relationship between royal and divine instructions. It is also extraordinarily revealing about the difference between the Jacobean and the modern attitude to authority. In Ancient Egypt, Pharaoh had ordered the Jewish midwives to kill all the male children born to the Jewish people. The midwives disobeyed these royal instructions and saved all the baby boys. Pharaoh wanted to know why. 'And the midwiues said vnto Pharaoh, Because the Hebrew women are not as the Egyptian women; for they are liuely, and are deliuered ere the midwiues come in vnto them.'

This was, of course, a lie. Jewish pregnancies came to precisely the same term as any other. The modern reaction would surely be to admire the midwives' courage in standing up to the Pharaoh and their presence of mind in telling a straightforward and quite convincing white lie. Their disobedience was brave and their deception clever. But the Genevan note ran as follows: 'Their disobedience in this was lawful, but their deception is evil.'

For James, their behaviour had been the essence of sedition. Their disobedience was wicked and their deception made it worse. It was clearly the midwives' duty to obey the royal instruction, to conform to the authority of the powers that be and to murder the babies. James would have been on Herod's side and no royally sanctioned translation of the Bible could tolerate any suggestion to the contrary.

He expanded on what he would like the new Bible to be like.

> His Highnesse wished, that some especiall pains should be taken in that behalf for one vniforme translation . . . and this to be done by the best learned of both the Vniversities, after them to be reuiewed by the Bishops, and the chiefe learned of the Church; from them to be presented to the Priuy Councell; and lastly to bee ratified by his Royall authority; to be read in the whole Church, and no other.

Everything implicit in the conference and in the competing constituencies in the country at large; everything that had been building up since Sir Robert Carey's ride to Edinburgh nine months earlier; and, in a wider way, everything involved in the long cultural revolution that had been rolling across Europe for the previous eighty-five years: all of that came to a point in James's response. Reynolds had wanted, when all the code was stripped away, a strict Puritan Bible, non-episcopal, the naked word of God, truly transmitted. And to that request James had said, in effect, 'Yes; I will give you the very opposite of what you ask.' A translation that was to be uniform (in other words with no contentious Geneva-style interpretations set alongside or within the text); with the learned authority of Oxford and Cambridge (which, at least in their upper echelons, were profoundly conservative institutions, both of which had sent to the king long and high-flown refutations of every point in the Puritans' Millenary Petition); to be revised by the bishops (the very influence that Reynolds did not want); then given, for goodness' sake, to the Privy Council, in effect a central censorship committee with which the government would ensure that its stamp was on the text, no deviationism or subversion allowed; and finally to James himself, whose hostility to any whiff of radicalism this afternoon had been clear enough. And this ferociously episcopal and monarchist Bible was to be the only translation that could be read in church: 'no other'. The treasured Geneva Bible would be forced to retreat into the privacy of people's homes and could no longer be used for public preaching.

The deep paradox and lasting value of the King James Bible is its response to both Reynolds's and James's instincts. Once the cantankerous and oddly hysterical atmosphere of the conference had faded, the deeper and slower rhythms of Jacobean royal ideology took control. Those were the rhythms of James's better side. His troubled upbringing had shaped a man with a divided nature. Later history, wanting to see him as a precursor for his son's catastrophe, has chosen only the ridiculous aspects of James: his extravagance, his vanity, his physical ugliness, his weakness for beautiful boys, his self-inflation, his self-congratulatory argumentativeness. Some of that had been in evidence at Hampton Court. But there was another side to James which breathed dignity and richness: a desire for wholeness and consensus, for inclusion and breadth, for a kind of majestic grace, lit by the clarity of a probing intelligence, rich with the love of dependable substance, for a reality that went beyond show, that was not duplicitous, that stood outside all the corruption and rot that glimmered around him. These were the elements in James and in Jacobean court culture that came to shape the Bible which bears his name.

FOUR

Faire and softly
goeth far

He that walketh with wise men shall be wise: but a companion
of fooles shall be destroyed.

Proverbs 13:20

he stricter Puritans were disappointed with the outcome of Hampton Court – no great change to the
church, and certainly no hint of revolution – but
at court an air of optimism prevailed. The English
Church would be unified, its Elizabethan squabbles forgotten.
England and Scotland would become one country. Peace would
be established in Europe. There would even be discussions with
the Pope about the reunification of the Roman and the Protestant
churches. Money and happiness would dance together through
the increasingly elegant streets of London. James's Arcadian
vision of untroubled togetherness would descend on the soul of
England like a balm.

Much of that looks like a joke now. The seventeenth century
would witness a civil war, in which a higher proportion of the
British population was killed than in any war before or since.
Throughout that century, attempts at imposing unity of belief
or government stimulated only anarchy, violence and revolt.
Scotland continued to loathe the very idea of a bishop and was
affronted by the semi-papist horrors of the Book of Common

Prayer. English suspicion of Scottish freeloaders remained as intense as ever and it was the Scots who eventually tipped Britain over into Civil War. In Ireland, native Catholics, treated as animals, were brutally replaced by incoming Scots and English settlers, and a mutually murderous history began which lasted into the twenty-first century. James's dream of a unified and peaceful realm, guaranteed by his own Solomonic wisdom, was perhaps a fantasy too far. The whole of Europe had been convulsed by violence and change since the 1530s, wars which would continue into 1640s. The same cultural and political currents were running on the European mainland as in Britain; it is perhaps a measure of the excellence of Jacobean government, or at least of the vitality of James's political ideals, that war in Britain did not break out until 1639.

Almost the only remnant of that dream, a piece of flotsam after the tide has passed, is the King James Bible. Its great and majestic beauties, a conscious heightening of the word of God (often far more grandly expressed in Jacobean English than in earlier English translations or in the Hebrew or Greek of the original) is a window on that moment of optimism, in which the light of understanding and the majesty of God could be united in a text to which the nation as a whole, Puritan and prelate, court and country, simple and educated, could subscribe.

As a sign of his willingness to consult with the representatives of the country, and not as any kind of duty, James summoned his first parliament of the reign in March. Bonhomie was not its mood. Most of its members were sympathetic to the Puritan cause and felt aggrieved at the lack of satisfaction the Puritan party had received at Hampton Court. James utterly mishandled them. He offered none of Elizabeth's honeyed words but instead lectures on the nature of kingship, on his own nearness to God and, most explosively of all, on the fact that the MPs' own privileges were not independent but derived from him. The witty, opinionated, sharp-edged talker in him torpedoed any kind of Solomonic judiciousness. The MPs, already deeply suspicious of the army of grasping Scots who had come down the Great North Road, would have nothing of any talk of union with Scotland. James might have commissioned himself an elaborate imperial crown, he might have himself described on coins as King of Great Britain, mountains of English gold might have ended up in the pockets of Scots courtiers, but the MPs knew they belonged to an English parliament. If they suddenly found themselves in a parliament of Great Britain, what would happen to their ancient and treasured privileges?

The relationship between king and parliament went nowhere. Bitter speeches were made on both sides, which James's late attempts at mollification did little to alleviate. Just along the Strand in London, peace negotiations were being conducted with a delegation of high-ruffed and black-suited Spaniards to bring the long war to an end. They moved easily towards their close in which every single one of the English negotiators, including Robert Cecil, received a handsome pension from the Spanish crown. But in the Palace of Westminster there was no such happy outcome. James scolded the members for their impertinence. The overwhelmingly difficult questions of finance, of tax in peacetime, of customs dues, were not resolved. Elysium seemed far less accessible than before and the parliament was dismissed in July. James's hopes for a happily reconciled nation looked very distant, at least in the political sphere, and his relationship with parliament would continue to alternate between expressions of love and loyalty, and unfettered arguments over money and their respective rights. A desired amity was scuppered, in other words, by a perfectly real clash of interests.

That political failure to achieve a sense of national unity, however, could, in a slightly paradoxical way, actually fuel James's efforts to bring peace and coherence to the church. The church, and its new Bible, could be driven towards the perfect condition which parliament was so obstinately refusing to adopt. And in pursuit of that goal, James found the perfect lieutenant in Richard Bancroft.

Old Archbishop Whitgift had died in February, after catching a cold travelling in his barge on the winter Thames. Bancroft was his nominated successor and would soon be elevated from London to Canterbury. Like any effective politician, he exuded the complexity of the age. He was a ferocious defender of the Church of England but was the readiest of servants and messengers for the king. He had pursued the Puritans with ferocity in the past and would now harry any Separatists out of the church, driving them to Amsterdam, Leiden and eventually America; and yet, in the matter of this new Bible, he created a team of Translators drawn from an extraordinarily wide spectrum, a generous slice of Jacobean England to be set to work on its central project. This is even more remarkable considering that Bancroft had objected violently to the idea of a new translation at all, having pleaded with James on his knees against it. But Bancroft was politician and monarchist enough to see that when James responded to the idea, the church should take the initiative and mould the new Bible to its own purposes.

That summer Bancroft was a whirl of energy. Letter after letter from his office begins with his 'verie hastie commendations': 'I have written so many letters about this matter of Translation,' he wrote to the Vice-Chancellor at Cambridge University, 'as keepinge no copies of them, I doe confound my self, forgetting what and to whom I have written.' All excuses that any possible Translator might have, he told the Vice-Chancellor, had to be 'sett aside'. This was the king's commission and James hovers in the background of every instruction. It was 'his Highness' who was busy drawing up the rules for the Translators to follow. It was 'his Majesties pleasure' that the most learned men should be drawn in. And to a set of Cambridge scholars he wrote at the end of July: 'I am persuaded his Royall mynde reioyceth more withe good hope, wch he hathe for the happy successe of that worke [the new Bible], then of his peace concluded with Spayne.'

This is going far beyond your average Jacobean formalities. Bancroft, it is quite clear, was doing his master's work and, as these letters reveal, the method, staffing and manner of the King James Bible stemmed from James himself. The Bible was to become part of the new royal ideology. Elizabeth had portrayed herself as a Protestant champion against the powers of Rome and Spain. That was now out of date. James, *Rex Pacificus*, was to make the Bible part of the large-scale redefinition of England. It had the potential to become, in the beautiful phrase of the time, an '*irenicon*', a thing of peace, a means by which the divisions of the church, and of the country as a whole, could be encompassed in one unifying fabric founded on the divine authority of the king.

It was from the beginning a tightly organised, tightly policed and tightly managed programme. In the arrangements for financing it, selecting and supervising the personnel and defining the methods and principles by which the translation was to be made, Bancroft performed his role as royal agent.

First, the money: there was very little of it to spare. Elizabeth, from her expenditure on the war against Catholicism in Ireland and the Netherlands, as well as at sea, had left the Exchequer destitute. James's own expectations of the riches of England were going to make things worse. In July, Bancroft wrote to his fellow bishops on the king's behalf. He had a set of Translators in mind but 'in this number *divers* of them have either no ecclesiastical preference at all, or else so very small, as the same is far unmeet for men of their deserts, and yet, We of OURSELF in any convenient time cannot well remedy it'. The bishops would have to pay for the translation themselves by finding livings for the Translators of £20 a year or upwards. Bancroft then wrote on his own behalf to explain the situation. The king, his loyal archbishop explained, had wanted to pay the costs himself, but his advisers had thought otherwise:

some of my lords, AS THINGS NOW GO, did hold it incon-
venient. I must require you in his Majesty's name, according
to his good pleasure in that behalf, as soon as possibly you
can, you send me word *what* shall be expected from you . . .
For I am to acquaint his Majesty with every man's liberality
towards this most godly work.

It is a glimpse of the underlying realities. At the conference
and at court the bishops may have kneeled and exaggerated the
language of deference. In sermon after sermon they may have
drawn crawling equivalencies between the majesty of God and
the excellence of the Stuarts, what Cordelia in *King Lear*, a play
Shakespeare was writing this same summer, calls 'that glib and
oily art/To speak and purpose not', but when it came to the rub,
money was not forthcoming. A single copy of Bancroft's begging
letter for the Bible survives – in the archives of the Bishop of
Norwich, noted as received by the bishop's office – but not a
single reply to it has ever been found.

It is difficult to tell whether the bishops contributed or not.
Certainly, Lancelot Andrewes, who became Bishop of Chichester
in 1605, and then of Ely in 1609, placed several of the Translators
either in parishes in his diocese or as prebendaries in his
cathedral. Other bishops directly involved in the translation did
the same. But the question is opaque and it may well be that
until other money, from commercial sources, came into the project several years later, as will emerge, the translation was short
of cash.

As with any complex project, all parts had to be advanced at
the same time. There could be no waiting for money before the
other elements – above all the organisation, the control and
checking systems – were put in place. Bancroft recognised from
the start that the translation had to be a joint enterprise. The
idea was far from unprecedented. Although the first sixteenth-
century translation of the scriptures into English was the work
of a solitary hero, William Tyndale, making his extraordinary

achievement on the run and in hiding in a string of German and Flemish cities, almost never breaking cover, applying himself with an unparalleled and solitary dedication to the task of bringing the scriptures, as he declared, 'to the English ploughboy', that had not been the general pattern. The 1539 Great Bible had been produced for Henry VIII by 'dyverse excellent learned men'. The Geneva Bible had been translated by a small team of three or four English divines. The Bishops' Bible had been translated (rather badly) by a team of fourteen bishops, appointed by the Archbishop of Canterbury, and each allocated three or four individual books. Even the English Roman Catholics, at their college in Rheims and then Douai, had applied a small team of men to the job.

Jointness was the acknowledged virtue of the age. Most of the plays performed in Jacobean England were written by more than one writer. A joint translation, by a large number of people, consulting the original manuscripts in both Greek and Hebrew, but relying carefully on much of the work which the sixteenth-century translators had done, was completely concordant with the ideology of the time. Lack of jointness, either through an overweening individuality or through simple dissolution, a falling apart, was considered an overriding error and a sin.

The age was stiff with an insistent individuality, an overwhelming demand for 'authorship', for being master of one's fate, for claiming an individual significance beyond the world and society in which you had your being. 'Every one vaunts himself,' Philip Stubbes the Puritan pamphleteer had wailed in *The anatomie of abuses*, 'crying with open mouth, I am a gentleman, I am worshipful, I am honorable, I am noble, and I cannot tell what; my father was this, my father was that; I am come of this house and I come of that.'

The jointness on which so many of the moralists of the time lay such emphasis was an attempt to mend the cracks which the eruptive egotism of the time was opening. It is the great and tragic theme of *King Lear*, that selfhood and disunity, a natural urge in man, nevertheless destroy the life they aim to elevate. Jointness, by contrast, was slow and careful. It required consultation, the gradual application of principles, not their violent banging in. Although the evidence is a little uncertain, these were probably the years in which woodscrews, made of brass, with the thread on them hand-cut, were first used in the making of furniture. The chairs and joint-stools made with screws – as well as with the more conventional oak pegs – became, in sermon after sermon, a symbol of coherence and propriety, of jointness. 'In reformations of great importance,' the church historian Thomas Fuller told his congregation, 'the violent driving in of the nail will either break the head or bow the point thereof, or rive and split that which should be fastened therewith. That may insensibly be screwed which may not be knocked into people. Fair and softly goeth far.'

Fair and softly goeth far: the irenicon of the new translation was to be a joint product. If Bancroft's words are to be trusted, and there is no reason why they shouldn't be, the extraordinary degree of jointness in the project was James's own idea.

Everything in the modern frame of mind, trained up on centuries of individualism, and on the overriding importance of individual freedoms, rebels against the idea. Joint committees know nothing of genius. They do not produce works of art. It is surely lonely martyrs who struggle for unacknowledged truths. Committees thrive on compromise and compromise produces fudge and muddle. Isn't the beautiful, we now think, to be identified with what is original, the previously unsaid, the unique vision of the individual mind? How can a joint enterprise of this sort produce anything valuable? There may be one or two modern examples of successful co-operative writing – Pound and Eliot, perhaps Auden and Isherwood – but the idea of a committee producing a work of genius? That today sounds like a joke.

Not in 1604. If you think of the King James Bible as the greatest creation of seventeenth-century England, a culture drenched in the word rather than the image, it is easy to see it as England's equivalent of the great baroque cathedral it never built, an enormous and magnificent verbal artifice, its huge structures embracing all 4 million Englishmen, its orderliness and richness a kind of national shrine built only of words. Considered like that, it is inconceivable that the project should have been put in the hands of any individual. It can be no surprise that the king, in whose speeches the word 'love' comes up in paragraph after paragraph, and for whom unity was an almost sacred watchword, should summon a huge committee to do the work; it is unthinkable that he should have done it in any other way. The only mind that could have produced the King James Bible was the mind of England itself.

The translating committee was to be divided into six sub-committees. Each was to be called a 'company', a powerful word in Elizabethan and Jacobean England, not only the name given to the groups of actors who performed in the London playhouses and at court, three of them now having acquired powerful patrons in the king, Queen Anne and Prince Henry, but of the great new imperialist enterprises with which England was reaching out to the commercial opportunities of the newly discovered world. The Muscovy Company, founded in 1555, was the first English joint-stock company: unlike previous enterprises, the money invested in its shares remained with the company between voyages instead of being repaid after every voyage. Its jointness was its virtue and its security. Other companies soon followed: the Eastland, for the Baltic, in 1579, the Levant, for the eastern Mediterranean and all its links to the great trade routes of Asia in 1581, the Guinea, for West Africa, founded in 1588 and finally the East India Company, founded in 1600, to deal with the sub-continent of India and the Spice Islands beyond it, and to bring back to England the cottons and silks, the saltpetre and indigo, and above all the spices which those exotic and dangerous coasts could provide.

Potency, enlargement, drama and success were all built into the idea of a company. The application of this idea, and this word, to Bible translation was a real innovation, as was the scale of it. The six companies, each with a 'director' – a title that surely also carries a hint of efficient, modern commercial organisation – were originally envisaged to have nine members each, a total of fifty-four, a body of men nearly four times the size of any previous Bible enterprise.

There is also a hint of numerological order to this arrangement. Six is the number of the Trinity (3) multiplied by the number of testaments (2). Each company was to have eight members, giving a total of forty-eight Translators, with six directors supervising them. This is nowhere made explicit, but forty-eight is the number of apostles (12) multiplied by the number of evangelists (4). It may be, in an age deeply intrigued by the mystery of mechanical toys, by the mathematical wonders of interlocking numbers and by the charm of ingenious mechanisms (Robert Cecil, for one, collected such things with a passion), that the system James and Bancroft were setting up was, like a piece of Jacobean architecture or decoration, designed to be richly and intricately interrelated, because that too felt like the right and civilised way to do it.

Bancroft then issued the letter of instructions to the Translators. It is the central document in the story, the template against which the text is to be measured. Again, if we are to take Bancroft's words seriously, these were the king's own rules, Bancroft merely the transmitter of them. They are a remarkable insight into the workings of the royal mind. But the instructions are deeply encoded, concealing as much as they reveal, assuming as much as they make explicit. Exactly what they mean will emerge, but what is obvious from the start is that they exude a habit of orderliness: numbered, coherent, managerial and modern. They give a rather different picture of James and his advisers than history has chosen to remember.

It is worth analysing these instructions in some detail. There is no hint of inspiration, or even of prayerfulness, no idea that the Translators are to be in the right frame of mind. These are exact directions, state orders, not literary or theological suggestions. It is not as if inspiration was unheard of. Inspiration was an established part of literary and theological thought. And wild, inspired Blakean prophets of course appear in the Bible itself, writing down, as a phrase in the apocryphal book of Esdras unforgettably describes it, 'the wonderfull visions of the night, that were told, which they knew not'.

There is none of that. This is a job to be done with immense care and attention to detail. There are strong hints about the kind of language they were to employ – it should be conservative – but no guide as to the rhetoric or musicality of the translation. For that, Bancroft would have to rely on the literary instincts of his chosen scholars. A copy of the instructions, now in the University Library in Cambridge, is entitled simply 'The rules to be obserued in translation'. The sixteen separate instructions on two sheets are the record of an extremely efficient administrator at work. They are the scaffolding within which the King James translation was erected.

Rules 1 to 5 (numbered with a flourish in the manuscript) are concerned with continuity, with maintaining but regularising the Bible habits of the Elizabethan church, much like the other canons Bancroft was drawing up at the same time. This was necessary politics. To suggest that anything done in England over the last fifty years was not in itself excellent would play into the hands of the Roman Catholics. Were the English now admitting they had been in error all this time? Were they conceding what their Roman Catholic critics had been saying all along, that the official English version of the scriptures was unsatisfactory? That would have been poor politics.

1. *The ordinary Bible read in Church commonly called the Bishopps Bible, to be followed, and as little altered as the Truth of the Originall will permitt.*

The Bishops' Bible was acknowledged by everyone to be not as good as the Geneva Bible, which the king hated because of its marginal notes, but the Bishops' Bible was the official Bible and as such had to be respected. Its language was heavy with latinisms and strange phraseology, loathed by Puritans (one said he would prefer to read 'the alKoran'), and avoided phrases like 'a pissing she-mule' which the bishops thought vulgar. But that was its problem. The Bishops' Bible was too elevated for its own good, cloth-eared and inaccessible. Famously, instead of 'Cast thy bread upon the waters', the bishops had written, 'Lay thy bread upon wet faces'. Pompous, obscure and often laughable, it was never loved.

One account, perhaps unreliably, maintains that forty copies of the Bishops' Bible were run off by Robert Barker, the king's printer, and the sheets distributed to the Translators, unbound, for them to mark or amend. A copy of the Bishops' Bible does survive in the Bodleian Library in Oxford, marked as if with notes by a seventeenth-century Translator, in ways, as will emerge later, that are particularly revealing about the methods used. But the task was too serious for Rule 1 to be taken at face value: the Translators absorbed, copied and adapted from any source they wanted (Rule 14 says as much) and the Bishops' Bible is thought to have contributed no more than about 8 per cent of its phraseology to the King James Version. Vast quantities of linguistic scholarship and skill were to be assembled on this project, with scholars more than capable of teasing nuance and subtle meaning from Hebrew, Greek and even Aramaic scripts. They were not going to be hobbled by the rather hurried production of the Elizabethan bishops.

> 2. *The names of the Profyts and the holie Wryters, with the other Names in the text to be retayned, as near as may be, according as they are vulgarly used.*

Some Puritans maintained that the names of the great figures in the scriptures, all of which signify something – Adam meant 'Red Earth', Timothy 'Fear-God' – should be translated. The Geneva Bible, which was an encyclopaedia of Calvinist thought, including maps and diagrams, had a list of those meanings at the back and, in imitation of those signifying names, Puritans, particularly in their heartlands of Northamptonshire and the Sussex Weald, had taken to naming their children after moral qualities. Ben Jonson included characters called Tribulation Wholesome, Zeal-of-the-Land Busy and Win-the-fight Littlewit in *The Alchemist* (1610) and *Bartholomew Fair* (1614), and Bancroft himself had written about the absurdity of calling your children 'The Lord-is-near, More-trial, Reformation, More-fruit, Dust and many other such-like'. These were not invented. Puritan children at Warbleton in Sussex, the heartland of the practice, laboured under the names of Eschew-evil, Lament, No-merit, Sorry-for-sin, Learn-wisdom, Faint-not, Give-thanks and, the most popular, Sin-deny, which was landed on ten children baptised in the parish between 1586 and 1596. One family, the children of the curate Thomas Hely, would have been introduced by their proud father as Much-mercy Hely, Increased Hely, Sin-deny Hely, Fear-not Hely and sweet little Constance Hely. Bancroft, and this royal translation of the Bible, could give no credit to that half-mad denial of tradition. It was one that travelled to America with the Pilgrim Fathers. Among William Brewster's own children, landing at Plymouth Rock, were Fear, Love, Patience and Wrestling Brewster. It is one of the ironies of America's relationship to the King James Bible that, at the very beginning of the Massachusetts colony, the thinking of the colonists and of the Bible, which would in time come to seem like their national text too, could not have been further apart. The Pilgrim Fathers would undoubtedly have taken the Geneva Bible with them.

> 3. *The ould ecclesiasticall words to be kept viz. as the Word Churche not to be translated Congregation &c.*

Bancroft, and almost certainly the king, was not prepared to give any ground in the language of the translation to the Presbyterians (who denied any scriptural authority to bishops) or Separatists (who would in time call themselves Independents and then Congregationalists). This was one of the oldest nubs of Bible translation. William Tyndale in his great 1526 groundbreaking translation of the New Testament had translated *ecclesia* not as 'church' but as 'congregation' and *presbyteros* not as 'priest' but as 'senior' (which he later changed, under pressure from Thomas More, to 'elder', as being the more English word). The entire meaning of the Reformation hinges on these differences. A presbyter, an elder, has no ancient priestly significance; he is not the conduit of God's grace, he does not interfere with the direct relationship of each soul to God, nor, in Luther's famous phrase, with the priesthood of all believers. If presbyter is what the scripture says, what need is there of bishops and archbishops? And if *ecclesia* means not church but congregation, what relevance to God can there be in the elaborate and expensive superstructure of an established church and the grotesque indulgences of its officers? Was the true meaning of the word *ecclesia* not a reproach to the habits of even such a godly bishop as Thomas Morton who when travelling by coach 'had always some choice or useful book, which he either read himself, or else caused a Chaplaine as his *Amanuensis* to reade unto him, who attended on his Journeying'? Did *ecclesia* really mean old men riding about the countryside as comfortably as if in a first-class railway compartment? And monopolising the funds of the true church to do so? It was to avoid questions of that kind, redolent of the profound political and social subversiveness which lies within the Reformation, that the old words had to be kept.

> 4. *When a word hath divers Significatons, that to be kept wch hath ben most commonly used by the most of the ancient Fathers being agreeable to the proprietie of ye place and the analogie of fayth.*

The Church of England, like the Church of Rome, but unlike the more fully reformed churches of Europe, relied for its understanding of the often complex texts of scripture on the ancient inherited traditions of Christianity, the statements and resolutions of the councils of the early church and the great body of patristic scholarship, in particular those church fathers – above all Jerome, St John Chrysostom, Augustine and Origen – of whom sixteenth-century English scholars, including several of the Translators, had made a particular study. This instruction is part of that widespread Reformation phenomenon, the search for primitive authenticity, for avoiding all hint of dreaded 'innovation', looking for true meaning in the most ancient and hence the most reliable texts. This too is a mark of the modern: a historical consciousness and a sense that the world now has fallen away from the more perfect state in which it once existed.

> 5. *The Division of the Chapters to be altered either not at all, or as little as may be if necessity soe requier.*

The king seals his first point: the new Bible is to look and feel as much as possible like the old.

Having established the grounds of continuity, the Rules then move on to deal with the question of commentary and explanation. The sixth instruction, repeating James's outburst at Hampton Court, was in many ways the richest:

> 6. *Noe marginal notes att all to be affixed, but only for ye explanation of ye Hebrew or Greeke Words, which cannot without some circumlocution soe breifly and fitly be expressed in ye Text.*

A full exploration of this fascinating rule must wait until later – so much flows from it – but its bones are clear. The kind of notes with which the Geneva Bible was littered, so violently disliked by James, were not to be admitted. But the crucial point is this: there were to be no marginal notes 'att all', not even those which might conform to the ideology of the established Jacobean church. The text, as all good Protestants might require, was to be presented clean and sufficient of itself, except where the actual words of the original were so opaque that a 'circumlocution' might not explain them within the text. 'Circumlocution' did not mean then quite what it means now. Thomas Wilson in *The arte of rhetorique*, published in 1553 and in use throughout the sixteenth century, had described circumlocution as 'a large description either to sett forth a thyng more gorgeouslie, or else to hyde it'. The words of this translation, then, could embrace both gorgeousness and ambiguity, did not have to settle into a single doctrinal mode but could embrace different meanings, either within the text itself or in the margins. This is the heart of the new Bible as an irenicon, an organism that absorbed and integrated difference, that included ambiguity and by doing so established peace. It is the central mechanism of the translation, one of immense lexical subtlety, a deliberate carrying of multiple meanings beneath the surface of a single text. This single rule lies behind the feeling which the King James Bible has always given its readers that the words are somehow extraordinarily freighted, with a richness which few other texts have ever equalled. Again and again, the Jacobean Translators chose a word not for its clarified straightforwardness (which had been Tyndale's focus in the 1520s and '30s, and the Geneva Calvinists' in the 1550s) but for its richness, its suggestiveness, its harmonic resonances. That is the heart of the irenicon: divergence held within a singularity, James's Arcadian vision made word.

> 7. *Such quotations of places to be marginally sett downe, as shall serve for fitt reference of one Scripture to an other.*

The Bible was to be seen, importantly, as one text. The Hebrew Scriptures of the Old Testament were a foretelling and a foreshadowing of the New. Each had their part, as James told his son Prince Henry:

> The whole Scripture is dyted [dictated] by Gods Spirit . . . to instruct and rule the whole Church militant to the end of the world: It is composed of two parts, the Olde and New Testament: The ground of the former is the Lawe, which sheweth our sinne, and containeth iustice: the ground of the other is Christ, who pardoning sinne containeth grace.

Any edition of the Bible, relying on the voluminous commentaries of the early Christian Fathers, needed to sew these parts together. Grace was to be seen in the light of justice, and vice versa.

Having established the role of continuity, and an atmosphere of non-contentiousness, the Rules then move on to the mechanics at the heart of the translation, the precise workings of the joint enterprise. Rules 8, 9 and 10 lay out the geography of co-operation, the precise system by which individual understanding and scholarship was to be integrated into a single scriptural whole. Can James's habit of thought be seen here? Perhaps. His years in Scotland had been devoted to reconciling warring interests, to getting factious parties to work together, and the reporting structures which the Rules establish are evidence of an almost obsessive need for agreement and unity. All the frustrations James was experiencing with a recalcitrant, unco-operative, fissive, argumentative and Anglocentric parliament could find their outlet here. The body of Translators was to be an academy of order, coherence and mutual respect.

The level of integration rises progressively through each of these three rules. The first, Rule 8, is about the workings within each of the six companies:

> 8. *Every particuler man of each company to take ye same chapter or chapters, and having translated or amended them severally by himselfe where he thinks good, all to meete together, confer what they have done, and agree for their Parts what shall stand.*

This was where the bulk of the work was to be done. Each member of each company, alone – 'severally by himselfe', no conferring allowed – was to translate or amend all the chapters in his allotted section. Only then were they to meet together, discuss the text and decide on their final submission. This too is a recipe for richness, a broadening of the mouth of the net before it narrows to a conclusion. It is the idea of a company at work, individual contributions tied to a common purpose and avoiding what would have been seen as either the Roman – over-heavy supervision from above – or the 'libertine' error, too great a release of unsupervised, individual energies. This Rule is, in other words, a portrait of the Jacobean ideal.

The next Rule then extends the principle:

> 9. *As one company hath dispatched any one booke in this manner they shall send it to the rest to be considered of seriously and judiciously: for His Majestie is verie carefull of this poynt.*

This was the only moment at which Bancroft's Rules mention the king. It implies something about their relationship. Bancroft is clearly the author of the Rules as they stand, but he had clearly had deep discussions with the king about what they should contain. They are in other words a translation and formalisation by Bancroft of the king's intentions.

The point James was particularly concerned with is an interesting one. Each company had to supervise the work of every other. What was the sub-text of that? It surely had some suspicion built into it. Not every company was to be relied on to do the work as the king would like it. In Rule 13, he would name Lancelot Andrewes, Dean of Westminster, as chairman or director of one of the six companies. His responsibility was to be the opening books of the Hebrew scriptures, from Genesis to the second Book of Kings. A second company, also based at Westminster, was to be chaired by William Barlow, Dean of Chester, royal chaplain, fulsome flatterer, the man Bancroft had already commissioned to produce an official account of the Hampton Court Conference. Barlow had skewed his account in the bishops' favour: another safe pair of hands. Barlow and his team were to translate the New Testament Epistles. Four other companies, two from Oxford and two from Cambridge, were to be chaired by the King's Professors of Hebrew (for the rest of the Old Testament) and of Greek (for the Apocrypha and the rest of the New Testament) in each place.

The king could clearly trust the two Westminster companies, chaired and directed by those loyal servants of the Crown. But what about the four Oxford and Cambridge companies? James would have known of Cambridge as the seed-bed of the English Presbyterian movement in the 1580s and '90s. Laurence Chaderton, Master of Emmanuel, whom he had attempted to humiliate at Hampton Court, was bound to be on one of the Cambridge committees. And he would be joined by others of his persuasion. The same would apply to John Reynolds at Oxford. Was this Rule 9, over which the king was so exercised, an attempt to keep those Puritans, moderate as they were, within bounds?

Bancroft then applied belt and braces to the mechanism of mutual supervision. There was, finally, to be a general meeting at which the final, final text could be agreed:

> 10. *If any Company, upon ye review of ye books so sent, really doubt, or differ uppon any place, to send them word thereof, note the place, and withal send their reasons; to which if they consent not, the difference to be compounded at ye generall meetinge, which is to be of the chiefe persons of each company, at ye ende of ye worke.*

By the time they emerged from the general meeting, the words of the King James Bible would have gone through at least four winnowing processes. Nothing was being left to chance.

Bancroft wasn't satisfied with that. His final clutch of Rules are thick with an anxiety that things might go wrong. Again and again he introduces the words of hierarchy and control.

> 11. *When any place of speciall obscuritie is doubted of, letters to be directed* by authority *to send to any learned man in the land, for his iudgment of such a place.*

'Every Bishopp', Rule 12, was to admonish his clergy and to ask for their 'particular observations'. He names the directors of each company (Rule 13) and then in Rule 14 the other sixteenth-century English translations that are to be consulted: 'Tindall's, Matthews, Coverdales, Whitchurch's, Geneva'. The Bishops' Bible is not mentioned because that is the ground against which all other translations are to be judged, but the list summarises the great tradition of English Reformation Bibles. 'Tindall' is of course William Tyndale, the pioneer in the 1520s and '30s, finally garrotted and burnt in 1536 on a Flemish bonfire, a martyr to the English scriptures. 'Matthews, Coverdales, Whitchurch's' are the three versions of the Bible, all heavily dependent on Tyndale, which the English Crown sponsored and approved of under Henry VIII and Edward VI. 'Geneva' is the English Calvinist edition first produced by Englishmen exiled by Queen Mary in the 1550s. The notion of jointness, of this translation being a national enterprise, extends beyond the limits of the early seventeenth century to embrace nearly eighty years of effort and scholarship. The list is unremarkable except for what it leaves out: no mention of the great translation made by the English Catholics in exile at Douai near Rheims. The Translators ignored this omission.

Finally, in Rule 15, the last element of control. Yet further 'Ancient and Grave Divines, in either of the Universities', were to ensure that passages and references translated one way in the Old Testament were translated concordantly in the New. There had been ferocious controversies throughout the sixteenth century over precisely this problem. Distressingly, in the New Testament, Christ and the apostles, when quoting from the Hebrew scriptures, tended to use not the original Hebrew texts themselves but the Greek words of the Septuagint, the translation of the Old Testament made at Alexandria in about 130 BC. Often, even in the best texts, the words of the Septuagint do not faithfully reproduce the meanings of the Hebrew scriptures. Could Christ and the apostles have been wrong? Could the omniscient God, in the form of Jesus, be ignorant of his own word? It was clear that the standard of scholarship among Christ's disciples was despicable. The Greek of the New Testament was coarse and clumsy, a steep descent from the heights of fifth-century Athenian elegance, 'countrified and simple' according to Erasmus, or apparently 'concocted', as Charles Bradlaugh, the Victorian atheist described the Gospels, 'by illiterate, half-starved visionaries in some dark corner of a Graeco-Syrian slum'. Paul garbled quotations from Isaiah, Mark muddled Isaiah with Malachi, Luke included the name of Canain in a genealogy which was not there in the Hebrew Genesis, Matthew left out three kings in his genealogy of Jesus, then misquoted both the Hebrew and the Septuagint before attributing something said by Zechariah to Jeremiah. In a text which was said to have been dictated by God, this was an agonising and difficult problem. 'One should tremble before each letter of the Bible', Luther had said, 'more than before the whole world.' God was in every syllable and 'no iota is in vain'. How modern scholarship could approach such a problem was something which only the most ancient and gravest divines could solve. It is a measure of James's and of Bancroft's joint ambition that they were willing to try. All that remained was to choose the men themselves.

FIVE

I am for the medium
in all things

For the word of God is quicke and powerfull, and sharper than
any two edged sword, pearcing euen to the diuiding asunder of
soule and spirit, and of the ioynts and marrowe, and is a discerner
of the thoughts and intents of the heart.

Hebrews 4:12

he new Jacobean atmosphere of tolerance, discussion
and openness – set within a frame of a new kind of
royal, gilded, fatherly divinity – had begun to have
its effect. A flood of English Roman Catholics started
to return from the European continent. In the summer of 1603,
a pair of futile, ill-conceived and half-related plots by Catholic
extremists had been foiled when English Catholics loyal to James
had betrayed them. The plotters and their friends were the luna-
tic fringe of Catholic opinion, and the mainstream, including
the Jesuits, considered the plots 'impudent folly': impudent
because they threatened the establishment of order in England;
foolish because persuasion and influence, the 'feigning, suing,
and such-like' at which the age excelled, was clearly the route
to success. It soon emerged that the Jesuits themselves had
betrayed the plotters to the Privy Council, having more allegiance to their own future prospects than to their co-religionists.

James was filled with gratitude. Although the Jesuit betrayal
of the plots was probably the result of a power struggle between

different groups of English Catholics, the effect was precisely the kind of inclusive politics James had always dreamed of. Here were Catholics displaying allegiance to a declaredly Protestant throne. It was a new world order, an irenic wholeness embracing them all. James's response was to give them a break. For a year they would no longer have to pay the £20 a month fines which was the Elizabethan penalty for not attending church. The new age might be dawning.

The state's reaction to the two plots is a map of the age: the plotters themselves were ruthlessly and uncompromisingly suppressed, some executed, others left to fester in the Tower. They included Robert Cecil's longstanding enemy, Sir Walter Raleigh, who by modern standards of evidence was clearly not guilty of involvement in either plot. But he was a rival to Cecil and as such was ruthlessly removed from the scene, ridiculed and abused by the Crown lawyers at a show trial in Winchester and condemned, finally, to seventeen years of imprisonment. Beyond the guilty and the dangerous, however, James held out the prospect of an all-encompassing embrace to anyone and anything that might fall within the dream of national community. Destroy the extremists, whether Catholic plotters or those Puritans who could not conform to the habits of the Church of England, embrace a broad stretch of middle ground. That is the heart of all Jacobean policy – it is what any well-managed, civilised government would do – and of that middle ground the new Bible was to become both the expression and the symbol, the code and guidebook to a rich, majestic and holy kingdom.

In the summer and autumn of 1604, after parliament had been prorogued, both parts of the strategy came into play. Bancroft, and at times James himself, goading on his bishops, began to harry those Puritans who would not sign up to the idea that the surplice, the cross, confirmation, the use of rings in weddings and all the other remnants of symbolic religion in the English Church were perfectly good and holy practices. Those who wouldn't sign, or 'subscribe' as the word at the time went, were expelled, a total of about eighty ministers from a body of about 8,000. Ninety-nine per cent of the Church of England, in other words, thought conformity the better path. Among the one per cent who did not were those who would in time become the leaders of the Pilgrim Fathers.

At the same time, Bancroft began to hire the men for the great translation and here it was breadth and inclusiveness which dictated the choice. The first Westminster company, charged with translating the first books of the Bible, had Lancelot Andrewes, Dean of Westminster Abbey, as its director. He was known as 'the Angell in the pulpitt', the man more versed in modern and ancient tongues than any other in England, who could serve, it was thought, as 'INTERPRETER-GENERAL' at the Day of Judgement, but he had other skills, and another track record, which confirmed him as a member of the core establishment and recommended him to Bancroft and the king.

He had been used before in important political work, some fifteen years earlier when Bancroft was working for Whitgift rooting out the Separatist congregations in London. Andrewes, then in his mid-thirties and already recognised as the coming man, and as the cleverest preacher in England, could be relied on to do Bancroft's work for him. Highly detailed accounts survive of what Andrewes did for the ecclesiastical establishment: a representation, in other words, of what Bancroft would have known of him, the grounds on which he chose him as one of the principal Translators. Once again, it is not a dignified picture: his governing qualities are those of a man who knows how to exercise power.

Through the second half of the 1580s, the more extreme Separatist puritans, who considered each congregation a self-sufficient church of Christ, became the target of a campaign led by Richard Bancroft. They were to be found in private houses all around London, holding private conventicles in which their inspirational preachers were, it was reported to Bancroft, 'esteemed as godds'. Bancroft, who in another life would clearly have been an excellent detective, had his spies in place. As a central player in the Crown establishment, he would have had an array of inducements to hand: money, prospects, threats, the persuasive words of a man with access to power. Those tools gave him access to all kinds of secret meetings. 'After the Minister hath saluted everie one, both man and woman, at theire comynge into the Chamber with a kysse', one report of such a Separatist meeting described, shocked at its impropriety,

> a large Table beinge prepared for the purpose (which holdeth fortie or fiftie persons) he taking the chayre at the end thereof, the rest sitt down everie one in order: . . . the Minister hymself having receaved [communion] in both kyndes: the breade and the wyne which is left, passeth downe, and everye man without more a doe is his owne Carver.

The state church could not tolerate the freedom or the priestlessness of such behaviour. Many Separatists – and they were overwhelmingly young, idealistic people, a tiny minority, perhaps no more than a couple of hundred in England as a whole – fled to the Netherlands but others were arrested and, eventually, some fifty-two were held for long periods in the string of hideous London gaols: the Clink, the Gatehouse, the Fleet, Newgate, the Counter Woodstreet, the Counter Poultry, Bridewell and the White Lion, some of the prisoners shut in the 'most noisome and vile dungeons', without 'bedds, or so much as strawe to lye upon . . . and all this, without once producing them, to anie Christian triall where they might have place given them, to defend themselves'. One of them, the eighteen-year-old Roger Waters, was kept in irons for more than a year.

Their leaders, honest, fierce men, the spiritual forebears of the future Massachusetts colonists, were to be interrogated (or 'conversed with' as Bancroft described it; the meetings were known among the Separatists themselves as 'Spanish conferences') by the more brilliant and trustworthy members of the Church of England. Andrewes was at their head. Bancroft instructed him to interrogate Henry Barrow, the leading Separatist who had been arrested in 1587 and kept in the Fleet.

Andrewes visited the gaol accompanied by another divine, William Hutchinson. Their descent into the Separatists' hell is a moment of sudden, film-like intensity, when the passionate realities of early modern England come starkly to life. The entire context of the King James Bible is dramatised in these prison meetings: holiness meets power, or at least one version of holiness meets another; the relative claims of society and the individual, and the legitimacy of those claims, clash; the individual conscience grates against the authority structures of an age which senses incipient anarchy at every turn and so is obsessed with order; the candid plays against the cynical, worldliness against a kind of stripped Puritan idealism; and the godly comes face to face with the political.

The purpose of the visiting churchmen, Barrow wrote later, was 'to fish from [him] som matter, wheruppon they might accuse them to their holy fathers the bishops'. This was true: a good interrogation would be a good career move. Other Translators were nosing around these ratty dungeons: Hadrian à Saravia, a major propagandist of the Divine Right of Kings, was interrogating a Separatist called Daniel Studley, also in the Fleet. The Thomas Sparkes who had so meekly and dumbly sat at the Hampton Court Conference was to be found at this time trying to convince the young Roger Waters of his sins, as he hung in chains in the worst of the stinking pits of Newgate gaol, known as the Limbo.

With Barrow, in March 1590, Hutchinson and Andrewes began kindly. They were sitting in the parlour of the Fleet prison (one of the better of the London prisons, 'fit for gentlemen'). Hutchinson told the Separatist that he wanted 'to confer brotherly with you concerning certain positions that you are said to hold'. It was a gentle beginning and Barrow responded in the same vein. He was keen 'to obtain such conference where the Book of God might peaceably decide all our controversy'.

That phrase, innocuous as it might sound, was salt in the eyes for Andrewes. It released a flood of hostile questions. All the issues of order and authority, the great political questions of the day, streamed out over his prisoner-conversant. 'Whie,' Andrewes said, 'the booke of God cannot speake, which way should that decide owr controversies?' That was the central question of the Reformation: did Christians not need a church to interpret God for them? Or could they have access to the godhead without help, with all the immediacy of the inspired? Barrow replied in the spirit of Luther: each soul could converse with God direct, unmediated by any worldly church, his thoughts and actions to be interpreted by the words of scripture itself.

> DR ANDREWES: But the spirits of men must be subject unto men, will you not subject your spirit to the judgment of men?
> BARROW: The spirit of the prophets must be subject to the prophets, yet must the prophets judge by the word of God. As for me I willingly submit my whole faith to be tried and judged by the word of God, of all men.
> DR ANDREWES: All men cannot judge, who then shal judge the Word?
> BARROW: The word, and let every one that judgeth take hede that he judge aright thereby; 'Wisdom is justified of her children.' (Matthew 11:19)

Andrewes thought he spotted error. 'This savoreth of a pryvat spyrit,' he said. Nothing was more damning in his lexicon than that phrase. The privateness of the Puritan spirit was its defining sin, its arrogance and withdrawal in the face of communal and inherited wisdom, treating the word of God, the scriptures, not as a common inheritance, whose significance could be understood only within the tradition that had grown and flowered around it, but as a private guidebook to a personal and selfish salvation. The heart of the Puritan error was that social divisiveness, that failure to join in, its stepping outside the necessity of order, its assumption that the Puritan himself was a member of God's elect, and the rest could look to the hindmost. How could a society be based on that predestinarian arrogance? Increasingly, for churchmen such as Andrewes, it seemed that the true church could only be inclusive, one in which God's grace would descend on believers not through some brutal predestinarian edict but through the sacraments, through the ceremony of the church.

Separateness was of course an unacceptable political position. It severed the links on which order relied and carried the seeds of anarchy within it. The fact that the words of Paul in his second letter to the Corinthians sanctioned such separatism was for Andrewes secondary. The Separatists quoted the passage at every turn: 'Come out from among them, and bee yee separate, saieth the Lord, and touch not the vncleane thing, and I will receiue you, And will bee a Father vnto you, and ye shall bee my sonnes and daughters, saith the Lord Almightie.' The response of Andrewes and Bancroft to the emphasis placed on those words, to its implication of God-sanctioned individual freedom, was brief: it was 'libertine', meaning the thought typical of a man 'loose in religion, one that thinks he may doe what he listeth', as a 1604 dictionary defined it.

Barrow responded sharply. It was not a private spirit but 'the spirit of Christ and his Apostles'. They had been happy to be judged by the word of God and so was Barrow. This, for Andrewes, so crushingly aware of his own sin, was too much.

DR ANDREWES: What, are you an apostle?
BARROW: No, but I have the spirit of the apostles.
DR ANDREWES: What, the spirit of the apostles?

BARROW: Yea, the spirit of the apostles.
DR ANDREWES: What, in that measure?
BARROW: In that measure that God hath imparted unto
me, though not in that measure that the apostles had,
by anie comparison, yet the same spirit. There is but
one spirit.

That was not an unreasonable answer: God had blown his spirit into Adam, and it was acceptable to think that the life of men was a divine gift. But Andrewes, revealing himself here in a way he would rarely do later in life, curiously narrowed and harsh like Bancroft at the conference, clung to his hostility. They argued over the difference between a schism and a sect. Then, in an emblematic moment of the English Reformation, angry, impassioned, pedantic, scholarly, they called for a dictionary. The heretic and his interrogator pored together over the Greek–Latin Lexicon of Joannes Scapula (Basel, 1580) to try and sort out the etymologies of the two words, but they could come to no shared conclusion.

Andrewes then uttered one of the most despicable remarks he ever made. Barrow said his imprisonment had been horrible. He had been there for three years and the loneliness of it, the sheer sensory deprivation, the nastiness of the conditions, had sunk him deep into depression. Andrewes's reply, witty, supercilious, a pastiche of the sympathetic confessor, is still shocking 400 years later: 'For close imprisonment', he told Barrow, 'you are most happie. The solitarie and contemplative life I hold the most blessed life. It is the life I would chuse.' It is Henry Barrow, martyr to his beliefs, who emerges from this confrontation as the holy man. 'You speak philosophically,' he told Andrewes with some self-control,

> but not Christianly. So sweete is the harmonie of God's grace
> unto me in the congregation, and the conversation of the
> saints at all times, as I think my self as a sparrow on the howse
> toppe when I am exiled thereby. But could you be content also,

Mr Androes, to be kept from exercise and ayre so long togeather? These are also necessarie to a natural body.

The poor man was lonely, longing for his friends and for a sight of the sky, from which the intolerance of the state had excluded him. Andrewes's breathtaking insouciance continued until the last. In conversation, he had used the word 'luck'. For fundamentalists such as Barrow, there was no such thing: all was ordained, everything from the death of a sparrow to the execution of a heretic was the working out of God's providence. Calvin had written, in a famous passage, that to believe in luck was a 'carnal' way to look at the world. Barrow told the departing Andrewes 'there was no fortune or *luck*. To proove *luck* [Andrewes] torned in my Testament to the 10 of Luke, verse 31, "By chance there went down a certain priest that way." And torned in a leafe uppon the place, and as he was going out willed me to consider of it.'

That folded-down page of the Puritan's Bible, Andrewes's all-too-complacent knowledge of the scriptural text, 'the poor worne bodie' of the prematurely aged Barrow (he was about thirty-seven, a couple of years older than Andrewes) standing in the room, silenced by the rising self-congratulatory confidence of the young Master of Pembroke College, prebendary of St Paul's, vicar of St Giles Cripplegate, a candidate for the bishopric of Salisbury, sweeping out of the prison parlour door, with his departing quip, his patronising flourish: could you ask for a more chilling indictment of established religion than that?

Three years later Barrow's life ended in execution, for denying the authority of bishops, for denying the holiness of the English Church and its liturgy and denying the authority over it of the queen. Andrewes saw him again on the eve of his death. The prisoner had been transferred to Newgate, to the Limbo itself, and he was high on his impending martyrdom. He was reminded by one of those present of the Englishmen who had been martyred by the Roman Catholics in the reign of Queen

Mary for their defence of the very church which Barrow now denied. '"These holy bonds of mine" he replied, (and therewith he shooke the fetters which he did wear) "are much more glorious than any of theirs."' Andrewes argued with him again over points in the Geneva Bible. Barrow would have none of it and he told his adversary that his 'time now was short unto this world, neyther were we to bestow it unto controversies'. He was finally executed early in the morning on 6 April at Tyburn, where the mallows and bulrushes were just sprouting in the ditches.

Andrewes could put the knife in. What little one can judge from contemporary portraits – the Jacobean image is so much less revealing than the Jacobean word – shows a narrow and shrewd face, a certain distance in the eyes, as if the person had withdrawn an inch or two below the surface of the skin, but that surface was *bien soigné*, a well-trimmed beard, a well-brushed moustache. He could look the church's adversaries in the eye, and he was clever enough to slalom around the complexities of theological dispute: not only a great scholar but a government man, aware of political realities, able to articulate the correct version of the truth. He was a trusty (a Jacobean word, used in that sense), and useful for his extensive network of connections. It is clear that in 1604 he played a large part in selecting the men for his, and perhaps also for Barlow's, company. Several themes emerge: there is a strong Cambridge connection (Andrewes had been an undergraduate and fellow there and was still Master of Pembroke College); an emphasis on scholarly brilliance – more so than in the other companies; a clear ideological bent in choosing none who could be accused of Puritanism, however mild, and several who would later emerge as leading anti-Calvinists in the struggles of the 1620s; there was also a connection with Westminster Abbey, where Andrewes had been appointed dean on the recommendation of Robert Cecil; and, stemming from that, a clear thread of Cecil influence. In this marrying of leverage and discrimination, it is a microcosm of the workings of Jacobean England: the right men were chosen and part of their qualifications for being chosen was their ability to work the systems of deference and power on which the society relied.

They met in the famous Jerusalem Chamber, the fourteenth-century room in what had been the abbot's lodgings at Westminster, where Henry IV had died; now it was part of Andrewes's deanery. It was where the chapter usually met, on which Andrewes had secured for his brother Nicholas the valuable post of registrar for life. Such nepotism was habitual and habitually condemned. Ten years before, Andrewes had preached at St Paul's (in Latin), lashing the indigent clergy for their corruption: 'You are extremely careful to enrich your own sons and daughters,' he had told them. 'You are so careful of the heirs of your flesh that you forget your successors.' One of the Translators, in the Cambridge company dealing with the central section of the Old Testament, was Andrewes's brother Roger. Judging by every other aspect of Roger's life we know of, he was almost certainly there on Lancelot's recommendation: when Lancelot had become Master of Pembroke, he made Roger a fellow; when he became Bishop of Chichester, he made Roger a prebendary, archdeacon and chancellor of the cathedral. When Lancelot moved on to Ely in 1609, Roger became a prebendary there and also Master of Jesus College, Cambridge, which was in the gift of the Bishop of Ely. At Jesus, Roger was not a success. He argued with the fellows, neglected the financial affairs of the college and was finally sacked in 1632 for stealing college funds. Meanwhile, when in 1616 his saintly brother was translated to Winchester, the richest see in England, Roger received another prebend there.

Roger was certainly on his brother's side against the reformists in the church and it is clear that Andrewes's selection for the first Westminster company was made at least partly on the basis of that kind of political orientation. Whom could he rely on not to make Puritan-style difficulties? One can make out several layers within the company. First, there are the high-level church politicians and apologists for the regime. Andrewes took on Hadrian à Saravia, a Protestant Fleming who, like Andrewes, had become a client of the Cecils, had interrogated Separatists in London gaols, had been appointed a prebendary at Westminster where Andrewes was dean, and, like Andrewes, held several other positions in the church guaranteeing a satisfactory income from which he could propagandise on behalf of church and Crown. Although Saravia was seventy-three in 1604, he and Andrewes were soulmates, sharing a view of government and the episcopate, deeply conservative, both authoritarian and inclusionist, and opposed both to revision and controversy.

The third member of this high-level leadership of the group was John Overall, Dean of St Paul's, one of Andrewes's most loyal supporters and friends. It is significant that neither he nor Saravia was acknowledged as a great Hebrew scholar. Saravia was a general linguist, Overall a classicist, who been a Greek lecturer and Regius Professor of Divinity at Cambridge; but both were members of the anti-Puritan party in the church and, at this leadership level, attitude mattered more than qualifications. Overall himself would later overstep the mark, arguing at the convocation of the church in 1606 that obedience by all subjects was owed to a king simply through the fact that he was the king, not through any right or legitimacy he might have. Overall, in other words, was perfectly happy to worship and obey power itself. Legitimacy mattered less than potency; he was a pure authoritarian. To James's own credit, the king repudiated such views. They were too extreme and took no account of the inclusive and fatherly nature of kingship. It is easy enough to portray James as an absolutist in waiting, but he wasn't. As James himself said, 'I am for the medium in all things.'

With these men, it is often difficult to penetrate beneath the slew of titles and appointments, of publicly declared positions and overt alliances, but a correspondence survives, not of Overall himself but of his secretary, John Cosin, who worked for him when Overall later became Bishop of Coventry and Lichfield and then of Norwich. Cosin would have his own famous career, as Bishop of Durham and Master of Peterhouse in Cambridge where 'A glorious new altar was set up, and mounted on steps, to which the master, fellowes, schollers, bowed, and were enjoyned to bow by Doctor Cosins. There were basins, candelstickes, tapers standing on it, a great crucifix hanging over it,' and other 'ceremonious and babylonish practices' which made Cosins one of the most loathed of all anti-Puritan churchmen during the Civil War. But there is one letter from his time as John Overall's secretary which is suddenly revealing of this world beneath its skin.

Overall had just been promoted from the relatively junior and impoverished see of Coventry and Lichfield to become Bishop of Lincoln, one of the plums of the English Church. Cosin wrote to his successor, the secretary of the new Bishop of Coventry and Lichfield, to tell him how to maximise his own revenue. (This new bishop, incidentally, was the saintly Thomas Morton who in 1603 had worked to save the lives of plague victims in York while Lancelot Andrewes was relaxing at Chiswick.) The occasion for Cosin's letter was the visitation, the moment, usually every three years, when the bishop investigated the state of affairs in his own diocese. Every minister had to appear before the diocesan registrar (or 'Register') to show him the licence by which he was allowed to preach. (The licence was a tool of conformity: it would be granted only if the minister had explicitly signed up to the canons which Richard Bancroft had drawn up for the English Church.) This was the moment at which the bishop's secretary could make his killing.

To my verie loving friend, Mr Baddeley, secretary to ye Rt. Reverend Father in God ye Ld. Bp. of Coven. & Lichfield, These in London.

MR BADDELEY

Your best course wilbe, as mine was, in your Lord's Visitation, when their instruments are consigned, to sit with the Register, and demaunde of every minister their license, whereby you shall deprehend them which you want. One secret I will tell you, which I must entreat you to make a secret stil: vjd. a piece you may demaunde of every one of them, either licensed or not, for the exhibition of their license, and keep the profit to your self, howsoever the Register may perhaps challenge it. But I'le assure you they never yet had it . . . Collect the mony your selfe, els you may have some of it detein'd, as we had at first . . . I heare you leave not London yet this long while. If upon better remembrance and leisure I may thinke on anything to instruct you better, I shall not neglect that office to so good a friende. Thus in much hast I bid you hartily farewell.

Your assured
Jo. Cosin.

Norwch. Bp's. Pallace, Aprill 4, 1619

This is a rare sight of one of the sinews of the Jacobean church in action: private extortion by a high-level and ambitious church official of a little bribe or *pourboire* from the impoverished, simple rural clergy; a man looking out for his own, passing on a little tip by which advantage can be gained and the beginnings of a fortune made; and an awareness, in the insistence on the tip being kept secret, that it was wrong, that it ran full against the requirements of pastoral care which one sermon after another required of a bishop and his servants.

It is in the light of that letter, and of the feeling of impotent contempt with which Puritans looked on at this world of corrupt bishops and their officials, that the most famous story told about

John Overall must be seen. It is recorded by John Aubrey, the great seventeenth-century gossip, and is the kind of joky, subversive anecdote which the powerless always tell about the powerful. Whether it is true or not matters less than its atmosphere, which is like the stories that used to be told in Soviet Russia about the Nomenklatura: a behind-the-hands snigger fuelled by power on one side and by resentment and envy on the other.

It is to do with John Overall's lust. The poor man, who was forty-four in 1604, found it easier, he told his friends, to preach in Latin, which he had studied so hard and so long, and that he found it 'troublesome to speak English as a continued oration'. Despite (or perhaps because of?) that rather unworldly removal from everyday discourse, the dean fell in love with and married the sexiest girl in London. Anne Orwell was irresistible:

> Face she had of filbert hue
>> And bosom'd like a swan.
> Back she had of bended ewe
>> And waisted by a span.
> Hair she had as black as crow
>> From her head unto her toe,
> Down, down all over her,
>> Hey nonny, nonny no.

Even now there is no mistaking the desire in that. The world couldn't help but imagine the Dean of St Paul's in bed with his marvellous girl.

Sadly, or excitingly to his contemporaries, Overall was unable to satisfy Anne's sexual appetite and she eloped with the rather more glamorous Yorkshire squire, Sir John Selby. Overall sent a posse after her.

> The Dean of St Paul's did search for his wife
> And where d'ye think he found her?
> Even upon Sir John Selby's bed,
> As flat as any flounder.

Overall had her forcibly brought back to the deanery at St Paul's. London had never heard anything so hilarious. And what became of Anne? No word survives.

Several of Andrewes's team remain little more than names: Richard Clarke, a fellow of Christ's College, Cambridge, whose collected sermons were said to be 'a continent of mud'; Robert Tighe, vicar of All Hallows, Barking, the church in which Lancelot Andrewes had been christened; Geoffrey King, another Christ's man, and in time professor of Hebrew at Cambridge; and Francis Burleigh, who had been a scholar at Pembroke, Andrewes's own college. Even among the obscure, the connections continued to work. Those four have the look of workhorses, men flattered to be included, who could be asked to do much of the legwork, of which, if one considers the endless genealogies, or the delineation of the territories allotted to the seven tribes of Israel, there was a great deal.

Beside them, however, there was something else. It shouldn't be surprising that as broad and complex a figure as Lancelot Andrewes should have an inclusive and eclectic taste in companions and colleagues. Alongside Overall and the exotic Saravia (his parentage was partly Spanish) were three other men who had pursued a far from straightforward course as theologians and divines. The most eccentric (although a committed member of Andrewes's ceremonious, anti-Puritan tendency in the church, later pilloried by the Puritans for it) was Richard Thomson, born in Holland of English parents, a brilliant linguist, which perhaps goes without saying, who would later be calumniated by William Prynne as 'a debosh'ed English Dutchman, who seldom went one night to bed sober'. Thomson lived hard and fast and, although a fellow of Clare Hall in Cambridge, was also part of much racier and riskier London set. Extraordinarily, for a Translator of the

King James Bible, he was known as one of the wittiest of all translators ('the great interpreter') of the wildly obscene epigrams written by the poet Martial in the Rome over which Nero presided. Something about the knowing, post-austerity cynicism and wickedness of Martial's world appealed to Jacobean England and many contemporary gallants tried their hand at English versions.

How does this sit alongside a career in the Church of England? It is a true conundrum, perhaps the sharpest of all the instances where the remarkable work of biblical translation comes out of lives that might have been designed not to produce it. But Martial has a great deal to teach any writer. Everything he composed was honed to exactness. Every sentiment he expressed had been examined by a fierce intelligence. There is nothing lax, soft or expected in Martial's epigrams: they are the product of a mind that has worked. Their satirical edge is created, as in all satire, not by the satirist but by the society that is being satirised.

Anyone who could match Martial in his art, who was also a man of the church, and an acknowledged linguist, with correspondents in Italy, France and Germany, was a man to have in your company. The disciple of Martial would not accept the second-rate; and his mind would be bright enough to summon the best. A revealing gap opens up here. Andrewes could happily see a good, God-fearing, straight-living, honest and candid man like Henry Barrow condemned to death; and a debauched, self-serving degenerate like Thomson elevated to the highest company. Why? Because Barrow's separatism was a corrosive that would rot the very bonds of Jacobean order; because that order was both natural and God-given; and because nothing could be more sinful than subversion of that kind. Goodness, in other words, was not a moral but a political quality and nothing in Thomson's failings could approach the depth of Barrow's wickedness.

Besides, Andrewes could never be accused of priggishness. His belief in mercy was too real and his awareness of his own failings too strong. God's majesty and love, his power of forgiveness, Andrewes said every week in his private prayers,

> is tender, sweet, better than life;
> hating nothing that it hath made,
> neglecting neither the young ravens,
> nor the sparrows,
> bringing back the lost sheep on the shoulder,
> sweeping the house for the piece of silver,
> binding up the wounds of the half-dead,
> opening Paradise to the thief
> who is standing at the door and knocking.

Those are the words of the man who would always have had Richard Thomson in his company. He clearly loved him. When Andrewes became Bishop of Ely in 1609 he gave Thomson the living of Snailwell, a pretty and comfortable village a few miles from Newmarket, in the diocese of Ely, a living that afforded pleasurable ease, in which, like Noah, Thomson could plant his vineyard, cultivate his vines and feel rewarded for his self-indulgent life.

The director drafted in two others with rich and specialist experience. William Bedwell was both a leading mathematician and, because his readings in medieval mathematical studies had led him down this path, an Arabist, one of England's first. He was no admirer of Islam, being the author of a vituperative book on '*the blasphemous seducer Mohammed*', but he was captivated by the theological, medical and mathematical genius of the Arabs. Arabic, he was also convinced, was an invaluable tool in the interpretation of Hebrew. Andrewes also provided him with a living, in the village of Tottenham, north of London, to add to the one he already had at St Ethelburgh's, just up from the docks in the city. There, in April 1607, Bedwell gave communion to Henry Hudson and his crew, about to embark on their voyage in search of the north-west passage to Cathay.

That stretching, expanding world had a still more intimate part to play in the making of the translation. John Layfield, another Cambridge man, a Greek scholar from Trinity, was an explorer and prose writer of real distinction, who left one of the most civil-minded and generous accounts ever written of the English arrival in the New World. Another Translator, the egregious George Abbot, who will appear later, gave another account of 'the Americans' which is as poisonous as Layfield's is graceful. There was a crucial difference between them: Layfield had been to the New World, Abbot never had.

In 1596, the Earl of Cumberland, a man in the mould of Essex or Raleigh, intensely Protestant, intensely brave and intensely patriotic, wanting to see England as a standard bearer for reformed truth across the world, led an expedition to Puerto Rico. Layfield was his chaplain and his chronicler. What Layfield brought to this exciting subject – it was a violent and dangerous expedition; hundreds died; Cumberland himself very nearly drowned in his armour as he lay, wounded, under Spanish fire, unable to lift himself from the shallow waters of a Puerto Rican rio – was an unabashed manliness of style, a smart, brisk way of telling a story in which piety or an adopted moralism had no part. Layfield is completely au fait with the details of navigation, ordnance and the science of fortification. Chaplain he might have been, but there was nothing diminished in that status. Even before they leave Portsmouth, Layfield displays his gift for clear and dramatic narrative, for instant characterisation, for a scene brought utterly alert. It is March on the south coast of England:

> While we were at morning prayer, his Lordship happens to see a gallant of the company (purposely I name him not) reading of Orlando Furioso; to whom himselfe in person went presently after Service, all the Company being by, and having told him that we might looke that God would serve us accordingly, if we served not him better; bad him be sure

that if againe he tooke him in the like manner, he would cast his Booke over-boord, and turne himselfe out of the Ship.

The task of the first Westminster company was to bring to life some of the great narratives of the Bible, the legends of creation, the lives of Abraham, Isaac, Jacob, Joseph, Moses, Saul and David, Solomon and Elijah. Of course a vital sense of narrative was a qualification for the work. Layfield's chronicle is as bright-coloured an adventure as anything by Robert Louis Stevenson, a journey 'running West and by south, but bearing still to the Westward', with flocks of flying fishes skittering around their hull, the southern cross appearing over the tropical horizon, the sea changing colour as they head out into the deep Atlantic, 'whereas before it was a cleere azure, it then began to incline to a deeper blacke'.

Nothing about Layfield is cynical or even prejudiced. He meets the indigenes of Dominica with an open mind, even if amazed by 'their red painting, laid so on that if you touch it, you shall finde it on your finger'. But he uses no violent or oppressive language and evinces no horror at these alien people: 'They are men of good proportion, strong and straight limmed, but few of them tall, their wits able to direct them, to things bodily profitable.' They will swop 'any of their Commodities for an old Waste-coate, or but a Cap, yea but a paire of Gloves'. They long to acquire the language of their visitors – and the wonderful sight jumps to mind of American Indians learning English at the source, the pure and beautiful English of John Layfield, who was quite clearly entranced by the beauties of the still untrammelled Caribbean, its wonderful first-growth woods and its cooling waterfalls, its 'Parrots and Parrachetoes as common as Crowes and Dawes in England', the extraordinary grace of the Spanish settlements in Puerto Rico, which despite the heat that melted the glue which held their books together, and turned the English sweets they had brought with them into a gooey liquid, were 'exceedingly delightful'. Everywhere you looked were 'Guiavas, as bigge as a Peach like a very ripe great white Plum', lemons and limes, 'the goodliest Orenges that ever I saw', plains and lawns, estancias, wind- and watermills, delicious 'papaies, wild grapes as great as a good Musket-bullet, figs, pomegranates, muske-millions, pomecitrons . . . and soft, squeezable pineapples' the taste of which, Layfield wrote in ecstasy, 'I cannot liken it in the palate to any (me thinks) better then to very ripe Strawberries and Creame'.

Layfield was among the men who translated the famous opening chapters of Genesis. He would have had a hand in writing this:

> And out of the ground made the LORD God to grow euery tree that is pleasant to the sight, and good for food: the tree of life also in the midst of the garden, and the tree of knowledge of good and euill. And a riuer went out of Eden to water the garden.

As he did so he would have had in mind those incomparable forests of Dominica, where 'the trees doe continually maintaine themselves in a greene-good liking' – extraordinary phrase – 'partly of many fine Rivers, which to requite the shadow and coolenesse they receive from the Trees, give them backe againe, a continuall refresshing of very sweete and tastie water'. The seventeenth-century English idea of Paradise, a vision of enveloping lushness, was formed by the seduction of an almost untouched Caribbean.

SIX

The danger never dreamt of,
that is the danger

> Yee are all the children of light, and the children of the day: we
> are not of the night, nor of darkenesse.
>   But let vs, who are of the day, bee sober, putting on the
> brestplate of faith and loue; and for an helmet, the hope of
> saluation.
>   For God hath not appointed vs to wrath, but to obtain salu-
> ation by our Lord Iesus Christ.
>
> 1 Thessalonians 5:5, 8–9

hen the cataclysm. The entire world of the translation, and of its hopes for the future, was rocked and
very nearly shattered by an event which fell – or,
to be exact, almost fell – on Jacobean England in
November 1605: the attempt by a group of desperate and mar-
ginalised Catholic renegades and romantics – terrorists is the word
we would now use – to blow up the king, queen, princes, peers and
other members of parliament at its opening on 5 November. It
would come to define Jacobean England as much as September 11
2001 would shape the attitudes, fears and methods of revenge of
the western world in the first decade of the twenty-first century.

Most Jacobean English Catholics, like most twenty-first century Muslims, would not have dreamt of upsetting a status quo
in which, on the whole, they thrived. But a small and alienated
set of them were dreaming of a form of salvation which the
everyday and rather smug ordinariness of establishment life could

not provide. The state had elaborate, overlapping and interlocking security arrangements which had identified and tracked
some of these subversives, had infiltrated their networks, but had
not thought the threat serious enough to act against them. They
had concocted small plots and conspiracies and committed minor
outrages in the previous few years, but those had felt like irritants,
midgebites, not, in the end, threatening. There was a desire or
a hope alive in the early years of James's reign, as at the turn of
the third millennium, that in some ways history was over, that
it was possible to accommodate all shades of opinion in one
mutually beneficial society, that the threat of the Roman Church,
and of Spain, its military arm, belonged to the past. Both the
English and the Spanish had happily signed a peace treaty in the
summer of 1604 and after it trade boomed and customs dues
had soared. (Cloth exports alone would surge by 25 per cent in
the five years after the peace was signed.) *Enrichissez-vous* – 'God
make me rich,' as Ben Jonson wrote in one masque for his patron
Robert Cecil – was at the heart of establishment thinking in
1605 as much as 2001.

The terrorist attack blew that complacency apart. The king,
his family, his councillors and the whole range of English government had been within a few hours of death (or at least so Robert
Cecil led them to imagine). The English became fixated on
homeland security. An inclusive, irenic ideal of mutual benefit
was replaced by a defensive/aggressive complex in which all
Catholics, of all shades, never mind their degree of enthusiasm
for the planned attack, were, at least for a time, identified as the
enemy and required to subscribe to an oath of allegiance which
made it clear that their duty as citizens of England far overrode
any duty towards the whore of Rome. Parliament, which until
then had been dominated by a suspicion of Stuart profligacy,
crypto-Catholicism and Scottishness, now fell over itself to provide money, loyalty and support for the king. The state had
invaded and taken over the English conscience.

November 5 1605 changed the world in which the translation was being made, but also confirmed the Translators in some of their most deeply held beliefs. The plot acted on the Jacobean imagination as a drama of everything that should not be, the theatre of the wrong. It seemed to emerge from a dark, subterranean place, threatening the well-being of the world above it. But that very threat strengthened the vision on which the new Bible was already founded: it became more important than ever that England, that upper, well-lit country, needed a version of the scriptures that would bind together its people, its church, and its king.

Blackness was well-established as a mark of vice. At the very beginning of 1605, the queen had asked Ben Jonson to write a masque, an entertainment-cum-drama-cum-court ball, to be performed in Whitehall on Twelfth Night, and to be called the *Masque of Blackness*. The queen and ten of her beautiful young English aristocratic companions were to appear as blackamoors, an Aethiop Queen and the Daughters of Niger. Their azure and silver dresses designed by Inigo Jones, all lit by glimmering lantern light, were excitingly transparent, their breasts visible beneath the gauze, 'their hayre thicke, and curled upright in tresses, lyke *Pyramids*'. The drama was arranged on 'an artificiall sea . . . raysed with waves', which seemed to move, and in some places the billow seemed to break.

The whole story of the masque hinged on the expunging of an awful blackness. The Daughters of Niger, it was explained – as the queen and her 'black' ladies sat silent in a giant shell where lights shimmered on the upper rim – had always imagined they were beautiful until a poet had revealed to them that their blackness was ugly. Only a message from the Moon had showed them what they could do. If they travelled to a country whose name ended in '-tania', they would find a man 'who formes all beauty with his sight'. So far, they had trekked to Mauritania, Lusitania and Aquitania but to no avail. Now they had heard of a place called 'Britania', also known as 'Albion', which meant 'the white country' and which was

> Rul'd by a Sunne, that to this height doth grace it:
> Whose beames shine day and night, and are of force
> To blanch an Aethiope, and revive a *Corse*.

England was the white country, the king a magical miracle worker, a source of light himself who could turn black into white, who could bring happiness and a kind of Protestant truth to the sad, blackened and benighted.

It was ridiculous, and certainly seemed ridiculous to the sceptical members of the audience at the time. After the show was over, and before the banquet – chaos: the tables collapsed under the weight of sugar-glazed syllabubs and lark-stuffed pasties – the Spanish Ambassador bent to kiss the hand of the queen and came away with a black smudge on his face and lips.

Ridiculous but significant: black was what England was not and the most revealing aspect of the plot was the extent to which the darkness of its origins were exaggerated. It remains uncertain to this day how much Robert Cecil or his spies knew of it in advance. Nor is it certain how much he encouraged its development, delaying any arrests until the plan was ripe enough to make its prevention the political triumph he required. He certainly loathed Catholics, Catholic priests and the Jesuits above all – 'I condemn their doctrine,' he had written to James when he was still in Scotland, 'I detest their conversation.' The Jesuits were 'a generation of vipers' who were happy to paddle their fingers in 'the blood and crowns of Princes'. But neither Cecil nor the king had been bloodthirsty persecutors of the Catholics. James would rather Catholics were banished than executed. 'I will never allow in my conscience', he had written to Cecil, 'that the blood of any man shall be shed for diversity of opinions in religion, but I should be sorry that Catholics should so multiply as they might be able to practise their old principles upon us.'

That was the old political point, as good for Catholics as for extremist Puritans: errors in faith could be tolerated as long as they didn't threaten the order of the kingdom. The idea of blowing up parliament, needless to say, stepped over the line.

Cecil's spies seem to have entirely manufactured an element of the story which has been central to it ever since: the long dark tunnel which the plotters – or 'Miners' as they were called – are supposed to have dug from their house in Westminster under the House of Lords, the conduit along which they could bring their gunpowder. No such tunnel ever existed. Guy Fawkes was subjected to days on end of torture, personally authorised by James. 'If he will not other wayes confesse,' the king wrote, 'the gentle torturs are to be first usid unto him, & sic per gradus ad ima tenditur.' Latin was always useful to conceal, as if from oneself, the worst of instructions: the phrase means 'and so by steps going on to the worst', meaning from the manacles, in which a man hung from his wrists while his body danced in pain, to the big oak-framed rack in the Tower (there was only one of these instruments in England) on which a man was slowly stretched until the confession was squeezed out of him, and his body was left permanently maimed. So terrifying was the prospect of the rack that many confessed when taken into the room and shown it. It is not clear if Fawkes was racked or not – it was generally assumed he was – but still he could not bring the invented tunnel to mind and in his deposition to the court, its route, described as leading 'to the cellar under the Upper House of Parliament', was written in by another hand.

Even the cellar in which, famously, Guy Fawkes and his co-plotters stored the powder with which to bring about their Catholic revolution, was not really a cellar. It was on the ground floor, with the chamber of the House of Lords on the first floor above it. This whole gamut of tunnel, darkness, cellar, the night-time discovery, in short, the whole operatic nocturnal of the plot, was nothing but the fantasy of dread at work. Here was the underside attempting to exact its revenge. And the Translators were there to play their part.

The egregious William Barlow, by now Bishop of Rochester and author of the anti-Puritan account of the Hampton Court Conference, preached at Paul's Cross, 'the tenth day of November, being the next Sunday after the Discouerie of this late Horrible Treason'. He was a government man, but he was also, as one of the bishops who made up a full quarter of the House of Lords, a potential victim of the plot, and as such delivered the first version of the new line. The enemy from below was satanic in its wickedness, the king, their hoped-for victim, an unqualifiedly good man, the archetype of the good man, virtually a Christ-figure, 'universal scholar, acute in arguing, subtle in distinguishing, logical in discussing'. All the attributes of civilisation belonged with him above ground; all the qualities of wickedness, including Catholicism, belonged below it. Light, majesty and truth had only just escaped being eclipsed by the satanic, the dark and the deceitful.

It was an ancient and powerful opposition, now given new and polarising life. Gunpowder sermons became a yearly ritual in Jacobean England. The fifth of November became the day, far more than any anniversary of the Armada, on which God had saved Protestant England from the forces of darkness. 'This Day of ours,' Lancelot Andrewes told the king and court at Whitehall the following year, 'this fifth of Nouember, [is] a day of God's *making*; that which was done upon it, was the Lord's *doing*.' It was to be 'consecrated to perpetuall memory, by a yearly acknowledgement to be made of it through out all generations'. And it was the hidden nature of the danger that made it so terrible. They knew nothing of the danger beforehand.

> We imagined no such thing; but that all had been safe, and we might haue gone to the Parliament, as secure as ever. The danger never dreamt of, that is the danger . . . Danger by *undermining*, digging deep *under ground*; that none could

discerne . . . the *danger* not to be descried, not to be escaped, that is the danger.

The plotters were 'a brood of vipers, *mordentes in silentio* [biting in silence]; *still*, not so much as a *hisse*, till the deadly blow had been given'. It was not men who had done this, 'Not men; no, not savage wilde men: the Hunnes, the Heruli, the Turcilingi, noted for inhumanity; never so inhumane. Even among those barbarous people, this fact would be accounted barbarous.' Not even beasts would have done it. 'This is more than brutish, What Tiger, though never so inraged, would have made the like havock.' No, this could only have been the devil's work:

> so much bloud, as would have made it raine bloud; so many baskets of heads, so many pieces of rent bodies cast up and downe, and scattered all over the face of the earth. It yrketh me to stand repeating these; . . . That ever age, or land, that our age, and this land should foster or breed such monsters!

For years, Andrewes and other lesser preachers like him stood repeating these execrations. The plot and plotters were 'black', 'foul', 'accursed', 'locusts from the nethermost hell'. Ten years after the plot had been discovered, the energy of loathing was undiminished. 'Would they make men's bowels fly up and down in the air?' Andrewes asked. 'Out with those bowels. Would they do it by fire? Into the fire with their bowels, before their faces. Would they make men's bones fly about like chips? Hew their bones in sunder . . . They are not worthy to be *inter opera Dei* "among God's works."' Andrewes, as the newly ordained Bishop of Chichester, would have been among those blown up by the plotters, but this rage, still so vital after so long, cannot be explained merely by the shock of a narrow escape. This conspiracy to destroy from below touched the most sensitive of places in the Jacobean psyche. Andrewes's nightmare – and it is the national nightmare; these sermons were bestsellers, printed and distributed across the whole of England – is of brokenness, the world in pieces, all coherence gone, the parts to be collected up in baskets. It is the terror of anarchy and the loss of order, driven by the sense that order is no more than a taut and anxious skin drawn over the bubbling chaos below.

Throughout the previous reign and on into this one, Jesuits and other Catholic priests had been imprisoned, often horribly tortured and executed. It is nowadays perfectly clear that the Jesuits did not in any way condone the Gunpowder Plot, but the accepted and convenient view held by the Jacobean political class – and Lord Burghley had reckoned that about 100 people were politically significant in England – was that the Jesuits were more implicated than any other group. Henry Garnet, a saintly, pacific man, with a sweet singing voice, was the Superior of the Order in England, a man hustled from one hiding place to the next along the clandestine networks and channels of Catholic England. (This secret life of priests living in hidden holes, squeezed into the gaps between walls and chimneys, lurking undetected in the dark within inches of those in the airy, well-lit rooms beside them, fuelled the vision of the Catholic as a man of darkness, his purposes unclear, his methods concealed, his whole existence dangerous.) Garnet had known, through the confessional, of the plotters' intent. He had attempted and failed to persuade them to abandon their plans, but the seal of the confessional did not allow him to pass on what he knew.

In the extreme atmosphere that followed the discovery of the plot, the distinctions between Catholics were erased and the distance Garnet had kept from the plot was given no credit. He was in fact seen as the chief seducer, the master plotter. As soon as the trap was sprung, Garnet went into hiding, finally ending up in January in Hindlip House, near Worcester, a secret Catholic refuge. The place was a warren of concealment. Walls were false, every room had a trap door or access to secret stairs. Many of the chimneys had double flues, one for the smoke, the other in which a priest could hide. The place was betrayed, the house searched and then occupied by government agents, who waited for the priests they guessed were hidden within its walls.

Only after eight days, on Monday 27 January 1606, did Garnet and his companion Father Oldcorne emerge from their hiding place. They looked half-dead and their appearance terrified the men who were there to arrest them. The hole they had been crouching in was too small for either of them to stand up, and Garnet's legs in particular were horribly swollen. One of the women of the house had given them sweet hot liquids through a straw that perforated the walls of the hole and they had some marmalade they had taken in there with them. But there was no means of drainage in the tiny closet; it was the smell of their own accumulating faeces which had finally driven the men into the open air. Their only option now was to put themselves in the hands of the Jacobean state, which would humiliate, torture, try and then kill them.

Mr Henry Garnet, as the officials of the English state insisted on calling him, was deemed guilty of knowing about the conspiracy beforehand without reporting the plotters to the authorities. Those authorities did not accept that the secrecy of the confessional could not be abused. The conflict between his duty as a Catholic priest and his duty as an English citizen they considered no conflict at all. His was a treacherous, unreliable, seditious and above all a lying heart. Among the papers and books of Francis Tresham, one of the plotters, had been a manuscript written by Garnet entitled *A Treatise on Equivocation*. In it Garnet had elaborated on the circumstances in which the Jesuits considered it lawful not to tell the whole truth. A priest, for example, could say, when asked, that he was not a priest because he was not a priest of Apollo; or that he had never been over the seas, because he had never been over the Indian seas.

These desperate measures were the product of scruple: only because Roman Catholics considered it a sin to lie, and only because the intolerance of the English Church and state made it necessary for them to lie, were they forced to descend to this kind of Jesuitical equivocation. For the officials of the English court, everything they most disliked about Roman Catholicism seemed to focus on Garnet's pitiable figure: he had known about the plot before it occurred but had said nothing; he had been intimate with the satanic and bestial figures of the plotters, had administered the sacrament to them, but had done nothing material to sway them from their path; he was a liar; he was a man of dark and hidden recesses; he was the agent of the supranational Roman Church which had excommunicated Queen Elizabeth and whose head was the Antichrist. This gentle, prematurely aged man, with grizzled, thinning hair and spectacles, was the figure through whom that terror of anarchy and wrongness had so nearly been visited on the kingdom. Of course he should be tortured (probably by sleep deprivation or perhaps drugged) and of course he must be executed. Cecil told him he didn't care if Garnet lived or died. The king held interviews with him about some of the finer points of Roman theory and practice, centring on the secrecy of the confessional and its limits. Garnet finally broke that seal and admitted his foreknowledge of the plot. He was tried, convicted of treason, and dragged through the streets of London from the Tower on a hurdle to St Paul's where a scaffold had been erected. This means of transport was part of the punishment because a traitor, as the words of his sentence described, was

> not worthy any more to tread upon the Face of the Earth whereof he was made: Also for that he hath been retrograde to Nature, therefore is he drawn backward at a Horse-Tail. And whereas God hath made the Head of Man the highest and most supreme Part, as being his chief Grace and Ornament; he must be drawn with his Head declining downward, and lying so near the Ground as may be, being thought unfit to take benefit of the common Air.

Two of the Translators, George Abbot and John Overall, were there waiting for him at St Paul's, ready to convert him even at the last to Protestantism. After everything he had gone through, Garnet of course refused. He expressed his horror at what the plotters had planned to do and asked all Catholics to accept their place in the kingdom, and to be quiet. Then the final absurdity. It was said, perhaps a Cecil-inspired rumour, that Garnet would confess the wrongfulness of his religion at the last moment. A man in the huge crowd shouted out, 'Mr Garnet, it is expected you should recant.'

Garnet said, 'God forbid, I never had any such meaning, but ever meant to die a true and perfect Catholic.'

The extraordinary Jacobean ability to dispute, to be witty on the brink of the precipice, at this of all moments, now came to the fore. John Overall, considering the claims of the Church of England to be the true primitive church, then said to the Jesuit, 'But Mr Garnet, we are all Catholics.' That curious reasonableness, Overall's clever, witty face, that conversational tone, all in the presence of a violent death, the noose ready, the axe leaning on the block: no dissociation of sensibility here. Garnet could not agree with Overall's suggestion – it is the sort of sally you would make at a dinner party – and his due punishment took its course.

He shall be strangled, being hanged up by the Neck between Heaven and Earth, as deemed unworthy of both, or either; as likewise, that the Eyes of Men may behold, and their Hearts contemn him. Then he is to be cut down alive, and to have his Privy Parts cut off and burnt before his Face, as being unworthily begotten, and unfit to leave any Generation after him. His Bowels and inlay'd Parts taken out and burnt, who inwardly had conceived and harboured in his heart such horrible Treason. After, to have his Head cut off, which had imagined the Mischief. And lastly, his Body to be quartered, and the Quarters set up in some high and eminent Place, to the View and Detestation of Men, and to become a Prey for the Fowls of the Air.

The punishment, in its exaggerations and its pedantry, may seem like a kind of madness to us now. But here too the spirit of the age was at work. To do this to a man was to make a sermon of his body. It was to make his sin, in all its dimensions, apparent. The multiple destruction of his body was a clarification of his faults. It was judicial anatomy and, if this is not too grotesque an analogy, a kind of translation of inner and hidden sinfulness into open and explicit justice. It was a form of letting in the light.

To show the world what he was made of, Garnet was strung up, and, exceptionally, was allowed to die by hanging before the executioner cut him down, castrated him, disembowelled him and quartered his body on the block. The crowd around this little party in St Paul's Churchyard is said to have groaned and mumbled at the sight, not because it was a death sentence – over seventy thieves and murderers were executed every year in Jacobean England – but because, quite clearly, this was a good man killed for no good reason.

SEVEN

O lett me bosome thee, lett me preserve thee next to my heart

Wash mee throughly from mine iniquitie, and clense me from my sinne.

Purge me with hyssope, and I shalbe cleane: wash me, and I shall be whiter than snow.

For thou desirest not sacrifice: else would I giue *it*: thou delightest not in burnt offering.

The sacrifices of God *are* a broken spirit: a broken and a contrite heart, O God, thou wilt not despise.

Psalm 51:2, 7, 16–17

s the judicial murder of Henry Garnet was being enacted in the late spring of 1606, preparations were under way for the most extravagant celebration of monarchy the reign would witness. James's brother-in-law, the vast, red, cream-tea-eating Christian IV, King of Denmark and Norway, the man who insisted that Danish beer should be stronger than any brewed in the world, was coming to visit his sister and her husband, newly elevated from the exigencies of Scotland to the lushness for which he had a famous appetite. James himself was something of a drinker – he liked the heady, sweet malmseys from southern Greece, a featherbed of a drink – but there was no keeping up with Christian and his Danes. They scandalised even the Jacobean court with the depth of unbuttoned drunkenness they unleashed on the capital. The peak of their wild career came towards the end of their visit on a four-day outing to Theobalds where Robert Cecil, now, thanks to James, Earl of Salisbury, and ever richer through various complex deals over customs dues which he had farmed out to a group of businessmen, taking a cut himself, doled out the luxury.

Nothing was too much for the Danish revels. An artificial oak tree, full size, was bedecked with leaves made of taffeta on each of which was written the word 'WELCOME'. Drink flowed, men and women wallowed 'in beastly delights'. It was, according to Sir John Harington, a vision to match 'Mahomets paradise'. But, for a measure of how far court life stood outside the sort of regulated strictness which Puritan and God-fearing Englishmen believed in, nothing can quite match the events of the evening at Theobalds on which the masque of Solomon and the Queen of Sheba was performed. Intended as a picture of wisdom and maturity – the plan for the entertainment had been Cecil's own – it turned into alcohol-sodden chaos. Harington gave a full account:

> After dinner, the representation of Solomon his temple and the coming of the Queen of Sheba was made, or (as I may better say) was meant to have been made, before their Majesties, by device of the earl of Salisbury and others. – But, alass! as all earthly things do fail to poor mortals in enjoyment, so did prove our presentment hereof. The Lady who did play the Queens part, did carry most precious gifts to both their Majesties; but forgetting the steppes arising to the canopy, overset her caskets into his Danish Maiesties lap, and fell at his feet, tho I rather think it was in his face. Much was the hurry and confusion; cloths and napkins were at hand to make all clean. His Majesty then got up and would dance with the Queen of Sheba; but he fell down and humbled himself before her, and was carried to an inner chamber and laid on a bed of state; which was not a little defiled with the presents of the queen which had been bestowed on his garments; such as wine, cream, jelly, beverage, cakes, spices and other good matters.

Faith, Hope and Charity then appeared one by one to make their speeches. Faith was so drunk she couldn't get a word out; Hope couldn't stand upright and had to withdraw; only Charity, clearly the greatest of these, could say what she had to say – that Christian IV already had all the gifts that heaven could bestow and so there was nothing more she could give him – before returning to the lower hall where she found both Hope and Faith 'sick and spewing.'

It isn't difficult to share the reaction of Puritans to such a world, particularly when the costs are considered. The royal household in the last year of Elizabeth's reign had cost £47,000. By 1606, that had risen to over £100,000. Other costs were dropping: the end of the war in Ireland saved £300,000 a year, the Spanish peace still more on ships and men, but even those savings couldn't counteract the gush of Jacobean largesse. The royal debt had stood at £422,749 on the death of Queen Elizabeth. By Michaelmas 1606, it had gone up by a third to £550,331. And still the fountain poured, £3,000 here, another £2,000 there. A handsome courtier called Sir Henry Rich, known as Harry, the younger son of the Earl of Warwick, was standing in Whitehall and saw £3,000 in coins being carried past him to the office of the Keeper of the Privy Purse, the royal household's finance director. Harry Rich whistled at the sight and muttered half to himself that he wished he had that much money. The king overheard him muttering, asked what he had said, and on hearing the reply, said 'Marry, shalt thou, Harry', and ordered the money to be taken to Rich's rooms. 'You think now you have a great Purchase,' the King said. 'But I am more delighted to think how much I have pleasured you in giving this money, than you can be in receiving it.' It was, as so often with James, a winning remark and betrays the instinct at the heart of all his extravagance: money was a love vehicle, a bond of patronage and gratitude, part of the dream of one nation in which the glory of royal riches bound the people to the throne.

Of course it did nothing of the kind. The court was corrupt and everyone knew it. Gentlemen were bankrupting themselves to acquire positions there – and in the satellite courts of Queen Anne and the young Prince Henry – and then milking those positions to earn back the investment. Contractors to the court, in one investigation, were found to be marking up their supplies 3,000 per cent. James was aware of the rottenness, telling the Venetian Ambassador that if, as the Doge did in Venice, he executed all those who defrauded the state, he would soon have no subjects left. And he made his own efforts at economy: ordinances went out that only twenty-four rather than the accustomed thirty dishes were to be presented to him at lunch; and only twelve gallons of sack, dry Spanish wine, were to be issued by the Sergeant of the Cellar each day, for medicinal purposes only, and only to noblemen and their ladies. But they were meaningless gestures: the riot, the indebtedness, the corruption, the sale of offices, the cheating both of and by suppliers to the household, the sheer impetuosity of James's giving, especially to a handsome face: it all raged on unchecked.

How could this Bible emerge from such a world? A form of propagandist history, intent on seeing in the reign of James I the roots of the English (and American) people's struggle for freedom from a degenerate and autocratic monarchy, will take the chaotic evening at Theobalds, the gross indulgence by James of his favourites, and the air of louche sexuality that hangs over it all, as evidence of a regime both out of touch and on the slide. What can one say of a king who on receiving £453,000 from a parliament in trauma after the Gunpowder Plot, immediately gave £44,000 of it to three of his Scottish friends who had lost too much money gambling? And another £800 on 'spangles' (little silver sequins) for his guard? The whole court was, as the satirist Thomas Dekker called them, a cluster of 'spangle-babies', men and women made juvenile by money.

There is a sense, though, in which nothing could be more wrong than this judgement. James's desire to hand out his riches; to get so spectacularly drunk; to put on a great show; to preside lovingly over the nation; to include as wide a variety of non-subversive opinion as possible in the church; and to make one non-divisive Bible – all were part of a single instinct to make whole, to bring peace, to act the father.

The king who could get so drunk with his brother-in-law was also the king who was anxious for an inclusive church and an inclusive Bible. It was the dream of civilisation and for that dream to work the moderate Puritans clearly had to be included in its making. No Separatists or declared Presbyterians were to be included among the Translators. The heart of their thinking was divisive, not part of the unifying national project. But moderate Puritans could be and needed to be central to it. As a result, at least half of the new translation was put in their hands. Both John Reynolds at Oxford and Laurence Chaderton at Cambridge, the leading 'plaintiffs' at Hampton Court, came to take leading roles in their respective companies. Between them, Reynolds and Chaderton had the responsibility for the whole of the Old Testament apart from those books translated by Andrewes's Westminster company. With them on board, no Puritan could claim this was not his Bible.

'Puritan': what did the word mean? It was of course an insult, a slur-word; no one would have claimed it for himself and its meaning was shifting, sometimes applied to extremists, sometimes to what was clearly the moral majority of Jacobean England. Puritanism, in short, was in the eye of the beholder. 'Concerning the name,' Giles Widdowes wrote in *The schysmaticall puritan*, 'it is ambiguous and so it is fallacious.' The difficulty is made worse because 'Puritanism' spreads effortlessly into so many different areas of seventeenth-century life: it could be said to involve daily habits and styles of dress; attitudes to the place of ceremonial in worship, and the relation of word to ceremony; fiercely held beliefs about the constitution of the church, what it should be, what it must not be, and the relationship of church to state; the question of what were called 'things indifferent' – those parts of Christian practice, such as the use of the surplice, which some might like and others abhor; and beliefs about the nature of God's universe, the place of man within it and, crucially, the role of pre-destination. Had God designated some people for heaven and some for hell from the beginning of time? Would their own behaviour on earth have any effect on that destiny? Surely not, it was suggested, if all was pre-ordained? Why then should anyone behave well? If our destiny was settled, and our destination neither a punishment nor a reward for how we had lived, then what should stop us behaving as wickedly as we liked? What purpose could there be in good works or a good life?

The Bible itself was the answer to all those questions. It was the word of God, an enormous, direct, vastly complicated, infinitely interpretable account of what God meant by and for his creation. It was accessible to the people as a whole either through the lessons read to them every Sunday in church, or through sermons, or, to the literate minority, through reading the good book themselves. In the mid-sixteenth century, perhaps 30 per cent of the English gentry had been illiterate. By the 1620s, that figure had dropped effectively to zero. Lower down in society, the figures were worse – 55 per cent were illiterate among small yeoman farmers in the 1640s, and as much as 95 per cent among labourers at the same time – but at all social levels, the trend towards literacy was upwards, particularly among men and particularly in London, soon stretching far ahead of the rest of Europe. This increasingly word-orientated section of the population was the seed-bed in which the highly intellectual, questioning and quizzing form of religion we know as Puritanism had its beginnings. A puritan ate and drank the word of God. That word was his world. If the Bible authorised anything, by definition that was in concordance with God's will and so by definition should be followed. Anything explicitly denied or disapproved of by the Bible should not be indulged. So, for example, Samuel Hieron, the Puritan pamphleteer and one of the organisers of the Millenary Petition, maintained that the Bible provided for the head of each household, 'direction for his apparel, his speech, his diet, his company, his disports, his labour, his buying and selling, yea and for his very sleep'.

Most people would have probably accepted that. The difficulty came in deciding on the lawfulness of religious behaviour and belief that were not mentioned in the Bible. If something wasn't mentioned, did that mean God had no view on it? Or if it wasn't mentioned, did that mean that God did not approve of it?

That was certainly the understanding of the holy Separatist Henry Barrow, a view for which he died. Fasting in Lent, clergy appointed by the state, or by any grandee who held no place in the church, any ceremonies that were not explicitly authorised by scripture: all of these Barrow considered unlawful. Other Separatists and Presbyterians, or even reformists who wished to remain within an improved Church of England, considered fasting, holy days, kneeling at communion, most church officials (certainly bishops and archbishops), the baptising of infants who didn't know what was happening to them, the churching of women after childbirth, getting married with a ring, all unlawful. Bancroft had an answer for them. There were no Christian kings mentioned in the Bible. Did that mean that Christian kings were unlawful? Didn't religion have to change, at least in its relatively inessential practices, as the habits and practices of society changed? If the king, whose authority was essentially divine and who was God's agent on earth, required it, then was it not the duty of every good man to obey, whatever the Bible said? The surplice was not mentioned in the Bible but the king wanted surplices to be used. It was obvious to Bancroft and the king that every God-fearing minister should therefore wear them.

This was the territory across which the insult 'Puritan' would fly. 'A puritan is such a one', the London lawyer John Manningham wrote in 1602, 'as loves God with all his soul, but hates his neighbour with all his heart.' Anyone who took a stricter line on the demands of scripture than the person speaking could be labelled a Puritan. The critical division between extreme and moderate was on the question of royal authority: moderate Puritans accepted the authority of the church, and of the king as its head, even if they cavilled over points of doctrine; radical Puritans denied the authority of that state and would in the end rather separate themselves from the royal church than accept doctrines which they loathed. It was not the conventional modern conflict of freedom against authority, nor even a struggle for freedom of conscience or belief. This was not the age of toleration: it was a conflict of different visions of authority. 'Let them chant what they will of prerogatives,' Milton would write much later, 'we shall tell them of Scripture; of custom, we of Scripture; of Acts and Statutes, still of Scripture, till ... the mighty weakness of the Gospel throw down the weak mightiness of man's reasoning.' That was written in the heat of the Civil War, but if not so polarised, at least in embryo, that division between the rival claims of divine and worldly authority is apparent in the first decade of the century.

It was a difference of emphasis that split the 'Puritans'. It was the very fissure which James and Bancroft quite deliberately and very adroitly managed to deepen in the first years of the reign, when they expelled those eighty or so Puritans from the church between 1604 and 1606. For James, it was effective and practical politics: a means of achieving unity and uniformity in the church by excluding a small proportion of extremists.

Those Puritans who were engaged on the new translation of the Bible were by definition moderates. They had accepted the royal commission which no dyed-in-the-wool Separatist could ever have done. But lurking under the skin of these conformists was a Puritan inheritance of a much fiercer kind.

One of the Translators appointed to the Cambridge panel working on the Apocrypha left behind one of the most famous of all Puritan documents: his diary. It is a small bound paper book, with ninety-five leaves in it, each page measuring 5 inches by 6, a private object, devoted to an agonised conversation between the diarist and his conscience. It was written, a decade or so before the new translation was commissioned, by a man in his mid-twenties, Samuel Ward, a fellow of Christ's College, Cambridge, later Milton's college, famous with Emmanuel as a breeding ground of Puritan ministers.

The diary gives an insight into the thought habits of at least one of the Translators, a puritan frame of mind to set alongside the riches of an Andrewes or the world-experience of a Layfield. The essence of the King James Bible lies precisely in the coming together of these mentalities, the enriched substance of Andrewes's supremely well-stocked mind lit by the fierce white light of Puritanism.

Ward was a Durham man, his father 'a gentleman of more ancientry than estate', and part of a large family, all of whom in their different ways continued to cadge off him as his career prospered. He became a friend and in many ways client of James Mountagu, the puritan dean who had whispered in the king's ear at Hampton Court and who himself became a powerful figure in court–church circles, editing the king's own works and publishing them in a splendid edition. Ward was also a friend of the physician William Harvey and sent him a petrified skull, which he thought might amuse the king.

For all this, he was never the most sophisticated of men. He had a stammer and spoke extremely slowly, as slowly, it was said, as Moses. This was an ambivalent compliment in an age when the essential task of a minister was to preach, and this disability caused Ward infinite heart-searching and long, laborious hours practising his sermons. But it is his diary, the most private of documents, which reveals the astonishing turbulence of his mind. He is tossed from one agony to the next, from one self-indulgence to the next, from one moment of self-loathing and despair to the next of exhaustion and failure.

The little manuscript notebook opens with some notes on a sermon by Laurence Chaderton. But then, undated, there is the plunge into the agonies of the Puritan mind:

> Prid, Desire of vaynglory, yea, in little things. Wearisomnes in Godes service. Non affection. No delite in Godes service. Non care of exhorting my brethren. Non boldness in the confessing of Godes name. No delite in hearing Godes word, or in prayer, or in receyving of the Sacramentes. Shame in serving God.

Poor man! Ward's own high standards make for an ever-present sense of failure. But one must be careful in reading this. For a preacher to weep in the pulpit was considered in the seventeenth century a sign of God's grace. It was an essential part of Protestant theology that in order to be saved you had to know you were damned. Behind the breast-beating – as every anti-Puritan play and libel endlessly repeated – there is an undertone, a subtle recognition, that these appalling failures are steps towards deliverance. For the Jacobean divine, as for the modern alcoholic, the road of regret always led to the palace of salvation.

There is no doubt, though, that it is more than a pose. The confessions are real, shaming and often ridiculous enough for there to be no hint that this is a public document. It is an endoscope into one of the Puritan Translators' hearts. Ward, to his own horror, is bored by one of Laurence Chaderton's sermons. He gets angry with Mr Newhouse, his tutor, for the inordinate length of his prayers. Carnal desires sweep over him.

'The adulterous thoughts', he writes cryptically on 11 May 1595.
A week later: 'Thy wandering mynd on herbals att prayer tyme
... Also thy gluttony the night before.' He has a squabble with
his roommate in Christ's and the diary feels shame at 'my excan-
descentia agaynst him in wordes'. The Puritan is no saint: that
is his sorrow; he is aware of it, and that is his gift. 'I must learne
to desyre more after the Sundays than the Mundayes,' Ward
wrote, and to restrict 'thy overmuch delite in these transitory
pleasures of this world'. Nothing about which he could feel
pleased gave him any pleasure. He was much too brilliant for
his own good and reproached himself for 'My overmuch quipping and desire of praise thereby'. It is surely significant that he
flicks like this from 'my' to 'thy' and back again, alternately
owning and disowning himself and his sins, both judge and
accused in the court of his own conscience.

June 14 1595, a Sunday, was a particularly disastrous day.
Ward began by not wanting to go to chapel and didn't listen to
the sermon when he got there. He didn't pray. He didn't talk
about holy things at dinner. He was appalled at his 'immoderate
use of Godes creatures' – too much of the roast beef on offer
in the college hall – and then went to sleep afterwards. He slept
through the first afternoon sermon and through the second.
He couldn't stop himself chatting with his friends after that. He
hadn't encouraged any of them to do anything worth doing,
unlike the good 'Mr Chadderton, who hath such a living affection
to the poor'. Ward failed to go to evening prayers and afterwards
supped much too liberally. He didn't take any left-overs to the
poor women of the city, he didn't encourage his fellow students
to pray, congratulated himself, silently, on how good he was at
Greek, laughed at others' mistakes when they tried to keep up
with him, was too pleased at his own skill in geometry, 'magnified
myself inwardly' and he was sluggish in prayer. The whole day
had been a cascade of error. 'Thus sin I dayly agaynst the,
O Lord,' he told his diary.

Ward was overflowing with a rumbustious Jacobean appetite for all forms of the world around him. He loved wine and beer, he ate far too much cheese, he laughed too much, he loved eavesdropping on other people's conversations, he lusted after women and had exciting dreams about 'the grievous sinnes in T[rinity] Colledg, which had a woman which was [?carried] from chamber in the night tyme', and was far too jolly. On 15 July 1595, he wrote with deep regret of 'My over great myrth as we went to Hynton', a village outside Cambridge. When a crocodile was brought on exhibition to the university, Ward went to see it with his friend, James Mountagu, but even this engendered 'proud thoughts'.

Late summer was a testing time for this troubled soul as the trees in the college orchard came into fruit. September 15: 'My *crapula* [surfeit] in eating peares in a morning.' The next summer, Ward had a crisis over the plums fattening so temptingly in the orchard. On 18 July, he ate too many. More the following day, as well as raisins and drinks, and a great bonanza of them the following week. He was still racked by the plum problem in August. The damsons were hanging in clusters off the Christ's College trees.

August 8
My longing after damsens. when I made the vow not to eat in the orchard. Oh that I could so long after Godes graces.

A week later he was still guzzling.

August 13
My intemperate eating of damzens. also my intemperate eating of cheese after supper.

Such a fatbelly was always finding himself dozing off in front of the Bible.

Ward in the end gave in to his love of plums. After 1608, he gathered them in, becoming first chaplain to the Bishop of Bath and Wells (his old friend James Mountagu), with a living at Yatton, worth £50, became Master of Sidney Sussex College (where Oliver Cromwell was his student), and Lady Margaret Professor of Divinity (£20 a year), tried to become Archdeacon of Bath (and failed), succeeded at Taunton (where he sublet a nice piece of church property to a Cambridge friend), became a prebendary at Wells, rector of Great Munden in Hertfordshire, a canon of York, rector of Terrington in Norfolk and a royal chaplain. It was a full flush. The agonised diary had long since ceased to be written. But people wrote to him, a little questioningly, about what was, in effect, Ward's lucrative cluster of non-executive directorships. One had heard of his spectacular pluralism and warned him of 'some of your friends, I know not whether they spake of it unto you, yet quipping at it behind your back, others of lower rankes wondrynge at it, and those whom I had thought never to have hard it, urginge your example to induce others to it'.

Ward's answer was that, like everything else, his material well-being was all God's doing. He had remained true to his beliefs: the altar in Sidney Sussex, for example, remained an unadorned table in the middle of the chapel, and that 'when I was unprouided (being only a fellow of Emmanuel) I could not neglect God's Providence and was advised hereunto by my best Friends'.

Friends, his appetite and God all told the older Ward the same thing: plums were delicious. Why let them rot on the tree? Besides, he deserved them. As he wrote in a consoling note to himself in 1614, when James Mountagu, Bishop of Bath and Wells, was deciding who might receive yet another juicy fruit from the tree of the Church of England, the post of canon residentiary at Wells Cathedral, 'My Lord [ie Mountagu] may have good pretence for making me Res[identiary]. First, I was his first Chaplain. 2. I have small means. 3. I am a Doctor and Master of a College. 4. I was a Translator. Mr Young [his rival for the post] may have one of the other Prebends . . .'

'I was a Translator': it is the sort of phrase you might have put on your grave. And he got the job.

Ward is, in a sense, an exception, only just part of the main-stream. His hero and mentor, Laurence Chaderton was central to it, the controlling figure, the node, of Cambridge Puritanism. He is one of the most charismatic of all the Translators, a man who seems to have been loved by all who knew him. He was already in his late sixties by the time of Bancroft's commission, but he would live almost another forty years. No one quite knew how old he was when he finally died, aged 102 or 103 or 104, in 1640. He loved games, taking his place at the archery butts, the tennis and fives courts throughout his life. He used to botanise in the fields around Cambridge and planted trees which, it was said, matured and decayed in his own lifetime.

By his mid-forties he had become established as one of the leading Puritans in Cambridge and when in 1584 the Chancellor of the Exchequer, Sir Walter Mildmay, decided to found a new college which would be a seminary for Puritan minis-ters, Chaderton was the obvious choice. He was reluctant but Mildmay forced his hand: if Chaderton wouldn't be the master, Mildmay wouldn't found the college. Chaderton suc-cumbed and Emmanuel came into being. The new college was on the site of a suppressed Dominican friary and it was to be a strict place: no plays to be performed, no feasting, no 'conver-sation'; future bishops were to be trained here and Emmanuel men have a way of floating up in any story. Henoch Clapham, who had pursued Andrewes over his disgraceful behaviour during the 1603 plague; Lewis Pickering, who had rushed to find James in Scotland and who had helped organise the Millenary Petition: both Emmanuel men. But Chaderton was subtler than his aco-lytes. He had been part of the radical push in the 1580s for a more thoroughly reformed church. Presbyterianism in 1580s Cambridge played the role of communism in the same 1930s colleges. All young men with any brilliance or vitality were part of the movement. Chaderton certainly was, as were his co-Emmanuel men and co-Translators, Francis Dillingham and Thomas Harrison. These young apostles were burning with the idea of a renewed, reformed and holy world. But Chaderton was subtle and never allowed his support for the deep reform, which Bancroft was striving so ingeniously to undermine, to emerge in public. There was clearly something canny about him and the entire strategy of the Emmanuel project was not open revolution but a silent seeding of the Church of England to bring it, as if by stealth, to a more reformed condition.

Not that there was anything very secret about what went on in the college. The hall where the twelve fellows and their scholars dined was on the site of the Dominican church, and their own chapel, which had never been consecrated was, scandalously for the bishops, aligned north–south. Bedrooms for the undergraduates were in its loft, the only stained glass it had were the arms of the Queen of England, there was nothing, of course, resembling a cross, and the only furniture was a pulpit, an hourglass, a plain table and some plain wooden benches. Other, more wicked colleges like Gonville and Caius went in for 'singing and organs'. Not at Emmanuel. Nor were there any surplices, or gowns, or corner-caps, and no kneeling for the sacrament, which they took sitting on benches around the communion table, passing both the bread and the wine from hand to hand, 'one drinking, as it were, to another, like good fellows', at least according to a hostile report smuggled out to Bancroft.

Chaderton seems to have fostered an astonishingly loving atmosphere at the college. A correspondence from his time as master survives in manuscript in the Bodleian Library in Oxford between two young Emmanuel students who were clearly in love with each other. There is no suggestion of sex but the passion between these boys is unmistakable. One of them, William Sancroft, shared his room with Arthur Bonnest, the son of a minor gentleman from Hertfordshire. They lived together, read together and slept together. Bonnest seems to have contracted TB and gone home.

Sancroft wrote to him: 'I had a colleague in my studies, with whom I could communicate both my reading and my doubts. But now I sitt alone. Friendships (as one well said) are but Elemented in an universitie, and soe was ours, but they are best tried in the countrie, in absence I meane.'

Bonnest replied: 'Thou art oftener in my thoughts than ever; thou art nearer mee then when I embraced thee. Thou saiest thou lovest me: good, well repeat it againe and againe.'

And Sancroft wrote back in kind: 'O lett me bosome thee, lett me preserve thee next to my heart and give thee so large an interest there, that nothing may supplant thee.'

It isn't known what became of Bonnest. Sancroft, Chaderton's star seedling, later became Archbishop of Canterbury, the only reason this correspondence has been preserved.

This extraordinary and passionate atmosphere is one of the governing qualities of the time. The age was at ease with unbridled but apparently quite unsexual love between men. Even Cecil, discussing the intimate relationship between the king and his principal adviser, wrote to a friend: 'As long as any matter of what weight soever, is handled only between the prince and the secretary, those counsels are compared to the mutual affection of two lovers, undiscovered to their friends.'

That sense of closeness, of the possibility and richness of an unmediated intimacy, plays a shaping role in the translation. Among the many wonderful books of the Old Testament which Chaderton's company translated was the Song of Songs, or the Song of Solomon, the great love lyric of the Bible. Some sixteenth-century reformers had been keen to exclude it, on the grounds of its immodesty and its fleshliness, but others, drawing on a long Jewish tradition, read it as an account of God's love for his people and his church. That is how the luscious verses of the song are annotated in the King James Version: 'A bundle of myrrhe is my welbeloued vnto me,' the girl sings; 'he shall lie all night betwixt my breasts.' And her lover replies, 'Behold, thou *art* faire, my loue: behold, thou *art* faire, thou *hast* doues eyes.' Chaderton calmly annotates: 'The Church and Christ congratulate one another.' The lover continues: 'Thy two breasts, *are* like two yong Roes, that are twinnes, which feed among the lillies.' (Chaderton: 'Christ setteth forth the graces of the Church.') 'Thy lips, O *my* spouse! drop *as* the hony combe: hony and milke *are* vnder thy tongue, and the smell of thy garments *is* like the smell of Lebanon. (Chaderton, inscrutable to the last: 'Christ sheweth his loue to the Church.')

That aching gap, between the ecstatic sexuality of the poem and of the rather helpful and interesting notes which the Translators provide, might make us smile now, but it was clearly not a comic effect that the Jacobean Translators were after. The modern reaction to their binding of the religious and the erotic experience is a measure of what Eliot called the 'dissociation of sensibility' that occurred to English consciousness at some time later in the seventeenth century. We can no longer imagine that erotic passion and religious intelligence can be bound together into one living fabric. All we see in the commentary of Chaderton's company is what looks like their prudishness, their refusal to see the erotic and the passionate for what it is. But in doing that, we patronise them, we assume they were trying to conceal what they were so clearly and so consciously making vital and present. The Sancroft–Bonnest correspondence, Andrewes's private prayers, Donne's sermons and sacred sonnets, the poetry of Herbert, Vaughan and Traherne, all show that a profoundly open 'passionality' is completely and immediately available to these men. Their lives and works are largely motivated by a frame of mind in which emotion, intellect, spirituality and desire do not exist in insulated compartments but feed and nourish each other in what Eliot might have called, but didn't, an 'association of sensibility', a self-communicativeness which we have lost.

Again and again, as the marginal alternatives make clear, they chose the more passionate, the more immediate, and the more exciting of the alternatives that were open to them. 'Thou hast ravished my heart', the lover tells his girl, not, as he might have done, 'Thou hast taken away my heart'. They called the myrrh she poured on him 'sweete smelling' and in the margin suggested it might mean 'running about' or very liquid. In the most direct moment of the whole enchanted seduction, they wrote, 'My beloued put in his hand by the hole *of the dore*, and my bowels were moved for him'. Although there is a euphemism here – the phrase '*of the dore*' is in italics because it is not to be found in the Hebrew – they nevertheless placed in the margin a note which would give the even more explicit 'and my bowels were moued in me for him'. Any close reader would realise that the fullest and most explicit statement they were suggesting was: 'My beloued put in his hand by the hole, and my bowels were moued in me for him.' This is not the work of people who are avoiding the rich and potent interpenetration of religion and flesh. It is in fact one of the greatest of all English celebrations of that union, culminating in the verse which the Translators entitled 'The vehemencie of loue'. The girl of the song, the church, declares, in language as magisterial, passionate and imposing as the translation gets: 'Set me as a seale vpon thine heart, as a seale vpon thine arme: for loue *is* strong as death, iealousie *is* cruel as the graue: the coales thereof *are* coales of fire, *which hath* a most vehement flame.'

That is language which emerges from a world in which William Sancroft, future Master of Emmanuel, future archbishop, can say to his beloved Arthur, 'O lett me bosome thee, lett me preserve thee next to my heart'. It is a world in which all divisions of existence – the bodily, the emotional, the intellectual and the spiritual – are one, and from which we are now utterly divorced.

For these Puritans, and in a way we can scarcely understand now, the words of the scriptures were thought to provide a direct, almost intravenous access to the divine.

Listen, for example, to an account given by a friend of the Translators, William Hinde, fellow of Queen's College, Oxford, of the last words and dying moments of his friend, another minister, John Bruen of Bruen Stapleford in Cheshire, whose life Hinde wrote. Bruen embodied the milieu from which this translation emerged. He was both the minister of his local church and squire of his local village, and every Sunday he used to walk through the fields the mile or so from his manor house to divine service, 'leaving neither butler nor cooke behind him', singing psalms as they went along the broad, fair path between the hedgerows, gathering his tenants and neighbours around him, 'as a leader of the Lord's host', preaching to them when he got there, and then afterwards leading them all back – more psalms 'and that psalme especially *How pleasant is thy dwelling place*' because he loved Bruen Stapleford above all places on earth – to have lunch with him at home.

Bruen took the word of God seriously, gave up the hunting and hawking he had loved as a young man, dispensed with his 'foureteene couple of great mouthed dogges', disparked his park, had the deer slaughtered and the cuts of meat distributed, demolished his hounds' kennels and the cockpit, made his packs of cards useless by burning the four knaves in every one and put his backgammon set, its dice and its thirty men 'into a burning oven which was then heating to bake pies'. In his house, instead of these entertainments, he had set up on desks, in his hall and in his parlour, 'two goodly faire bibles of the best edition, and largest volume' for his family and servants to read as 'continuall residentaries'.

When Bruen knew he was dying, he told Hinde that, hugely loved as he was, he wanted no elaborate mourning. 'I wil have no blacks [mourning dress]. I love not any proud or pompous funerals.' He didn't want any show, nothing in other words beyond the verbal. And then, as he felt death coming on, he said this, the passionate erotic love poetry of the Song of Songs, melded in his mind with the words of Christ on the cross, rising effortlessly to his lips:

> 'Come Lord Jesus, and kisse me with the kisses of thy mouth, and embrace me with the armes of thy love. Into thy hands do I commend my spirit; O come now, and take me to thine owne selfe; O come, lord Jesus, come quickly. O come, O come, O come.' And so his spirit fainting and his speech failing, he lay quiet and still, for a little season.

That strange, intense, distant, scarcely English world, made distant above all by the passion of its religious experience, is the one in which the familiar phrases of the King James Bible were made.

EIGHT

We have twice and thrice so much scope for oure earthlie peregrination . . .

> Now I haue prepared with all my might for the house of my God, the gold for *things to be made of* gold, and the siluer for *things* of siluer, and the brasse for *things* of brasse, the yron for *things* of yron, and wood for *things* of wood; onix stones, and stones to be set, glistering stones, and of diuers colours, and all maner of precious stones, and marble stones in abundance.
>
> *Euen* three thousand talents of gold, of the gold of Ophir, and seuen thousand talents of refined siluer, to ouerlay the walls of the houses withal:
>
> 1 Chronicles 29:2, 4

n 22 May 1607, in the great gallery at Theobalds, Robert Cecil, the all-smiling secretary, who liked to pad silently from room to room, affecting invisibility, acting the part of the impresario who was nothing in himself but revealed all in the glamour of his productions, staged yet another show for the king and queen. He had hired Ben Jonson and Inigo Jones as writer and stage designer. The entertainment was intended to mark the most astonishing gesture of love and generosity from a subject to a king which the world had ever seen: to James (or, as the play pretended, to the queen, Anne) Cecil was giving his father's enormous gilded palace in which they were all assembled, the family's proudest possession. Emerging through a scene, designed by Inigo Jones, of 'Columnes and Architrabe, Freeze, and Coronice', a series of figures announced that the making of the gift would be a disaster to his own successors. But that didn't matter. What was important was absolute loyalty and obedience to the king, to the idea of majesty he represented, and the greater 'design' – God's institution of order in the world – of which kingship was the essential part. What were mere windows and walls next to that?

Quite a lot, as it turned out. Ben Jonson did not write about this, nor Inigo Jones make it part of his *mis-en-scène*, but Cecil had been negotiating long and hard with the king over Theobalds. James had loved it and lusted after it ever since his first sunlit arrival in England four years before. He had often returned to its comforts and its glories and had been pressing Cecil to give it to him. The secretary now exacted his price: eighteen manors, including the huge old royal palace at Hatfield, only nine miles away, just as convenient for London, a mile or two off the Great North Road which James habitually took to go hunting at Royston and Newmarket. Through a series of subtle negotiations, Cecil established that in addition to the old medieval palace (all but one side of which he would demolish), Hatfield would come with a vast acreage around it. His father's park at Burghley near Stamford was twice the size of Monaco, and the son was intent on matching the father. Well before the ceremonies at Theobalds, he had visited the site at Hatfield and had begun planning his palatial new house there. Of course, at this ceremony, he could look on his king with the most humble and beneficent smile.

Unlike Theobalds, of which only a staircase remains, ripped out, sold off and reinserted in Herstmonceux Castle in Sussex, Cecil's great house at Hatfield, which was built in under four years, still survives. And although Hatfield is not quite unaltered – there have been fires and redecorations – for the most part its great rooms are still so like their original condition that to walk around them is like entering the world in which the King James Bible was made.

The building, for which the first foundations were dug that August, and which cost £10,000 to build, another £28,000 to decorate – at a time when you could get a design by Inigo Jones for £10 and a Yorkshire gentleman would happily live on £100 a year – was complete by the spring of 1611. It is, in other words, the King James Bible's exact contemporary, the product of precisely the same cultural moment, produced from precisely the same court culture, with precisely the same intention of celebrating and in a certain sense 'housing' James I and his dream of majesty. Can Hatfield House, then, be read as a companion to the Bible whose genesis is so close to its own?

This is scarcely what conventional historians of Jacobean England have done, but it is possible to see some connections here. Enter Hatfield and all the ingredients of Jacobean court mentality hit you like a wave. First, there is a certain anti-quarianism. Although the house is planned in a new way – no courtyards, a clustering of rooms into large and massy blocks, an open Italian loggia on the ground floor over which the Long Gallery runs – there is a recognisable medieval pattern in one's arrival into a screens passage, with the great hall on one side and the kitchens on the other. The great Marble Hall itself reproduces the heart of a medieval house, and the staircase beyond it leads to the richer and more private rooms of the Cecils themselves. This is a deeply traditional arrangement of a great man's house; no break here with the antiquity of England.

But the place is dripping in Jacobean style, governed above all by the sheer love of stuff, the early modern lust for substance. Every element of the Marble Hall, with its screen at each end and its original tables and benches still in situ, is carved and enriched as no later taste would have contemplated. Bushy-bearded and vast-breasted hermaphrodites stare out from the hugely enriched screens. On the great staircase beyond it, every post is carved with intricate decoration, every pillar surmounted by a figure, heraldic lion or almost-classical, slightly disproportionate boy, playing the bagpipes or holding aloft not quite spherical spheres. In the seventeenth century both boys and lions were gilded, as was the huge carved pendant which hangs from the ceiling above them. Even the gates at the foot of the staircase, put there to prevent dogs from going upstairs, are pimpled and bobbled, no line left uncurled, no surface plain. In the long gallery on the floor above, to which the staircase gave access, yard after yard of decorated joinery extends in a long disappearing perspective in front of you, the ceiling patterned in interlocking arabesques, the painted fireplaces a display of the classical orders, many of the gilt and jewelled, rock crystal and pearl treasures on show collected by the Jacobean Cecils to decorate this place: it is the most beautiful surviving room of Jacobean England.

Enrichment was all and that is one of the keys to Jacobean England: love of decorated stuff. In 1609 Cecil would set up England's first shopping mall on the Strand, called Britain's Burse, in tribute to his sovereign's dream of unification. The world of Britain's Burse was the world 'Cecil-Hatfield' (as its creator wanted it called) was intended to crown and was also the milieu from which the King James Bible would emerge. The country and the world were growing and bursting at the seams. The explorers of the previous century had 'so muche enlarged the boundes of the Worlde, that now we have twice and thrice so much scope for oure earthlie peregrination'. The globe had suddenly become elastic and from all the new corners came the delicious luxuries. Things had never been so rich. Goods were pouring into England: silks, lace, Venetian glass, tin-glazed ceramics, fine thick Italian paper, German swords and armour, Turkish carpets and Venetian instruments, metal-threaded textiles like the wonderful Italian silk worn by James's Queen Anne, in which the peacock eyes sparkle across its glimmered surface. They came from the other end of the earth. 'What doe you lacke?' one of Ben Jonson's sales boys asked, 'What is't you buy? Veary fine China stuffes, of all kindes and quallityes? China chaynes, China braceletts, China scarfes, China fannes, China girdles, China knives, China boxes, China cabinetts.'

At the grand opening of the Burse – with celebratory text by Ben Jonson – Cecil provided a special shop for the king and his wife and children over whose door was written: 'All other places give for money, here all is given for love.' Delicious and perfect presents were provided for the king and queen and princes. Throughout the little stalls of the Burse (no hammering of metals and no sale of vegetables, no dogs, no fighting and no whores allowed) all the most modern and glamorous objects of the mercantile world were on sale: eastern satins, golden bracelets, fans, umbrellas, sundials, silk-flowers, perspectives (precursors of the telescope), musical instruments, toy automata and singing birds were all on sale. Everything seemed to be from China or Virginia. For the true elite, England in the first decade of the seventeenth century was life on satin pillows.

It was a culture of repetition, of piling richness on richness, in love with the exotic and with the exotic enriched. It wasn't enough to have a china bowl; it should be set in a gilded mount. It wasn't enough to have a wonderful dress; it should be slashed to show the more wonderful material beneath. Every surface was to be alive with decoration and illustration. Embroidery was to overlace richness. Plainness was poverty and unless courtiers looked glorious, they, or what they were seeking, could scarcely be considered. The Earl of Suffolk wrote to Sir John Harington with sage advice on coming to court:

> I would wish you to bee well trimmed; get a new jerkin well bordered, and not too short; the king saith, he liketh a flowing garment; be sure it not be all of one sort, but diversely coloured, the collar falling somewhat down, and your ruff well stiffened and brisky. We have lately had many gallants who failed in their suits for want of due observance of these matters. The King is nicely heedfull of such points, and dwelleth on good looks and handsome accoutrements.

This love of variegation, of the multiplicity of things, overlay something else: an appetite for the undeniably solid. The hunger for substance was Victorian in its intensity. There is no Augustan or eighteenth-century conception of fineness or slenderness. Chippendale would not have thrived in Jacobean England. What was valuable to a Jacobean was robust and huge. Tables and sideboards sprouted fat melons clamped to their legs. From the high, plain and virginal concealment of Elizabethan taste, women's necklines plunged through the first decade of the century to a deep, bosom-revealing immodesty. At court masques, the queen and her attendant ladies would appear dressed in nothing but the finest silk gauze.

The two tastes lay within each other: a love of stuff, of the material thing, was wrapped in a baroque entrancement with the flickering, the dramatic, the elaborated and the enriched. The interplay of these two aesthetic principles, of show and, in Hamlet's famous phrase to his mother, of 'that within which passeth show', is one of the governing tensions of the great Jacobean translation of the Bible. Beauty was about firmness but it was also about brilliance; clarity vied with glitter; candour with bitter irony; simplicity with complexity; a vision of the pure with a relishing of the lush.

In public the grandees who would have filled the rooms of Hatfield wore the strict and dignified blacks of the statesman (it was said to be a Spanish habit, a sober, imperial style). In private, all controls were off. The Earl of Northampton, the Henry Howard who had been Cecil's go-between with James before the accession, a complex, political self-promoter, retired from a day dressed in nothing but black to sleep in a bed of Chinese lacquer, overdecorated with silver branches and his own coat of arms on the headpiece, with 'the toppe and valance of purple velvett striped downe with silver laces and knottes of silver, the frindge blewe silke and silver with 8 cuppes and plumes spangled suteable, the 5 curtanes of purple taffeta with buttones and lace of silver, the counterpoint of purple damaske suteable laced.' To wash, at night and in the morning, he had a generous silver basin, in the form of a shell, and a ewer in the shape of a mermaid. The rosewater sprang out into the bowl through the mermaid's large and protuberant nipples.

At Hatfield, Cecil also had a sumptuous bed, with its tester, valance and headpiece of crimson velvet, embroidered with his arms. But that lushness and fullness of Jacobean decor, of the Jacobean sense of the beautiful, required one further element: illumination. No buildings in English history until the twentieth century had such enormous light-admitting windows as these great private prodigy houses. The rooms encrusted with the beloved substantiality were also flooded with the all-revealing light. 'Light', Thomas Fuller, the church historian, wrote, was 'God's eldest daughter [and] a principall beauty in a building'. All rooms were arranged with a thought to how the light from the windows would fall into them at different times of the day. Modern conservators, struggling to preserve the gorgeousness of fabrics in vastly overlit rooms, are grappling with precisely the combination of qualities Jacobean taste required. Outside the walls of London, north of the Tower, enormous factories were set up to satisfy the demand for glass. Experts in glass were brought in from the Netherlands. And the grandees who commissioned the glass palaces had their portraits painted in the total, flattening light those windows provided.

That depthlessness of Jacobean portraiture, in which there is no chiaroscuro, no moulding shadow, is often seen as a simple technical failure, the chasm between Holbein and Van Dyck. Cecil, like James, hated being painted, which is why nearly all images of him repeat the same, copied pose, in which his flat white face seems to lack definition, or even a third dimension. In portrait after portrait at Hatfield, as elsewhere, his face, with its unresponsive eyes, looks like an oval cut out of paper. But perhaps this two-dimensionality is a symptom of something else:

here, even with the luxury and thickness of the Turkey carpet underfoot and the Venetian silk velvets on the table, the ostrich feathers in the band of the hat, the Indian pearls at its brim, the jewelled pommel of the German sword on its embroidered hanger at the waist, still there is, washing over it all, the clarity of a pure, unshadowed, Protestant light.

One can read almost everything from this visual and aesthetic amalgam into the making of the King James Bible. Precious light is what the Translators of the King James Bible thought, at least in part, they were bringing to their readers. James himself had written that 'it is one of the golden Sentences, which Christ our Sauiour vttered to his Apostles, that there is nothing so couered, that shal not be reuealed, neither so hidde, that shall not be knowen; and whatsoeuer they haue spoken in darkenesse, should be heard in the light'. Light was understanding. 'Translation it is that openeth the window, to let in the light,' wrote Miles Smith, the author of the Preface to the Bible, 'that breaketh the shell, that we may eat the kernel; that putteth aside the curtain, that we may look into the most Holy place; that removeth the cover of the well, that we may come by the water.'

The light of understanding was one of the qualities which Christ had brought to the world. Smith's wonderful words, easy and without pretension; sensuous without affectation; profoundly generous, shaped by a desire to reveal the innermost secrets to all, might stand as representative for the underlying aim of all the Translators. When Lancelot Andrewes died, William Laud, his disciple and admirer, then Bishop of London, wrote simply in his diary, that Andrewes had been 'the great light of the Christian world'.

It may be difficult to think of an age in which multiple and apparently contradictory qualities are rubbed so closely together but the multiplicity – and the love of *mixture*, which took such striking form in the hugely exaggerated hermaphrodites which decorated so many of the great Jacobean interiors – was something from which the King James Bible would draw its vitality. The flat, overall illumination of Protestant ideology was all very well but for these sophisticates, pure, simple plainness was not enough. Francis Bacon, corrupt, brilliant and unlikeable, builder of his own great pair of houses, now disappeared, not far away at St Albans, famous for the pale-faced catamites he kept to warm his bed, the inventor of the English essay, later to be Lord Chancellor, and, later still, accused of corruption, to be thrown to parliament as a sop to their demands, defined in his essay 'On Truth' the subtle and shifting Jacobean relationship to light and beauty, to plainness and richness, to clarity and sparkle. 'This same Truth', he wrote,

> is a Naked, and Open day light, that doth not shew the Masques, and Mummeries, and Triumphs of the world, halfe so Stately, and daintily, as candlelights. Truth may perhaps come to the price of a pearle, that sheweth best by day: But it will not rise to the price of a Diamond, or Carbuncle, that sheweth best in varied lights. A mixture of a Lie doth ever adde Pleasure.

That shifting, layered sensibility is also, in part, the world into which the King James Bible was born. The king's instructions were perfectly explicit: they were to use 'circumlocution', in other words language in which meaning was to be 'sett forth gorgeously'. There was no terror of richness in this. Richness, as King David had known when he decorated the temple for God, was one of the attributes of God. Majesty, honour and power were gorgeous in themselves and the Jacobean sense of the beautiful loved both pearls and diamonds, both openness and ceremony. Miles Smith referred in his Preface to 'the Sun of righteousness, the Son of God', and it was the beams of that sun which the King James Translators would bring to the people.

But the sense of clarity and directness was sewn and fused to those other Jacobean virtues: a pattern of order and authority; the majestic substance, the 'meat' of the word of God; the great ceremonial atmosphere of its long, carefully organised, musical rhythms, a ceremony of the word; an atmosphere both godly and kingly; both rich and pure, both multiplicitous and plain. This Bible, in other words, would absorb the full aesthetics of the age. You only have to read the Translators at full flood, feeling behind them the sense of unstoppable divine authority, to hear the immense, gilded majesty of the translation. In describing God's assembling of the armies of a vengeful justice, they reached their apogee:

> And he will lift vp an ensigne to the nations from farre, and will hisse vnto them from the end of the earth: and behold they shall come with speed and swiftly.
>
> None shalbe weary, nor stumble amongst them: none shall slumber nor sleepe, neither shall the girdle of their loynes be loosed, nor the latchet of their shooes be broken.
>
> Their roaring *shalbe* like a lyon, they shall roare like yong lions: yea they shal roare and lay hold of the pray, and shall carie *it* away safe, and shall deliuer *it*.
>
> And in that day they shall roare against them, like the roaring of the sea: and if *one* looke vnto the land, behold darkenesse *and* sorrow, and the light is darkened in the heauens therof.

NINE

When we do luxuriate and grow riotous in the gallantnesse of this world

And I will break the pride of your power; and I will make your heaven as iron, and your earth as brass:

And if ye walk contrary unto me, and will not hearken unto me; I will bring seven times more plagues upon you according to your sins.

I will also send wild beasts among you, which shall rob you of your children, and destroy your cattle, and make you few in number; and your highways shall be desolate.

And if ye will not be reformed by me by these things, but will walk contrary unto me;

Then will I also walk contrary unto you, and will punish you yet seven times for your sins.

Leviticus 26:19, 21–4

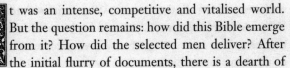t was an intense, competitive and vitalised world. But the question remains: how did this Bible emerge from it? How did the selected men deliver? After the initial flurry of documents, there is a dearth of evidence almost until the final printed volume appeared in 1611. Once the king had decided it should happen; once Bancroft had disseminated the Rules; and once the Translators had been chosen, almost the entire process drops from view. A few tiny glimpses remain. In November 1604, the ubiquitous Lancelot Andrewes was asked to attend a meeting of the Society of Antiquaries to which he had been elected in the summer. He sent a note to Mr Hartwell, secretary of the society, to excuse

his absence because 'this afternoon is our translation time'. As the Oxford antiquary, Anthony à Wood, recorded, some of the Oxford translators began meeting once a week in John Reynolds's rooms in Corpus Christi College, and 'there as 'tis said, perfected the work, not withstanding the said Doctor, who had the chief hand in it, and all the while sorely afflicted with gout'. Beyond that, of the beginning of the process, there was for centuries almost nothing to say. More recently, though, scholars have made discoveries which throw some real light on the process, in particular three long-hidden manuscripts.

The first is a vellum-bound book, of about 125 pages, the page size slightly smaller than foolscap, the paper gratifyingly thick and substantial. It belonged at one stage of its life to William Sancroft, the passionate Emmanuel undergraduate who later became Archbishop of Canterbury. He gave it to the library housed above the cloisters of the archbishop's London palace at Lambeth, where Richard Bancroft had established it – England's first public access library – in 1610.

This manuscript, number 98, remained in the library, uninspected and unvalued, until a Californian scholar, E. E. Willoughby, recognised it for what it was in 1955. It is still there today and can be requested from the shelves by anyone who walks in off the Embankment. Why is it not more famous? Why not more treasured? It should be, because this, very nearly uniquely, is as near as any of us will ever come to a manuscript of the King James Bible.

Its title is *An English Translation of the Epistles of Paule the Apostle*, and each page is ruled out in red ink into double columns with a margin to left and right. Only the left-hand column and margin are used; throughout the book the right-hand column, and its margin, remain blank. Except for one or two italic notes, the entire text is written in the spiky, cursive manner of the secretary-hand, the style of handwriting used in English legal documents from the fifteenth to the seventeenth centuries. And that gives a hint to its character. Any tendency to believe that the creation of this Bible was an act of passionate inspiration; or that somehow in the age of Shakespeare and Donne, the making of this book was a wild eruption of untutored genius – that fantasy is dispelled within seconds of opening the manuscript. It is like an accountant's document, businesslike, its double-ruled columns more like a ledger than a work of literature. It is a version of the Epistles, prepared by the second Westminster company under William Barlow before being circulated, according to Bancroft's Rules, to the other companies and to other learned men in the kingdom. There is no telling which of Barlow's company wrote it, but the manuscript has clearly gone through several hands. Missing words have been supplied, letters added, spelling corrected, punctuation changed. It has an air of carefulness, efficiency, good government, not of inspiration: it exudes a particularly bureaucratic kind of holiness.

There must once have been many such manuscript books, prepared for circulation, the second blank column awaiting the remarks of other scholars and divines. We know this, because another remarkable discovery has been made: a letter requesting the return of such a manuscript book when it was needed for the final editing process. The letter was written on 5 December 1608 by William Eyre, a fellow of Emmanuel, who has no other known connection with the translation, to James Ussher, then the young Chancellor of St Patrick's Cathedral in Dublin and later a great scholar, owner of the Book of Kells, who employed agents to scour the Middle East for ancient manuscripts, and famous, along with the puritan preacher John Lightfoot of Cambridge, as the man who calculated that God had created the earth on Sunday 23 October 4004 BC, at nine o'clock in the morning, London time, or midnight in the Garden of Eden.

Eyre's letter to Ussher brings one close to the atmosphere surrounding the work. 'In my absence from Cambridge,' he wrote, 'there was an order taken from the Kings Matie by the Arch B. of Canterb. that the translation of the Bible shalbe finished and printed as soone as may be.'

It has often been suggested that James played no part in the translation after commissioning it. All the documents of the Privy Council between 1600 and 1613 were destroyed in a Whitehall fire and, apart from this and Bancroft's early letters, there is no official record of James's interest. Protestant and anti-royalist historians have jumped on this. The king may, in a passing fancy, have begun the process, they have maintained, but he didn't have anything to do with its completion or coming forth. In fact, given how thin any kind of surviving evidence is, it is remarkable how often James's concern for the project appears, and always with the same note of urgency and concern to get it right and get it done 'as soone as may be', not to lose the project in the swamps of academic indigence.

Eyre continued: 'Hereupon I am earnestly requested to gett agayne that copy of our part wch I lent you for D. Daniel his use.' What Eyre means by 'our part' is not clear, but it is at least likely that these are the books of the Old Testament translated by Laurence Chaderton and his company. Nor does anyone know who D. Daniel is. That is not a name associated with the translation. Clearly, the whole process was spread more widely through the intellectual community of the British isles than any document records.

'[F]or albeit there be 2 fayer written copies out of it; yet there will be use of it because I noted in the margent ... the places wch were doubted of. And this marking of places that want consideration is not in the others.' Eyre was anxious that Ussher should send the annotated copy back 'so soone as you can after my letters come to your hands'.

This is the world in which the Lambeth MS. 98 has its being. It is very modern: company life, a memo that has gone astray, the chairman requiring a report, a project which had been stalled a little, with too many opinions canvassed from too many experts, needing now to be wrapped up and delivered.

The third document is more intimate with the process of translation than either the Lambeth manuscript or the Eyre letter. It is a record of a scholar in the very process of translating. It too had been lying ignored for centuries in a famous British library and it too was discovered by the indefatigable Dr Willoughby on his great 1950s trawl. He found it in the Bodleian Library in Oxford, James's favourite place in England. On his famous visit to the library in August 1605, surrounded by the chained-up books, he told the assembled dons, with all the eloquence and charm of which he was capable:

> Were I not a King, I would be a University-man. And I could
> wish, if ever it be my lot to be carried captive, to be shut up
> in this prison, to be bound with these chains, and to spend
> my life with these fellow captives which stand here chained.

The book which Dr Willoughby discovered was an edition of the Bishops' Bible printed in 1602. This, of course, was the Elizabethan version of the English Bible on which Bancroft's Rules required the Translators to base their own. Forty copies, in unbound sheets, were said to have been acquired for their use and distributed to them. The Bodleian volume was probably one of those sets, later bound together. It was acquired by the library in 1646 for 13s 4d and catalogued as 'a large Bible wherein is written down all the Alterations of the last translacōn'. What no one realised at the time, or for another three centuries, was that this Bible was not only an account of the alterations made; it was an instrument in the translation itself.

As another American scholar, Dr Ward Allen, has shown, one can trace in this Bible the very heart of the process. Marked on its pages are the first suggestions of an individual Translator who had this Bible in his rooms. He would then have taken it to the weekly meeting of his company, where the others would discuss and analyse his choices and decisions. Their comments and corrections were then added. One can read it now like an oscilloscope trace of the very act of translation itself.

This is not the place for a long analysis, but it is instructive to look at one example from Luke. In Luke 1:57, the moment when Elizabeth, the mother of John the Baptist, the herald of Christ, gives birth, the Bishops' Bible text reads:

> Elizabeths time came that she should bee delivered, and she brought forth a son.

This, incidentally, is almost exactly the wording of William Tyndale's 1526 New Testament. It is an uncomplicated and straightforward moment, almost certainly too prosaic for Jacobean taste and, in one minute particular, inaccurate. The King James Translator on his own in his room marked the verse very carefully with Greek letters, as follows:

> κElizabeths time λcame that she should bee delivered, and she brought forth a son.

and in the margin beside it wrote 'κ *Now*' and 'λ *was fulfilled*', with the intention presumably that the verse should read:

> Now Elizabeths time was fulfilled that she should bee delivered, and she brought forth a son.

That is the suggestion he took to the weekly meeting. His co-Translators didn't entirely like what he had done. They accepted his inclusion 'Now', translating a word which is in the Greek, and giving an extra flick both of vitality and of conversational engagement to the verse, the storyteller drawing you in. But his other suggestion was rejected. The phrase '*was fulfilled*' was a brave attempt at just the kind of lexical enrichment the Jacobeans enjoyed, and on which the King James Bible, almost subliminally, often relies. It carries a double hidden pun: not only had the time come for Elizabeth's son to be born, but she was both filled full with the child in her womb and fulfilled in her role and duty as the mother of the Baptist.

The idea is marvellous but the word is not quite right, a little dense, even a little technical. So *'was fulfilled'* is crossed out in the margin and replaced with *'full time came'*. As a result, the reading in the King James Bible, with which the English-speaking world has been familiar ever since, is Tyndale plus first Oxford Translator plus revision by the Oxford company:

> Now Elizabeths full time came that she should bee deliuered, and she brought forth a sonne.

It is undoubtedly the best, more accurate for its inclusion of 'Now' and wonderfully subtle in the phrase they landed on. 'Full time came' is irreproachably English, simple, accessible, conceptually rich, as full of potent and resonant meanings as Elizabeth was with child. In Jacobean English, full can mean plump, perfect and overbrimming, and all of those meanings are here. It is difficult to imagine anything being better done, but it wasn't thought good enough for the twentieth-century translators of the New English Bible. They settled on:

> Now the time came for Elizabeth's child to be born, and she gave birth to a son.

That is a descent to dreariness, to a level of banality below Tyndale's, perhaps even unaware of what the second Oxford company's subtle minds had given them. The modern world had lost the thing which informs every act and gesture of Hatfield, of the King James Bible, and of that incomparable age: a sense of encompassing richness which stretches unbroken from the divine to the sculptural, from theology to cushions, from a sense of the beauty of the created world to the extraordinary capabilities of language to embody it.

This is about more than mere sonority or the beeswaxed heritage-appeal of antique vocabulary and grammar. The flattening of language is a flattening of meaning. Language which

is not taut with a sense of its own significance, which is apologetic
in its desire to be acceptable to a modern consciousness, language
in other words which submits to its audience, rather than in-
structing, informing, moving, challenging and even entertaining
them, is no longer a language which can carry the freight the
Bible requires. It has, in short, lost all authority. The language
of the King James Bible is the language of Hatfield, of patriarchy,
of an instructed order, of richness as a form of beauty, of authority as a form of good; the New English Bible is motivated by
the opposite, an anxiety not to bore or intimidate. It is driven,
in other words, by the desire to please and, in that way, is a form
of language which has died.

That group of Oxford Translators was meeting in Merton, the
oldest college in Oxford. The college register had noted them
gathering there first on 13 February 1605, a good fire going,
books summoned for consultation from the college library. They
represented the heart of the translation process, given the responsibility for some of the key Christian texts: the Gospels, the
Acts of the Apostles and Revelation, a book of such violence and
inflammatory imagery that many sixteenth-century Protestants
had wished it excluded from the Bible. Only the Epistles, which
were given to the second Westminster company, under the control of Bancroft's hyper-loyalist William Barlow, were of anything like equal importance. This was the solid core of the
Jacobean church establishment, and no one with any hint of
dissension from it was allowed near these texts. There were, as
usual, the workhorses on the committee: a fellow of St John's
called John Peryn (or Pern) who resigned his other posts to
concentrate on the translation; another called Ralph Ravens, a
country vicar of whom little is known beyond his name; John
Harmar, warden of Winchester College; and Dr Hutten, canon

James VI, king of Scotland, in a portrait attributed to Adrian Vanson, painted in 1595 when he was 29. His wary, covert look was the product of a difficult and often desperate youth.

SERO, SED SERIO

Robert Cecil, Secretary of State, soon to be earl of Salisbury,
a hunchback and a busy man, who loathed having his picture painted.
This portrait was made by John de Critz the elder in 1602 as Cecil
was organising James's succession to the English throne. *Sero Sed Serio*
is the Cecil motto, *Late but in earnest*, the watchword of the modest
but loyal secretary.

SETTINGS FOR THE TRANSLATION
Part of a slightly sanitised panorama of London made by Claes van
Visscher in 1616. From the ramshackle Palace of Whitehall on the left,
a string of aristocratic palaces stretches along the north bank of the
Thames. On the south bank is the Swan, the theatre where Thomas
Middleton's 'A Chaste Maid in Cheapside' was often performed.

Anthonis van den Wyngaerde's depiction of Hampton Court Palace,
drawn in about 1544, where the idea for the King James Bible was born
in early 1604. An airy palace and garden to which the court had escaped
from the plague-infested capital.

THE TRANSLATION TEAM
Richard Bancroft, Archbishop of Canterbury and principal
organiser of the King James Bible, by an unknown artist, his face
worn by decades of struggle against the extreme puritans, a
lifetime's mission which had 'hardened the hands of his soul.'

Lancelot Andrewes, chief Translator, Bishop in succession of
Chichester, Ely and Winchester, host of £3,000 banquets for
his king, prose writer of genius, who spent five hours every
morning at prayer, much of it in tears, weeping for
the miserableness of his soul.

Sir Henry Savile, by far the most glamorous of the Translators,
buccaneer-scholar, the only Translator not to take Holy
Orders. When this portrait was painted in 1594 by the Fleming
Hieronimo Custodis, Savile was 45, Warden of Merton
College, Oxford, and soon to be Provost of Eton.

LEFT John Overall, Translator and Bishop of Norwich, in a portrait engraved by Wenceslaus Hollar. Overall's raised eyebrow is a conventional signal in portraits of Reformation churchmen, a sign of enquiring protestant intelligence rather than papist credulity.

BELOW James Montagu or Mountagu, Translator and Bishop of Bath and Wells, one of James's favourite churchmen and the patron of many ministers who shared his own clear and uncompromising Calvinist convictions.

Vera Effigies. Reverendi in Cristo
Patris Dñi: IOH: OVERALL.
Episcopi Norwicensis.

ABOVE Miles Smith, Bishop of Gloucester, Translator and author of the great preface to the King James Bible, who famously walked out of one sermon which bored him to go to the pub.

LEFT George Abbot, Archbishop of Canterbury in succession to Richard Bancroft, Translator and churchman of unremitting seriousness.

RIGHT Figures of the night I:
A costume design for a
blacked-up English Countess in
Ben Jonson's and Inigo Jones's
'Masque of Blacknesse'. At the
dénouement, the pure light of
James's own presence would
turn her white.

BELOW Figures of the night II:
The Gunpowder conspirators
of 1605, portrayed in a contemporary handbill as men of
darkness, alive with whispered
secrets.

CONCILIVM SEPTEM NOBILIVM ANGLORVM CONIVRANTIVM IN NECEM IACOBI · I·
MAGNÆ BRITANNIÆ REGIS TOTIVSQ · ANGLICI CONVOCATI PARLEMENTI ·

...ates   Robert
Winter

Christopher
Wright

Iohn
Wright

Thomas
Percy

Guido
Fawkes

Robert
Catesby

Thomas
Winter

RIGHT Love of the flesh I: The deep décolletage of Frances Howard, Countess of Somerset, is a mark not of her own degeneracy but of a Jacobean court fashion in an age which valued lusciousness.

BELOW Love of the flesh II: Christian IV of Denmark, James's brother-in-law, the most pleasure-loving man in Europe, whose visit to England in 1606 witnessed scenes of debauchery at which even the Jacobean courtiers blanched.

William Sancroft, later Archbishop of Canterbury when still the young master of Emmanuel College, Cambridge. Few faces show more clearly the atmosphere of passionate puritanism engendered at Emmanuel by its first Master, the Translator Laurence Chaderton.

The holiness of simplicity: Loughwood Meeting House,
near Axminster in Devon, although built in about 1653,
is a capsule of the puritan aesthetic: the elevation of the
word in the dominance of the pulpit, no enrichment,
the all-revealing light.

The aesthetics of richness: the King's Closet at Knole in Kent
was a dressing room, hung with a 17th-century mohair cloth,
watered and stamped to look like damask, part of the
consciously glorious visual environment in which
the King James Bible was made.

A reconstruction of Theobalds, the Elizabethan
prodigy house with which Robert Cecil
dazzled his new king on James's first journey into England,
a display of glass unrivalled until the 20th century.
Theobalds was demolished after the Civil War.

RIGHT Hatfield House, the Marble Hall: the height of
Jacobean taste, precisely contemporary with the King James Bible.
Both building and translation were retrospective in
the mimicking of the past and superbly modern in the deep
lusciousness of their textures.

OVERLEAF Hatfield House, the stained glass in
the Chapel (1610): the first stained glass windows
installed in England since the Reformation seventy years
before, a radical return towards richness as a route to God.

of Christ Church. All were learned Greek scholars, they had connections with the great – Harmar, a committed Calvinist, translator of the sermons of Beza, Calvin's successor in Geneva, had been a client and protégé of the Earl of Leicester – but they were not of the same standing as the heavy-hitting power-players who surrounded them.

The men at the core of this Oxford group were deeply engaged with the realities of money and power. That political involvement brought a worldliness and glamour which provided a certain steel. And that raises an intriguing question: was the King James Bible so alive precisely because the Translators weren't entirely good?

George Abbot was perhaps the ugliest of them all, a morose, intemperate man, whose portraits exude a sullen rage. Even in death, he was portrayed on his tomb in Holy Trinity, Guildford, as a man of immense weight, with heavy, wrinkled brow and coldly open, staring eyes. He looks like a bruiser, a man of such conviction and seriousness that anyone would think twice about crossing him. What was it that made George Abbot so angry?

Much of it can be put down to what he would have learned from his parents of their suffering when young. They had been poor people, living in a small cottage next to the bridge in Guildford. His father was a clothworker – a member of one of the educated, urban trades which, along with printers, bookbinders and booksellers, upholsterers, pewterers, barbers and cooks, provided the seed-bed in which early Protestantism grew in England, as in the rest of Europe. Both Abbot parents, the church historian Thomas Fuller recorded, 'embraced the truth of the Gospel in King Edward's days and were persecuted for it in Queen Mary's reign'. The precise nature of their suffering is not recorded.

They were certainly a brilliant and ambitious family. One of George Abbot's brothers became Master of Balliol and then Bishop of Salisbury, another Lord Mayor of London and

Governor of the East India Company, where he made a nabob's fortune, in 1614 alone earning 60 pounds in weight of gold from the import of Indian commodities. George himself became Archbishop of Canterbury. He was the cleverest and the gloomiest, fiercely Calvinist, anti-papist, anti-ceremony, but in equal measure, anti-Separatist and anti-libertarian. He of course supported the idea of bishops, but only as what was called 'a superintending pastorate', in the eyes of God indistinguishable from any other minister. He could be the most crawling of royal supplicants, saying in one pamphlet of James's life that it was 'so immaculate and unspotted that even malice itself could never find true blemish in it'. The king, in Abbot's opinion, could be compared in virtue, intelligence, wisdom and wit to David, Solomon, Josiah, Constantine the Great, Moses, Hezekiah and Theodosius. Abbot devoted a paragraph each to these comparisons. But this was a bluff. In his heart, Abbot was no courtier, and when it came to a conflict between royal and divine authority (over the famous divorce case of Lady Essex in the following decade) he, unlike other more intensely royalist bishops such as Lancelot Andrewes, voted for what he saw as God's interest (no divorce) over the king's explicit desire for a divorce to be granted.

Abbot tried his hand at court manipulation. James was always vulnerable to male charm and beauty and Abbot had a part in introducing to him the most entrancingly beautiful boy, George Villiers, soon to be Duke of Buckingham, hoping that advantage would flow from such a lovely connection. Villiers, however, soon learned to ignore him and Abbot entered the last period of his life alienated from the court and in disgrace. Shooting deer in Hampshire one Tuesday in July 1621, he killed a gamekeeper by mistake. One Tuesday every month, he fasted, denying himself the meat pies he loved, in penance. He died in 1633, an outmoded and isolated figure.

It is easy enough to misinterpret men like George Abbot. He was stern, intransigent and charmless. He had no modern virtues and in a modern light can look absurd. Early every Thursday morning from 1594 to 1599, he preached a sermon on a part of the Book of Jonah. That is 260 Thursdays devoted to a book which, even if it is one of the jewels of the Old Testament – a strange, witty, surreal short story – is precisely four chapters long, a total of forty-eight verses. Abbot devoted over five sermons to each of them. (He was not alone in that; his brother Robert was the author of a vast commentary on Paul's Epistle to the Romans of such tedium that it remains in manuscript to this day; Arthur Hildersham, one of the pushiest of the Puritans, wrote 152 lectures on Psalm 51: if the Word of God encompassed everything, as these men sincerely believed, then no balloon of commentary or analysis could ever be enough. The age had word-inflation built into it.)

Abbot could be brutal as well as verbose. He once had 140 Oxford undergraduates arrested for not taking their hats off when he entered St Mary's Church. He had another man arrested at dinner in Christ Church 'for publicly in the hall making a very offensive declaration in the cause of the late Earl of Essex'. He had religious pictures burned in the Oxford marketplace and a stained-glass window in Balliol, showing a crucifix, before which an undergraduate had been praying and beating his breast, pulled down and destroyed. He would not hesitate, later in his career, to use torture against miscreants, nor to execute Separatists. And he was not indifferent to worldly things. In March 1600, he was told that the deanery of Winchester, the richest of all English sees, was vacant 'and to be had for £600'. Abbot considered it overnight and in the morning 'the £600 was paid, and Dr Abbot was made Dean'. It was an enormous investment but a good one and as he advanced up the episcopal ladder, Abbot habitually wore one gold ring 'with a turkoyse in it' and another 'with a West Indian sapphire' in which his coat of arms was cut. His collection of antique coins and of gold and silver pieces, of curious cups and other elaborate vessels made of serpentine, and 'a great silver hourglass for preaching' were all kept in a large and beautiful inlaid cabinet.

A wicked, mean, greedy, self-indulgent, vituperative, pompous bishop? It is certainly possible, before one reads a word that Abbot wrote, to see him as that, an obdurate brute, coarsened by rage and the worst of the Protestant inheritance.

There is more to him. He could joke about his devotions to Jonah. 'Before that I can come to this fourth chapter,' he wrote, 'the fourth year has now expired.' He could write lyrically and movingly about the fading of earthly life: 'remember how that every winter the glory of the trees and all the woods is decayed; their leaves lie in the dust, their cheerful green is but blackness – the sap and life is held in the root within the ground – all the tree doth seem dead'. That is not far from what John Donne might have written. Or on sin, which

> is like a smoke, like fire, it mounteth upward, and comes even before God to accuse us; it is like a serpent in our bosom, still ready to sting us; it is the devil's daughter. A woman hath her pains in travail and delivery but rejoiceth when she seeth a child is born; but the birth of sin is of a contrary fashion; for all the pleasure is in the bringing forth, but when it is finished and brought forth, it tormenteth us continually; they haunt us like tragicall furies.

Eloquence, though, is not the preserve of the virtuous – or even the entertaining. A version of Abbot's interminable disquisitions on the tale of Jonah was published in 1600 and a copy of it is preserved in the Cambridge University Library. An early-seventeenth-century reader, pen in hand, began to pick his way through it.

> When we do luxuriate and grow riotous [Abbot began one magnificent passage] in the gallantnesse of this world . . . and with the vntamed heyfer which is full fed, and growne perfectly wanton, we kicke against the sole author of our happinesse and beatitude; with the Magnificoes of the world, and

great-mouthed Gloriosoes we do both contemn our brethren, and speake against the Highest.

The reader, alerted perhaps by the marvellous vigour of this Puritan contempt for those he is accusing of contempt, starts to write in the margin. But then the grandeur of the language begins to lose him. Abbot relishes the word 'audacitie'. The margin notes: 'audacitie is boldnes'. From then on the reader is reduced to parsing for himself, converting Abbot's Latinisms into English. For Abbot's 'defigrement' he writes 'illes', for 'impetuous' 'violent', for 'alacritie' 'cheerfulnes' and finally for Abbot's baffling 'inculcating' and 'insinuation' there are just stars and underlinings. What on earth could these words have meant? And after page 43, the seventeenth-century reader gives up. Abbot is boring and the remaining 592 pages are entirely unmarked. Along with the other oceans and continents of Jacobean biblical exegesis, they had never been read.

It isn't difficult to see how the King James Bible emerges from this pattern of thought and language. There is an immense and sonorous dignity to Abbot's style, a torque towards grandeur, a natural majesty, but also an understanding of metaphor, of the sudden vitalising presence of the autumn leaves, the smoke, the woman in labour, the heifer kicking and dancing around the early summer meadow, fat with new grass, as happy as the Magnificoes and Gloriosoes even then parading at court. The gift of this language-moment, the great Jacobean habit of mind on which the King James Bible rides for chapter after chapter and book after book, is this swinging between majesty and tangibility, the setting of the actual and perceptible within an enormous and enriching frame, the sense of intimacy between great and small, the embodiment of the most universal ideas in the most humble of forms, the sense in other words that the universe, from God to heifer, is one connected fabric.

Amazingly, Abbot was also the author of a bestselling guide to the world, which remained in print for sixty-five years, going through five editions, the last in 1664. This work, intended for his pupils, probably envisaged by him as a spare time entertainment, far less significant than the great work on Jonah, turns out to be the place in which one can come closest to George Abbot, to see behind the gauze of the man in the pulpit, the church administrator, the court politician. Off his guard, he reveals himself and by extension his age and its curious mixture of openness, inquiry and blinkered hostility.

A briefe Description of the whole worlde is in many ways a wonderful and humane book, full of enthusiasm. France 'is one of the most rich and absolute Monarchies of the world'. Civilisation is not a European phenomenon: 'The people of *Chyna* are learned in almost all artes. No Country yeeldeth more precious Marcandize, then the workmanship of them.' There is no grandeur of language here, nor any romance in Abbot's description of the world, but an exact, plain, reliable and unvitriolic appreciation of the virtues of others. It's the Calvinist on tour. If the Africans are 'exceedingly blacke', that is no mark against them. In fact, Africa, as Pliny had said, is a source of marvels and here, remarkably, from one of the most conservative of all those involved in the translation, is a straightforward denial of creationism:

> Often times new and strange shapes of Beasts are brought foorth there: the reason whereof is, that the Countrie being hott and full of Wildernesses, which haue in them litle water, the Beastes of all sortes are enforced to meete at those few watering places that be, where often times contrary kinds haue coniunction the one with the other: so that there ariseth new kinds of species, which taketh part of both.

Abbot's astonishing theory of the origin of species – God's creation is not immutable; the changes in that creation come about through the influence of the environment; sex is the crucial transmitter and transformer of genetic identity – does not quite stumble on the theory of natural selection but is moving in that direction. The King James Bible is the work of people who were dazzlingly open, at least in some parts of their minds, to the new spirit of scientific inquiry.

Elsewhere, a more familiar Abbot appears. The Irish are 'rude, and superstitious', the Scots 'barbarous' and the Jesuits filled with a 'blind zeal'. But what he had heard of the native Americans – having never been there, and clearly not having discussed them with his fellow Translator John Layfield, who had – left him quivering with shock and rage. They were

> naked, vnciuill, some of them deuourers of mans flesh, ignorant of shipping, without all kinde of learning, hauing no remembrance of historie or writing among them: never hauing hard of any such religion as in other places of the world is knowne: but being utterly ignorant of Scripture, & *Christ* or *Moses*, or any God: neither hauing among them any token of crosse, Church, temple, or deuotion, agreeing with other nations.

As one part of the background to the King James Bible, this is an important passage. The Americans encountered by Europeans on arrival were to be condemned because they weren't *literate*: 'There was no sort of good Literature to bee found amongst them,' Abbot wrote. Not only were they not like the English, they were not like the people of the Old World, who, for all their differences, were united from here to China by this one thread: they all wrote and read. Even if God was English, the Bible was not. It had come from the riches of the Mediterranean culture which Abbot and all cultivated Englishmen deeply admired. As scholars and linguists, they were not in any way xenophobic; but the textlessness of the Americans, that was a radical and shocking difference. Abbot could only imagine that it was the work of the devil:

> In all ages it hath appeared, that Sathan hath vsed ignorance as one of the chiefest meanes, whereby to encrease idolatrie, and consequently to enlarge his kingdome: it were otherwise

incredible, that any who have in them reason and the shape of men, should be so bruitishly ignorant of all kinde of true religion, and understanding deuotion.

Lying behind that are the famous words of St Paul – the rubric scalded into every Puritan's heart – 'In understanding be men', and much of the coming English experience in America will stem from it: as people of the book, of rationality, of text, of translation, of the Bible, eventually of this Bible, of the word, they are of their essence set against other human beings, or at least beings with the shape of men, who are in thrall to Satan precisely because they do not possess or understand the word. The American Indians had, Abbot recognised, some virtues. They could be kind, affable and hospitable to strangers but, in the light of everything else, those qualities were not enough: they did not possess the one thing it was essential to possess. They were shut out from the truth.

Alongside Abbot in this second Oxford company were three of the most powerful of all the Translators. No company had a greater density of egos than this. James Mountagu, the Dean of the Chapel Royal who had whispered so intimately in the king's ear at the Hampton Court Conference, found his place in this all-important company, as did Thomas Ravis, first Bishop of Gloucester, and then of London. Ravis was another uncompromisingly political bishop, a man who had out-Bancrofted Bancroft in his pursuit of the seditious Nonconformists with whom Gloucester was stuffed. It was his enthusiasm in search of the quarry that recommended him to the archbishop and landed him the London job. Christianity was not a religion of love and forgiveness for these men and Ravis arrived in London brimming over with an appetite to nail his enemies. Of all places in England, London had the largest proportion of Nonconformists, both

Presbyterians who wanted to remain part of the church but could not accept that everything in the Book of Common Prayer was sanctioned by scripture; and the most deeply entrenched Separatists, who were unwilling to submit to the authority of any established church at all.

These distinguished and powerful men gathered together to translate the key passages of the New Testament in the rooms of the most glamorous of the Translators, Sir Henry Savile. He stands out from the rest, a scholar, courtier, politician, educationalist, mathematician and astronomer. If Laurence Chaderton had the sweetest nature, Lancelot Andrewes the most passionate soul, John Layfield the most charming manner and George Abbot the most alarming glare, then Henry Savile undoubtedly had the most exotic and alluring presence. He was, according to the indefatigable gossip John Aubrey, 'an extraordinary handsome man, no lady having a finer complexion'. That must have been when he was young. The earliest portrait that survives of him, a superb picture by the Fleming Hieronimo Custodis, was painted in 1594 when he was forty-five, mid-career, and it is a strikingly manly image: one hand on hip, in the self-proclaiming way of the Renaissance courtier, the other hanging easily at the side of his basket-hilted sword, a doublet both black (the colour of statesmanship) and richly embroidered (no denier of the world). Beside him a blank folio book lies open on a table, an enigmatic symbol: yet to be written in? Savile's own uninscribed future? But it is Savile's head, that great intellectual instrument, held above a huge simple ruff, which draws one's attention. He looks like a buccaneer, a scratchy beard and moustache, his thinning hair pushed roughly back across his ears, a big aggressive vigour in his stance. If this man was the greatest scholar of his age, there is not a whiff of the library about him. At the heart of the portrait are the eyes, curiously painted, their look slewed a little sideways, avoiding the viewer's own, inescapably duplicitous, on the make.

He was born in 1549 in a family of poor Yorkshire gentry.

It was his cousins who owned the land outside London on which Savile Row would be built. But Henry Savile was brilliant and he thrived on his intellect. He entered Brasenose College, Oxford, in 1561 and was elected a fellow of Merton in 1565. When he took his Master of Arts degree in October 1570, the lectures he gave were on Ptolemy's *Almagest*, the great Greek text describing the world-centred cosmology which had shaped the European vision of the universe since it was written in Alexandria in about AD 130. Lectures on the *Almagest* had been an Oxford staple for centuries, but Savile put a modern and characteristic twist on an old subject. His notes for the lectures survive and they are marked by an appetite for the new. The lectures are, in fact, a manifesto for the new learning. Oxford, he told his audience, was hopelessly adrift from what was going on in Europe. Why did they not read the works of Regiomontanus, the great fifteenth-century German geometrician, he asked, nor of Copernicus, 'Mathematicorum Modernorum Princeps', the prince of modern mathematicians, who had revolutionised the understanding of the solar system? The undergraduates at Oxford did not understand the importance of mathematics, let alone astronomy, mechanics, optics or trigonometry. They had no teachers who could guide them on their way. This was not a case of training up navigators: there was a far grander Renaissance vision at work. The study of mathematics, Savile argued, turns a man into an educated, civilised human being. Did they not remember the story of Aristippus who, on being shipwrecked on Rhodes, realised that the inhabitants were civilised men when he saw a mathematical figure drawn in the sand? If any stranger came nowadays to England's shores, they would think they had landed in Barbary. When Giordano Bruno, the Italian free-thinker, rejected by both Geneva and Rome for his theories, had visited Oxford in 1588, he had 'talked of the new astronomy and infinite worlds, the sun dying of its own heat, the planets decaying into atomic mist'.

But Oxford wasn't quite ready for such a strong draught. Bruno found it 'a constellation of ignorant, obstinate pedants: a herd of donkeys and swine'. That is what Savile meant; but he was not a man for rudeness.

It was a flourish of challenges, from someone who felt he had a great deal to teach the world. Colleges at Oxford and Cambridge often sent their promising young fellows abroad to buy books for their libraries (which were tiny; it was thought a great achievement during Savile's time at Merton that he increased their number of printed books from 300 to 1,000), and in 1578 Savile was sent out on a long European tour. Merton paid for it, £6 13s 4d, and with him went a small party of other brilliant young intellectual and aristocratic Elizabethans: Henry Neville, later a Jacobean diplomatist; George Carew, another Jacobean statesman; and Philip Sidney's younger brother Robert, all founder members of the Society of Antiquaries. They went to France, Poland; Bohemia, Germany, Austria and Italy, including Rome, visiting and impressing the greatest European humanists, scholars and astronomers with their sophisticated, multilingual charm and cleverness. Robert Sidney seems to have decided to split from Savile, who was acting as something of a tutor to him. His brother Philip sent him a letter:

> I have written to Mr Savile, I wish you kept still together, he is an excellent man ... and for your sake I perceive he will do much, and if ever I be able I will deserve it of him ... Now (dear brother) take delight likewise in the mathematics, Mr Savile is excellent in them.

These were blue-chip connections into the heart of the English cultural and political establishment and Savile must have felt that the wind was in his sails. The commonplace book he kept on this early version of the Grand Tour (bound in limp vellum, with Italian paper) has also survived and it is full of the life-loving and self-admiring brio of a brilliant young man abroad. In

Poland, he announces the subject of the following notes first in Greek, '*Περὶ τησ των πολονων πολιτε΄ιασ*', of the political structures of the Poles, then in French '*et des droits roiaux*', of the royal prerogatives, and finally in Italian, '*la forma del governo*'.

The smugness of Henry Savile found its source not only in his own cleverness but also in the welcome he was getting from the great scholars of Renaissance Europe – one wrote to a friend recommending him as '*praestantissimi iuvenis*', in the first rank of youth – and the sheer delight he was taking in the pleasures around him and the company he kept. For years afterwards, he would get letters (in Latin) from his Italian and German friends reminiscing over the days when they 'used to converse so delightfully together in Venice'. Any idea that the culture from which the King James Bible emerged was parochial or insular, the great statement of an embattled island nation cut off from the corrupt and worldly currents of a degenerate continent, could not be further from the truth. A river of European influences runs through it, and through no more open a conduit than Henry Savile.

He was already intrigued by the works and figure of St John Chrysostom, the great fourth-century patriarch of Constantinople, whose elegant, conversational, witty and morally fierce sermons often left the Byzantine aristocrats in his congregation caught between laughter and dread at his ridicule of their wealth and pretensions. Chrysostom is a Jacobean figure, in his immediacy, his tendency to dramatise rather than to analyse and desiccate, his conjuring the vision, for example, at the Day of Judgement, of the poor calmly waiting for heaven, their small bags packed and ready beside them, while the rich 'in great perplexity, are wandering about, looking for a place to bury their gold, or someone they can leave it with! Why, O man, dost thou seek thy fellow slaves?'

This is just the perplexity, and just the divided consciousness, of the Jacobean rich, and Chrysostom's taunting voice is calculated to appeal to the sophistication of a Savile. By the 1580s he had already hired a professional researcher from Chania in Crete – there was a Venetian connection – to search for the oldest and purest of the Chrysostom manuscripts and to buy them. Savile recommended the agent look in Patmos, the beautiful island in the eastern Aegean where the monastery of St John was said to harbour the greatest treasures, and to acquire what he could. It was a lifelong fascination for Savile which culminated in his great edition of Chrysostom's work, printed and published between 1610 and 1612 at the appalling cost of £8,000. By then, Savile had assembled 15,800 sheets of manuscript (which he presented to the Bodleian Library in Oxford). All the great libraries of Europe had been searched, not only in Mount Athos, Constantinople and the island of Chalce, but in Paris, Vienna, Augsburg and Munich. To copy, analyse and translate, Savile hired some of the best scholars in England, including John Bois and Andrew Downes, Cambridge Greek scholars working on the Apocrypha for the King James translation. It is typical of the man that he consulted, and acknowledged, two of the great Jesuit scholars, Andreas Schott and Fronton du Duc, with no narrow-minded sectarian thought that their allegiance to the pope disqualified them from the task. The work was published in eight beautiful volumes, and was a commercial disaster, mounds of copies remaining unsold, even when reduced from the original £9 (about half the annual salary of a country vicar) to a knockdown £4 or even £3. But perhaps Savile was not concerned with commerce. Forget, as he would have wished, the copies mouldering in the Eton store (his contemporaries gossiped about little else) and remember instead the set still to be found in the great Sansovino library in Venice, which Savile sent to the Doge in January 1614, each volume bound in crimson satin.

Savile's edition of Chrysostom has been called 'the one great work of Renaissance scholarship carried out in England'. But there is no need to be too naive about the point and purpose of the scheme. It is a self-erected monument to a cosmopolitan, glorious and vain-spirited man who had climbed hard. On his return to England in 1582, the queen 'taking a liking to his parts and person' first made him her tutor in Greek and three years later procured him the wardenship of Merton. Savile had arrived. Lord Burghley and Francis Walsingham were his patrons, the Earl of Essex his intimate. A famous moment of Savile's wit is preserved from a conversation with Essex. The earl asked him what he thought of poets. 'They are the best of writers,' Savile said, 'next to them that write prose.'

Savile never took holy orders – he was the only one of the Translators not to – and that proved a problem when his eye settled on the next plum to be picked from the establishment tree. The provostship of Eton, with a fountain of patronage flowing from it, was, according to the statutes of the college, only to be held by a minister of the church. Savile wanted it. He manoeuvred hard to get it. Essex pressed his case but failed. The queen, responding to her favourite's requests on Savile's behalf, made Savile her secretary of the Latin tongue, and Dean of Carlisle 'in order to stop his mouth from importuning her any more for the provostship of Eton'. Savile then shamelessly turned to Essex's rival, Robert Cecil, to press his case. 'The man that may do most in this matter', he wrote to him, 'is your father [Lord Burghley], from whom one commendation in cold blood and seeming to proceed of judgement, shall more prevail with the Queen than all the affectionate speech that my lord of Essex can use.' When it was pointed out that Savile was unqualified for the post because of the statutes, he replied 'the queen has always the right of dispensing with statutes'.

Savile, perhaps the pushiest of the Translators, that bucca-neer spirit bursting out around the edges of the scholar, won the case. In 1596, he became, despite all the regulations, Provost of Eton. It was there that he gathered all the Hellenists and all the documents for his monumental edition of Chrysostom. He didn't renounce Merton. Far from it. Merton, which he had already beautified with a new library and lodgings, which he had elevated into a college full of distinguished men by carefully seeking out the most promising of the undergraduates to be fellows, was now to be his milch-cow. He transferred his favourites to Eton, conveniently near Windsor so that when the court came down, gloriosoes and grandees could visit and discourse learnedly with the fellows there. And he used all of Merton's resources to his own ends.

The Merton fellows considered themselves betrayed by their high-flying warden who 'hath been negligent and unprofitable by his personall absence from the colledge for the most parte of the years he hath been warden ther'. He had accepted money from a benefactor's will which had been meant to go towards improving the fellows' 'commons' and had taken a long time to hand on the benefits; he had let out a college manor to a friend on very favourable terms and had kept back some of the rent for himself; and had taken 'secret bribes or fines for the leases and turning the same to private use, to the common hinderance of the society'. Savile had, in other words, squeezed Merton for all it was worth. A brilliant man, a handsome man, a man of enormous energies and breadth of interests (he would, among all this, found the first chairs in geometry and astronomy at Oxford): all that is undeniable. But was this Translator of the Holy Bible a good man? There is not much evidence of that.

He was, of course, a reader of Machiavelli. He knew how to negotiate the shoals and rapids of court life. But there was a moment – and he is the only Translator of whom this is true – when he very nearly came adrift. Lurking beneath this surface brilliance and careful self-promotion within the double world of university and court, there is another faintly subversive layer. When he was still a young fellow of Merton in the 1570s, acting as second bursar, Savile had given disquisitions on two strikingly non-establishment themes: *Terra movetur circulariter* – the

Copernican clarion call, earth moves in a circular path around the sun, something almost no one would have accepted in England at the time; and, even more astonishingly, the at least mock-seditious *Democratia est optimus status reipublicae* (Rule by the people is the best condition for a state). In the early 1590s, Savile published the first English translation of the works of the Roman historian Tacitus. Savile was no great stylist and, even though, as will emerge, sixteenth- and seventeenth-century translation theory allowed translators quite freely to adapt and transform the original they were working on, his book is not an elegant thing. But in it there is an astonishing encomium on the rebellion of a late Roman republican Julius Vindex, governor of Gaul, against the tyrannical emperor Nero. The purpose of Vindex's rebellion, Savile wrote admiringly, was 'not to establish his owne souveraignety . . . but to redeeme his cuntrye from tyranny and bondage, which onely respect he regarded so much that in respect he regarded nothing his owne life or security'. Those rather clumsy words are not in Tacitus; they are Savile's elaboration and expansion on the text. And they would mean little if they had remained no more than academic theorising on the nature of legitimate government and its relation to popular consent. But it is utterly characteristic of Savile that a great deal more hinges on these words. He was already part of the circle around the Earl of Essex, the chivalrous, intelligent, eloquent and courtly hero of one part of the English establishment, a passionate Protestant, and deeply opposed to the careful, conservative, unwarlike and unglamorous policies of Burghley and his son. Cold Cecil rationality may have been useful in pressing suits but it was not an ideal to which Savile could devote his life. Already, lurking just beneath the surface of the 1590s, is a stirring of rebellion, at least in embryo. If the queen, or so the argument went, failed to pursue the path of Essex's noble, warlike and Christian crusade against Spain and the Catholics, and if instead she surrendered herself, her government and her country to the cautious and riskless policies of the Cecils – this is the argument over appeasement – then surely, according to Tacitus, it was the duty of someone in the position of the Earl of Essex to rebel, 'not to establish his owne souveraignety . . . but to redeeme his cuntrye from tyranny and bondage'. And the tyranny and bondage was not that of the queen but of the loathed Cecils who, it was believed in the Essex camp, held the queen in thrall.

Savile's great friend, a west country Greek scholar called Henry Cuffe, whom he had made a fellow at Merton, became Essex's private secretary. Cuffe wrote regularly to Savile at Eton or Merton, reporting on the secrets and the fears of the Essex circle. Their fevered plottings for an anti-Cecil coup came to a head in the spring of 1601, when Essex made his hopeless attempt on the throne in London. He had surprisingly wide support, including five earls, three barons and sixteen knights. James VI in Scotland had written to him encouragingly, but Cuffe had burnt the letter out of loyalty to his master. Cuffe and Savile were both implicated. Savile himself had all his papers impounded and was held under house arrest in the provost's rooms at Eton, but Cuffe was in far more deeply. Many of those whom he had attempted to woo on Essex's behalf gave evidence against him. Savile, who was never as subversive-minded as either Essex or his secretary, slipped smoothly out of any noose. Cuffe? He hardly knew the man, had never discussed anything of the kind with him. Savile kept his valuable posts. He would in time – it was said for £1,000 – get himself a knighthood. Cuffe was condemned to death and in his will left £500 to the Henry Neville, now Sir Henry, with whom Savile had gone gallivanting around Europe thirty years before, and

> With the like affection I desire that there may be given to my true and dear friend, Sir Henry Savile, £100; and I beseech him to continue the memory of his unfortunate friend, and ever to think charitably of him, however some endeavour to ruin and deface as well his name as his estate.

There is no evidence that Savile did anything to have Cuffe remembered with either honour or dignity. The Jacobean court could afford few such luxuries. Instead, perhaps, as the Oxford company translated St John's Gospel, Savile might have reflected on loyalty, on the fate of Cuffe and Essex, on his own standing in the Jacobean world, his comfortable place by its warming fires, and Peter's denial of Christ:

> Then saith the damosell that kept the doore vnto Peter, Art thou not also one of this mans disciples? He sayth, I am not.
>   And the seruants and officers stood there, who had made a fire of coales, (for it was colde) and they warmed themselues: and Peter stood with them, and warmed himselfe.

TEN

True Religion is in no way
a *gargalisme* only

It is the Spirit that quickeneth, the flesh profiteth nothing: the
wordes that I speake vnto you, they are Spirit, and they are life.

John 6:63

y 1608, the campaign by the Church of England
and its bishops against radical Nonconformists had
reached something of a lull. The pursuit and expul-
sion of Puritans had peaked two or three years before.
Many, on financial grounds, had signed the necessary documents
of conformity and been allowed to keep their places. At the same
time, the threat of international Catholicism had faded after the
imagined horrors summoned by the Gunpowder Plot had turned
out largely to be phantoms and mirages. A Europe-wide debate
was now going on, at least in print and among the elite, over
the competing claims of religion and state, obedience to the
pope or to the king, loyalty to God or nation – and in the course
of it Lancelot Andrewes defended the English Church against
the attacks of Roman cardinals – but it was an intellectual affair,
hardly troubling the everyday lives of the English people.

There were, of course, arguments: between the respective
rights of Crown and parliament, over money as ever and the
king's ability to impose customs dues, over the power and
jurisdictions of common law and the ecclesiastical courts. But

England was not on any high road to civil war. These were the digestive rumblings of a complex, old and mature society going through its motions. Essentially, for all the extravagance of the king and parliament's voluble assertion of its ancient rights, peace reigned. In diocese after diocese in England, the records show that neither Catholics nor extreme Puritans were being hunted down. Pax and Concordia reigned rather sleepily over the country and, on the whole, in quiet corners, without much intervention or harassment, English men and women were getting on with their lives and their religion. Revolution, martyrdom, the heroism of exile – these hardly featured in the landscape. The country was relatively fat on a series of good harvests, pursuing its interests, in many ways sharing a common idea of what was good: a Christian, orderly commonwealth.

As if on cue, in 1608, golf was introduced from Scotland for the first time, played around a 5-hole course on Blackheath, south of London. The leather balls, stuffed with feathers, lasted no more than one game each, particularly if it rained. At 5 shillings a time, it was a ruinously expensive but a strangely consoling pursuit, fitted to a country replete with contentment.

That is not how it looks from America. For Americans, the spring and summer of 1608 burns in the history of religious belief and the struggle for freedom of conscience as the months in which those Separatists who would later sail for New Plymouth on the *Mayflower*, known to us (but never to them) as the Pilgrim Fathers, finally gave up the struggle of living in England, unable to tolerate its oppressions any longer, and left, after great travails, for the freedoms of Amsterdam and then Leiden.

How can this be explained? How can one of the most pacific moments in English history be the source of something which, in retrospect, looks like one of its greatest ruptures? It is, in part, a question of scale and of perspective. From the point of view of the English establishment, the events in the small agricultural communities around Scrooby and Gainsborough, on the borders of Lincolnshire and Nottinghamshire, were no more than minor irritations at the outer edge of their concerns. There was a tiny cell of radical thinking here – with strong Cambridge connections, a stream of fire-breathing preachers coming north from the university city – wedded to all those extreme Puritan beliefs which the broadly tolerant English Church and state felt unable to accommodate. The Separatists' model was the ancient church of Antioch, in which there had been neither bishop nor clergy of any kind, and which was ruled 'by the Spirit', manifesting itself through the congregation. It was the congregation that appointed and ordained its own pastors, teachers, lay elders and deacons. In these gatherings, often in stables and outhouses, away from the sight of the church authorities, the priesthood of all believers was a living reality. Their services might last four hours, much of which was spent in prayer, often extempore, with no help from any prayer book, an unregulated, private spirit guiding the prophesyings of the faithful. Anyone, whether artisan or peasant, could expound the meaning of the scriptures. They held as their guiding sign the words of St Peter to all members of the church: 'But yee are a chosen generation, a royall Priesthood, an holy nation, a peculiar people, that yee should shewe forth the praises of him, who hath called you out of darknes into his marueilous light.' The accompanying note in the Geneva Bible, which the Scrooby Separatists would have read, makes it quite clear. People like them, it reassured them, were God's elect. They were the true believers and the rest of the world, who clearly did not attend as closely as they did to the very word of God, would be damned to hell. 'And lest any man should doubt whether he is chosen or not, the apostle calls us back to the voice of the gospel sounding both in our ears and minds.' Listen to the words of the Bible and you will be saved. Nothing else is necessary. It is that singularity of conviction which drove the Puritan and pilgrim experience.

Of course, those words of Peter's carry an explosively

subversive charge. A congregation of ploughmen and farriers to be described as 'a royal priesthood'? Labourers and carters God's own people? Where did that leave the institutions of king, bishop and church? Floundering in the wilderness or swallowed up, as a Separatist would have said, in a tide of their own corruption. Such Puritans would have felt themselves adrift in a world of wickedness. Earlier in 1607, when a flood invaded the low-lying moors of Somerset, it had been a sudden physical confirmation of everything that was wrong with England. 'Sinne overflowes our soules,' an anonymous pamphleteer had crooned, 'the Seas of all strange impieties have rusht in upon us: we are covered with the waves of abhomination and uncleannes: we are drowned in the black puddles of iniquity: wee swim up to the throates, nay even above the chins in Covetousness.'

That is not a frame of mind any government would happily condone, and clearly a coherently managed state church, with its necessary belief in a God-ordained central order and authority, could not tolerate the survival of such a Separatist cell. From time to time, ever since Bancroft's campaign had begun in 1604, one or two of the Scrooby Separatists had been summoned to account for their practices and beliefs, held in town lock-ups and fined. But this was no Stalinist state, and it was far from being a ferocious campaign of extermination. Matthew Hutton, Archbishop of York, had even written to Cecil to suggest that the Puritan clergy in his archdiocese should be given more time to conform. In 1606, Hutton died and was succeeded by a genial and slightly lackadaisical man called Tobias Matthew, famous for his courtesy and his lack of interest in church administration, more concerned with preaching than anything else, a pattern in many ways of the Jacobean churchman. And it is this gentle and scholarly man who has been portrayed by American Puritan historians, beginning with William Bradford, the great early governor of the Plymouth Settlement, who had grown up as a boy in Lincolnshire, as the Jacobean Antichrist itself.

The archbishop, beginning his term of office with some un-accustomed vigour, offered three alternatives to the Separatists – subscription to the rule of the church, imprisonment or exile – terms which in a liberal age might seem monstrous but which in the seventeenth century were a model of reasonable government. But reasonableness was not the medium of this encounter. 'The ceremonies and service book, and other popish and anti-christian stuff' seemed to the Separatists 'the plague of England'. The bishops, Bradford thought, were consumed with 'inveterate hatred against the holy discipline of Christ in his church', perse-cuting those who 'would not submit to their ceremonies and become slaves to them and their popish trash, which have no ground in the word of God'.

The Scrooby Separatists were indeed looked for, arrested when they could be found, imprisoned and more often than not soon released to go into exile. But the community was put under severe strain by this treatment, as was the intention. Bradford put it more colourfully:

> They could not continue in any peaceable condition, but were hunted and persecuted on every side, so as their former afflictions were but as flea-bitings of those which now came upon them. For some were taken and clapped up in prison, others had their houses beset and watched night and day, and hardly escaped their hands; and the most were fain to flee and leave their houses and habitations, and the means of their livelihoods.

In the summer of 1607, about fifty of them, having sold up their possessions, made their way to Boston on the Lincolnshire coast where a boat had been hired to take them to Amsterdam. But, in a scene with intense biblical resonances, echoing partly the Exodus out of Egypt, partly Jesus's betrayal by Judas, the captain of the ship revealed their presence and intentions to the authorities. The town constables of Boston 'rifled and ransacked them, searching them to their shirts for money, yea even the women further then became modesty; and then carried them back into the town, and made them a spectacle and wonder to the multitude, which came flocking on all sides to behold them'.

It was a catastrophe. Events then took a significant turn. In contrast to everything that had been done to the Jesuits in London two years earlier, the essential civility of Jacobean England came to the fore. A large number of people in Boston were sympathetic to Puritan ideas – many from the port would emigrate to Massachusetts Bay in the 1630s – and these poor refugee Separatists were treated quite properly. Of course they were held, but even Bradford says they were 'used courteously' and with 'favor'. The Privy Council in London, 120 miles away, had to be consulted, at a time when even royal mail travelled at two miles an hour but, after a delay of a month, the entire party except for seven of its leaders was released and sent back to Scrooby. Soon enough, the leaders were also released on bail.

Clearly, the Separatists had to try again, and this second attempt in the spring of 1608, leaving from the site of Immingham dock on the Humber, also very nearly failed. More boats, more payments, more chaos, the men in one craft, women and children in another, a muddle over tides, the two halves of the party becoming separated, the menfolk already underway, running before the tide with a panicky captain, suddenly seeing their women and children stranded on the shore, descended on by an armed party of constables, arrested and taken away, with no one able to help them. It was a disaster: the men had all the money with them. Their families were left penniless in a hostile England and under arrest. A fearsome south-westerly storm got up and blew the men's ship almost to the coast of Norway – Jonah and St Paul in their minds, the sailors despairing of life, the Separatists crying out, 'Yet Lord thou canst save, yet Lord thou canst save!' – fourteen days of terror before the storm at last dropped and they could make their way, chastened and convinced of God's intervention, to the Low Countries, all the time uncertain of the fate of their families.

Meanwhile, in England, their women were in pitiful distress, 'weeping and crying on every side', as Bradford wrote, 'some for their husbands, that were carried away in the ship; others not knowing what should become of them, and their little ones; others again melted in tears, seeing their poor little ones hanging about them, crying for fear, and quaking with cold'.

Again, even on the evidence of such a hostile witness as William Bradford, some sense of fairness and justice in the English judicial system came into play. No one quite knew what to do with the abandoned families,

> for to imprison so many women and innocent children for no other cause (many of them) but that they must go with their husbands, seemed to be unreasonable and all would cry out of them; and to send them home again was as difficult, for they alleged, as the truth was, they had no homes to go to.

And so they too were let go, to emigrate to the Low Countries, where 'in the end, notwithstanding all these storms of opposition, they all got over at length, some at one time and some at another, and some in one place and some in another, and met together again according to their desires, with no small rejoicing'.

This moving story of a small group of people, driven by a passionate belief in the strict purity of their devotion to the word of God and an equally passionate rejection of worldly authority in favour of a divinely sanctioned life, scarcely registered on the consciousness of England. The most authoritative modern history of the Jacobean church and its bishops devotes a single dismissive sentence to the episode: 'One of the few signal successes of the York commission [a church tribunal] in these years', Dr Kenneth Fincham wrote recently, 'was the destruction of a Separatist cell at Scrooby in Nottinghamshire.' Nothing more, and that, in effect, is how Jacobean England would have seen it too: a pimple scratched, an annoyance excised, some trouble-makers gone abroad so that the real business of the country could be allowed to continue. Puritan America had its origins in a small and unimportant piece of church administration, by which the church's own presiding officer was frankly bored.

It may have been a marginal incident but it was in many ways a central and symbolic moment in the history of the English Reformation and of Jacobean England. Reduced to essentials, the struggle at the heart of the European Reformation had been the conflicting claims of word and of ceremony, of the verbal and the visual, of a naked and direct relationship to God through scripture against a mediated, elaborated and socialised approach through an ancient church, guided by tradition. And that was precisely the conflict that was in play at Scrooby. Surplices, the cross, bishops, authority, kneeling and all the elaboration of a symbolic religion were rejected in favour of the word. It was the word that drove them into prison, near-shipwreck, exile, and later, for many of them, struggle and an early death in the New World.

The sheer wordiness of the Separatists' religion was extra-ordinary. In each four-hour service, several passages would be read from the Geneva Bible and then long, analytical expla-nations given of what they meant. Before any psalms were sung (without accompaniment) they too would be explained. Prose expanded to fill the time. After the psalms and after the readings, members of the congregation would then give their own in-terpretation of what the texts meant. All this was done standing up, after the practice of the primitive church. Very occasionally, a simplified form of communion and of adult baptism for new members of the church would be enacted but no Separatist was ever married in church, because there is no hint of a marriage ceremony in scripture and the primitive church had not considered marriage a sacrament before AD 537.

The words of scripture, and an intellectual consideration of them, were the essence of Separatist Christianity and in many ways of Protestant Christianity itself. Some Separatist pastors took this one step further: if the Bible was the word of God, it was intended to be conveyed to men in its original languages. Every translation, however good, was bound to contain errors and so by definition could not be used. If God had spoken in Hebrew, Greek and Aramaic, then those were the languages in which he should be heard. John Smyth, originally from Gainsborough, but by 1608 pastor of the Brethren of the Separation of the Second English Church at Amsterdam, its congregation made up of Lincolnshire farmers, decided that they needed to hear the scriptures in the original. One can only imagine the effect on the poor exiles from Gainsborough: hour on hour of Smyth reading out passages of Hebrew and Greek of which they had not the faintest understanding, desperately looking for the sanctity in this.

Smyth was an eccentric – after realising that no other ecclesiastical authority could be as pure as himself, he dunked himself in holy water and became famous as the Se-Baptizer or Self-Baptist – but his position is only a distortion and exaggeration of what everyone in Protestant Europe believed. John Reynolds, the moderate Oxford Puritan, had encouraged his students to read 'the Worde of God, and that, if it may be, ovt of the uerie well-spring, not out of the brookes of translacyons'. But even in translation, the word ruled. In early seventeenth-century England, endlessly and repetitively, the word of God was preached in the 8,000 or so pulpits across England. It was the ocean in which everyone swam. Attendance at sermons was compulsory. Many people would hear two or three on a Sunday in which every last echo of meaning would be squeezed from the words of the Bible. And week after week, preachers would occupy their

pulpits, analysing texts, pursuing moral and theological arguments, exercising the difficult and demanding skills that hold a
congregation's attention. They were clearly good at it. Laurence
Chaderton, the moderate Puritan leader, once paused after two
hours of a Cambridge sermon. The entire congregation stood up
and shouted, 'For God's sake go on!' He gave them another hour.

There can never have been a time in which Englishmen were
so thoroughly drenched in the word. James I used to sleep, it
was said, with Lancelot Andrewes's sermons under his pillow.
Andrewes himself could speak for an hour, to an enraptured
audience, on the multiple significances of a single word. He
could, as T. S. Eliot said in admiration, 'derive the world from
a word', squeezing it, stretching it, crushing and contorting it,
so that every conceivable facet of its meaning could be made
apparent. Not until the tortured analyses of twentieth-century
literary criticism was so much applied to so little.

But it wasn't little! At moments of intensity and crisis, the
natural direction a man's thoughts took would not be, as it now
might, towards the inarticulate, drowning in the struggle to
express the extremities of experience in a language that seems
scarcely adequate or sufficient for the task, but to the words of
scripture from which they had all drawn their sense of reality,
their sense of how the world was, for their entire conscious lives.
In a sense that almost no one now understands, the words of
the Bible were the ultimate and encompassing truth itself. That
depth of belief in the sufficiency of language is also one of the
shaping forces of the King James Bible.

The king himself was obsessed with words. He was a book
man to his core. He commissioned an elaborate history of his
mother's reign; he dictated every word of every royal proclamation himself; he loved epigrams, tales and long analyses of
theological problems; he wrote endless letters; with Bancroft's
help he had drawn up the instructions for the Translators himself. Words, as instruments of government, were part of a king's

service to God. He was the only person ever to have occupied the English throne to have his works collected – political treatises, designed to guide his sons towards good government, blasts against tobacco and witches, translations of the Psalms, endless theological tracts – bound in a magnificent edition published in 1616. In earlier times, his loyal editor James Mountagu wrote, a king might have been more at home with a pike. This one wielded a pen, just as Moses, David and Solomon had done. England was a kingdom of the word. On the frontispiece to his *Workes*, James stands beside a table on which there is a book inscribed with the words *Verbum Dei*. Government would have been impossible and unthinkable without it.

If the words of the Bible were the foundation of all under-standing, nothing could be more important than a text which was both accurate and intelligible. Precision in Bible scholarship and in translation was the foundation stone of the Reformation. High fidelity reproduction was a moral as well as a technical quality and it was axiomatic that Translators and scholars could approach the text only in a mood of humility and service. 'He who does not believe even one part of it,' Luther had said, 'cannot believe any of it.'

This attitude had stiffened and deepened as the Reformation had taken hold and it was Calvin who, in a typically passionate and forthright passage in his great and often revised work, *The Institutes of Christian Religion*, set the word of God on its throne. He wrote of it as earlier churchmen would have spoken of the pope. The words of the Bible should compel

> all the virtue, glory, wisdom, and rank of the world to yield
> and obey its majesty; to command all from the highest to the
> lowest trusting to its power to build up the house of Christ
> and overthrow the house of Satan. The apostles and their
> successors were sure and authentic *amanuenses* of the Holy
> Spirit; and, therefore, their writings are to be regarded as the
> oracles of God.

Those who originally wrote the words of the Bible had been God's secretaries, as loyal, as self-suppressing, as utterly disposed to the uses of the divine will as those royal secretaries, the Cecils, had so conspicuously been to Elizabeth and James. Self-abnegation in the service of greatness was the ideal.

Secretaryship is one of the great shaping forces behind the King James Bible. There is no authorship involved here. Authorship is egotistical, an assumption that you might have something new worth saying. You don't. Every iota of the Bible counts but without it you count for nothing. The secretary knows that. Like Robert Cecil, he can be clever, canny, resourceful and energetic but, for all the frustrations, he does not distort the source of his authority. A secretary, whether of God or of king, is in a position of dependent power. He has no authority independent of his master, but he executes that authority without hesitation or compromise. He is nothing without his master but everything through him. Loyalty is power and submission control. For this reason, biblical translation, like royal service, could only be utterly faithful. Without faithfulness, it became meaningless.

By the early seventeenth century, a crucial difference had developed in translation theory between sacred and non-sacred texts. Anyone thinking of translating history, poetry, foreign tales or works of classical rhetoric, taking their cue from Cicero and a couple of words of Horace, would despise the literalist as a plodding, and scarcely civilised pedant. Any well-educated man would take a text in a foreign tongue and absorb its meaning so that he could reproduce something like it in his own language. Literalism, a word for word translation, would do nothing more than transfer the corpse of the original into a new language, not the living thing. Cicero, when translating Demosthenes and other great Athenian orators, 'did not translate them as an interpreter', he wrote, 'but as an orator myself, keeping the same ideas and forms, or as one might say, the "figures" of thought, but in language which is more suitable to the way we speak'.

This, of course, was also a question of authority. Cicero did not consider himself subservient to the Greeks he was translating. He was at least their equal. Why, then, should he suppress his own eloquence on their behalf? Luther, fascinatingly, the grandfather of all Reformation translators, had taken a Ciceronian view of his task. When faced with translating a Bible text, he had written, 'You've got to go out and ask the mother in her house, the children in the street, the ordinary man at the market. Watch their mouths move when they talk, and translate that way. Then they'll understand you and realise that you are speaking *German* to them.' His whole idea, he said, was 'to make Moses so German that no one would suspect he was a Jew'.

Of course, the King James Translators were heir to this double and in some ways contradictory tradition. Lutheran accessibility ran directly counter to Calvinist secretarial strictness. It was a problem the Translators had to navigate, as will emerge. But there is another, all-important element which comes into play in the first decade of the seventeenth century in England and which had a shaping influence on the translation: a growing love of ceremonial, of a sense of religion which goes beyond the merely verbal and begins to take up the more luscious, musical and sensuous elements which extreme Puritanism would reject as popish trash.

There are all sorts of signals in the air. In Westminster Abbey, Jacobean churchmen, encouraged by the king, started to enrich the way services were held, in a manner no Puritan could have tolerated. Rich old copes and canopies, showing images of Christ and Mary, probably from before the Reformation, were bought out and dusted down. Effigies of all the kings of England were 'repayred, robed and furnished at the King's Majestie his charge' (£70) and rehoused in a specially built 'presse of wainscott'. Christian IV, between the parties, was taken to see them. A royal tomb was built for Elizabeth and an elaborate second funeral was held for James's mother, Mary, Queen of Scots, when she was reinterred in the Henry VII chapel, the royal sepulchre of the Tudor dynasty. Money was found for a new organ, a better choir, and a body of clerks to copy out sheet music for the choir to sing. Anthems were commissioned to be sung every day at morning prayer. Tudor England had never seen anything like it.

At Hatfield, Robert Cecil was clearly moving in the same direction. He was utterly entranced by music and had at least two vastly expensive and beautifully decorated organs made for the house. No stained- or painted-glass windows had been commissioned or installed in England since the 1530s. Everything about stained glass – its distortion of clear pure light; its reliance on imagery rather than the word; its sense of ecclesiastical luxury – ran against the essential mood of Puritan and even Protestant ideas. Yet despite this, and ground-breakingly, Cecil's new palace included an elaborate and luxurious scheme for a highly coloured and heavily decorated chapel, not only with a beautiful and expensive organ, but with the most gorgeous set of painted glass windows ever commissioned in Jacobean England. They are still there, their blues, yellows and reds as brilliant as ever, their Old Testament stories set within painted scenes that somehow elide the ancient (semi-classical, semi-medieval) with the realities of the seventeenth-century landscape: the passover in a house with glazed and diamond-leaded windows, well-coursed brickwork, with oak beams and ceilings; Moses and his bulrushes by a Hertfordshire stream, next to a house with dormer windows and obelisks in the garden. This is not what the congregations at Scrooby or Amsterdam would have admired. Nor, though, are they a sign of a return to Roman Catholicism. Cecil and the administrators of the Abbey were all fierce anti-Catholics. Instead, these are signs of something that hadn't happened before, an enriching and ceremonialising of the English Church, a subtle shift away from the dominance of the word, and an embracing of the idea that majesty, godliness, enrichment and ceremony could all be part of one new vision.

Nowhere does this new ceremonialising instinct appear more clearly than in the figure of Lancelot Andrewes. It is easy to portray him in an unflattering light, as a machine politician, crushing the spirit of individualists such as Henry Barrow. But there is far more to Andrewes than that, a depth and a delicacy to him, a tenderness and a kind of humane sagacity which goes beyond the sometimes violent polarisations of the age. His sermons were famous at the time and, after his death, at the command of Charles I, they were published in a handsome folio volume. His editors were his disciples, William Laud, then Bishop of London, and John Buckeridge, Bishop of Ely. And from their immense, complex fabric one repeated warning emerges. Words are not enough. A Puritan religion dependent on dry analysis is insufficient. As Buckeridge said in the preface: 'true Religion is in no way a *gargalisme* only, to wash the tongue and mouth, to speake good words; it must root in the heart, and then fructifie it in the hand; els it will not clense the whole man'.

Andrewes had devoted his life to the word, but he distrusted it. It was his whole existence, he had been obsessed by his studies as a boy in a way which even his contemporaries thought a little unnatural – he never played a game – and his sermons picked up and toyed with the words of scripture, 'crumbling' them as George Herbert would later say, teasing them apart for the meanings they might bear, but still the word was not enough. The sermons to which the English were exposed every week should not be the only route to God. 'All our "holiness" is in hearing,' he had lectured the court in one sermon, 'all our service ear-service.' But human beings should be more than their ears.

His own practice was different. When Archbishop Laud finally fell, was arrested and tried in 1643–44, mounds of papers were produced by parliamentarians who had searched his rooms for evidence that he had been leading the Church of England on the path to Rome. Among them, to Puritan horror-cum-delight, was a description of the chapel that had been furnished by Bishop Andrewes, then long dead. It is a measure, in secret, of the kind of religion to which Andrewes felt most deeply drawn. It is richness and heaviness itself, an embroidered, brocaded, gilt-thickened and hidden world. You must imagine it in an England of stark wooden clothless tables placed in the clear-lit naves of English churches, the ten commandments up on the wall, no images, no crucifixes, no atmosphere beyond the pro-claimed word. It is as if Andrewes's chapel was the only place in colour. On the altar were two large candlesticks, a dish for alms and a cushion on which the prayer book rested. There was a silver canister for the communion wafers, a 'tonne' or little barrel for the wine, a round basin with spouts for the water, two patens or plates on which the bread was put during the Eucharist, and a chalice 'having on the outside of the bowl Christ with the lost sheep on his shoulders; on the top of the cover, the wise man's star'. There was a basin, ewer and towel for the priest to wash his hands, and five copes, two altar cloths and 'a cloth to lay over the chalice, wrought with coloured silk'. Most remarkable of all, the furniture of this gilded shrine included a three-sided 'censer, wherein the clerk putteth frankincense at the reading of the first lesson'.

That too is scarcely what people imagine when they think of the circumstances in which the King James Bible, the great monument of English and North American Protestantism, was made. Andrewes, as ever, justified this by an appeal to the practice of the primitive church. Incense was not papist, it was apostolic. 'Our religion you miscall modern sectarian opinions,' he once told the Roman Cardinal Bellarmine in a famous exchange of pamphlets made just as the King James Bible was being prepared: 'I tell you if they are modern, they are not ours; our appeal is to antiquity, yea even to the most extreme antiquity. We do not innovate; it may be we renovate what was customary with those same ancients, but with you has disappeared in novelties.'

The 'novelties' Andrewes was referring to were the creation of an all-powerful and dominant papacy some thousand years before. Incense, and the other practices in his chapel, reeked of antiquity and showed the world, as Andrewes wrote to one Roman Catholic, that he and his chaplains and co-communicants were 'the sons and successors of those ancient christians who in former times had used them'.

A belief in the primitive is allied in Andrewes to a love of the royal. This is another foundation stone. One of the King James Bible's most consistent driving forces is the idea of majesty. Its method and its voice are far more regal than demotic. Its archaic formulations, its consistent attention to a grand and heavily musical rhythm are the vehicles by which that majesty is infused into the body of the text. Its qualities are those of grace, stateliness, scale, power. There is no desire to please here; only a belief in the enormous and overwhelming divine authority, of which royal authority, 'the powers that be' as they translated the words of St Paul, was an adjunct and extension. James once told parliament that he had about him 'sparkles of the divinity'. The Translators of the Bible clearly believed that and the majesty of their translation stems from its loyal belief in that divine-cum-regal authority.

Andrewes was perfectly explicit about this in many of the long series of Christmas sermons he delivered at court. On Christmas Day 1620, Andrewes was at the height of his powers. He wore a small, pointed beard. Linen ruffs stood out at his neck and wrists and the sleeves of his cambric chimere ballooned over the pulpit balustrade. Each sleeve was as wide as his body. Carrying only his Bible, he began his sermon to the Jacobean court. The king sat before him, impatient and querulous as ever, his blue eyes bulbous, his cheeks as red as the silk of his doublet. (He may well have suffered from porphyria, a hereditary disease which makes the face go blotchy and has symptoms, at times, identical to those of drunkenness.) James had brought other men's sermons to a halt in mid-flow, bored or irritated by them, coughing the preacher to silence. Andrewes stilled him with the story of the coming of the Magi:

> But heer come a troope of men of great Place, high account in their country: And withall, of great *Learned men* (their name gives them for no lesse). This (lo) falls somewhat proper to this Place and Presence, that will be glad to heare it . . . *wealth*, *worth* or *wisedome* shall hinder none, but they may have their parte in CHRIST's *birth*, as well as those of low degree. It is not only *Stella Gentium*, but Stella Magorum: the Great Mens, the *Wisemens Starr*, this.

You can imagine a little shuffling in the seats at this, confronting head on one of the Jacobean bogeys, that God and money, God and greatness, did not mix. But Andrewes went on: 'CHRIST is not only for russet clokes, Shepheards and such; shewes himself to none but such. But even the *Grandez*, Great States such as these.'

One can imagine, with that last phrase, Andrewes's large, strong hand, the episcopal rings glittering on the fingers, sweeping out across his privileged congregation, the gesture a physical cousin of the verbal puns of which he was so fond. Surely 'Great States such as these' means not only the Magi he has been discussing for the last half an hour, but James, Anne, Charles, the dukes and earls, the *Grandez* arrayed below him?

This is the context in which to read Andrewes's most famous words. They were not famous at the time he spoke them, again in the Chapel Royal, at Christmas 1622, but they enjoyed a resurrection when in 1927 T. S. Eliot, entranced by the idea of a form of English religion whose language was both sensuous and exact, began a poem with a version of them. 'It was no *Summer Progresse*', the Bishop said, subtly, flatteringly, a royal reference for a royal audience.

> A cold comming they had of it, at this time of the yeare: just, the worst time of the yeare, to take a iourney, and specially a long iourney, in. The waies deep, the weather sharp, the daies short, the sunn farthest off *in solstitio brumali*, the very dead of winter.

Everything you find in the great translation of the Bible prepared for James I is in those words: immediacy, dignity, a sense of deep, musical rhythm, an intuitive and poetic under-standing of the connection between the present and the past, a tangible empathy, a precision, 'an ordonnance' to use Eliot's word, a careful elaboration of arrangement and structure. The court audience would have known about the agonies of winter travel and would have grasped the implications of 'no summer progress', with its chastening hint of luxury now, seriousness then. (Some might have reflected that this solemn and ascetic figure had often enjoyed one or two days' racing with the king at Newmarket and Royston.) The sermon, like the translation of the Bible, is shaped by learning (Andrewes is familiar with the workings of a modern Copernican solar system where in the course of each year the earth moves from its perigee to its apogee, nearer and further from the sun) but infused with an imaginative sympathy. There is an urgent sense not only that the Christmas story of the Magi is something which was as alive then as it had been 1,620 years before, but that the language itself is an adventure, that the story can be remade in the modern world.

In 1608, according to royal instructions, Andrewes, as direc-tor of the first Westminster company, would have been bringing their work to a conclusion before sending it on to the final revising committee which the king's instructions had long envis-aged. There is a tiny fragment of evidence that Andrewes did not think much of his co-Translators. 'Most of our company are negligent,' he had written to the secretary of the Society of Antiquaries in late 1604. 'Negligent' is hardly the word that one has come to expect from this passionate age, or these brilliant men, or the vital and central importance of the task, a royal commission, a profound honour, attending to the fulcrum of the universe. But perhaps one can understand Andrewes using it. Of his company, there was John Overall, Dean of St Paul's, whose beautiful wife Anne had just run off with Sir John Selby. It wouldn't be surprising if Overall was a little distracted. The ancient Hadrian à Saravia, a royal favourite, was perhaps rather exhausted at seventy-three. John Layfield the adventurer was more a Greek than a Hebrew scholar. The eccentric Bedwell, and the drunk pornographer Thomson, were perhaps not entirely to be relied on. The others in his company – Tighe, Burleigh, King and Clarke – were more strait-laced, but the impression emerges from this brief remark of the busy, stretched and impatient dean. If most of his company were negligent, does that mean that Lancelot Andrewes himself was the translator of most of the opening books of the Bible?

It is at least a possibility. In no other company was the director quite so dominant over his fellows; in no other were complaints made of the laziness of the majority; and in no other was there a man who was acknowledged as one of the great preachers of the age. If there is an author of the opening books of the Bible, was it Andrewes?

Certainly, one has only to look at the first page of Genesis to see and feel in intimate detail something very like the mind of Andrewes at work. In the version of the Old Testament which the lonely Protestant martyr, William Tyndale, made in the 1530s, he began like this:

> In the beginnyng God created heauen and erth. The erth
> was voyde and emptye, and darcknesse was vpon the depe,
> & the spirite of God moued upon the water.

As an opening, it is already dramatic and enormous, its resonant bass notes – void, empty, dark, deep – infused with a heroic directness and, despite their scale, simplicity. Tyndale was indebted to Luther's translation, which to a large extent he copied, and this first modern English version is an extremely Protestant one, accessible, useful, clarifying, less interested in the grandeur of its music than the light it brings.

The Geneva Bible, a far more sophisticated and professional job, performed by a small team of English Calvinists in Geneva in the late 1550s, had taken Tyndale's bare bones and made something a little more fluent of them:

> In the beginning God created the heauen and the earth.
> And the earth *was* without form and void, and darknesse was upon the deep, and the Spirit of God moved upon the waters.

Andrewes takes those qualities, that openness, loses none of it, and incorporates it into something larger, more three-dimensional, more operatic, making of these opening words what is in effect a baroque form:

> In the beginning God created the Heauen, and the Earth.
> And the earth was without forme, and voyd, and darkenesse was vpon the face of the deepe: and the Spirit of God mooued vpon the face of the waters.

These are slight and marvellous changes. Some are almost purely rhythmic. To say 'the Heaven' and 'the Earth', which he borrowed from the Genevans, allows an easier run than Tyndale's harsher and more naked substantives. The commas after 'Heauen' and in the second verse are signs to pause in the reading of it, and the colon after 'deep' marks a slightly longer rest. In these slightest of ways, Andrewes introduces two new qualities to add to Tyndale's: an aural fluency and the sense of ease which comes from that; and, allied to that ease, a pace of deliberate and magisterial slowness, no hurry here, pausing in its hugeness, those bass colours in the vocabulary matched by a heavy, soft drumming of the rhythm. It is as solemn and orderly as the beginning of a steady and majestic march.

Of course there is more. Twice, Andrewes inserts the same beautiful phrase: 'upon the face of the deep/upon the face of the waters'. There is a word which means 'surface' in the Hebrew but Tyndale had avoided any mention of it. 'Surface' is what a modern and flattened version such as the World English Bible chooses to say:

> Now the earth was formless and empty. Darkness was on the surface of the deep. God's Spirit was hovering over the surface of the waters.

Why did Andrewes choose 'face' and not 'surface'? At least partly because, in 1611, 'surface' was still a technical word, borrowed from the French. Its first appearance in English is in Randle Cotgrave's 1611 French–English dictionary, where it is defined as 'the superficies or vpper part', and it was an explicit part of the king's instructions that strange and inaccessible words were not to be used. Instead, 'face' has a rich, plain Englishness to it, and in using it Andrewes is more accurate than Tyndale (as is 'waters' in the plural). But it is also, in its physicality, more stirring. The spirit of God moving on the face of the waters has a mysterious and ghostly humanity to it which neither the modern translations nor Tyndale's blankness can match. The face of the waters carries a subliminal suggestion that the face of God is reflected in them. That too is a baroque suggestion, a scene from Michelangelo or Blake. In this first, archaic darkness a connection already exists between God and his creation. The universe from the moment of its making is human and divine, almost as if, purely by this one lexical gesture, James's Translators are foreshadowing the whole long story which will unfold from that first moment.

But how did this feeling for enrichment, and a layered, dense, baroque sensibility, sit alongside those other contemporary demands for secretarial exactness and clarity? This could not be a Bible for the elite. If it was to play its role as the national irenicon, it had to bridge the categories of rich and clear. Fascinatingly, one can detect this double imperative work in precise detail.

Ninety years before, Luther had produced a famous example of how not to do Bible translation:

> In Mark 14.4 the traitor Judas says *Ut quid perditio ista unguenti facta est?* If I followed those lemmings the literalists, I'd have to render that 'Why was this waste of the ointment made?' What kind of talk is that? Whoever talks about 'making a waste of the ointment'? You make a mess not a waste, and anybody who heard you talking about making a waste would naturally think you were actually making something, when in fact you were unmaking it – though that still sounds pretty vague (nobody unmakes a waste either). What a real person would say, of course, is 'What a waste!'

Turn from this postcard from the front line of the Reformation to the words of the King James Bible, and what do you find? The King James Translators do exactly what Luther had described as absurd: they mimic precisely the form of the original. No searching for the language of mothers, or the man at the market stall. They acted, in other words, according to Calvin's injunction, as God's secretaries:

> There came a woman, hauing an Alabaster boxe of oyntment of spikenard very precious, and shee brake the boxe, and powred it on his head.
>
> And there were some that had indignation within themselues, and said, Why was this waste of the oyntment made?
>
> For it might haue bene solde for more then three hundred pence, and haue bene giuen to the poore: and they murmured against her.

The New English Bible follows Luther: 'Why this waste?' they have the disgruntled apostles ask.

God is in the details and it is worth looking a little more closely at exactly what is happening here. This is a particularly resonant and revealing passage about the way in which the King James Bible works. The private ritual of the woman with the spikenard is cloaked in an air of what can only be called holiness. Her bringing the oil of spikenard (an aromatic plant, sometimes identified with lavender) carries echoes of the Magi bringing their precious substances to the child in the stable, and the words these translators chose also carry forward-echoes of the Last Supper, now only hours away ('and shee brake the boxe, and powred it on his head', 'Iesus tooke bread, and brake it'). This atmosphere of holiness is made to reside in the strange, formal, ritualised language of the seventeenth-century Bible (which also happens to be an intimately exact translation of the original). These heightened atmospherics are not there in Luther, nor in the twentieth-century version. 'Why was this waste of the oint-ment made?' is not only a beautiful line in English, subtle in its variations of dactylic and iambic rhythms, but it answers all Luther's objections about the meaninglessness of something being made when in fact it was spilled. The spilling of the oil of spikenard was essential to the making of the ceremonial moment, the pre-anointing of Jesus for his gave.

In this sentence, one can see the extraordinary phenomenon of the King James Bible conforming both to Protestant and to pre-Protestant ideas about the nature of Christianity. It is both clear and rich. It both makes an exact and almost literal transla-tion of the original and infuses that translation with a sense of beauty and ceremony. It has that peculiarly Jacobean combination of light and richness, the huge windows illuminating the densely decorated room, the unfamiliar amalgam of the court–Puritan, both strict and grand. No one could fault the Translators in their meticulous attention to the detail of the original texts; and yet in doing so, more than any other English translators, they enshrined a high moment of Christian meaning. You only have to compare it with Tyndale, the English Lutheran, to see how far beyond Tyndale they took the atmospherics of the translation.

> There cam a woman with an alablaster [sic] boxe of oyntment, called narde, that was pure and costly, and she brake the boxe and powred it on his heed. There were some that disdayned in themselves, and sayde: what neded this waste of oyntment? For it myght have bene soolde for more then two houndred pens, and bene geven unto the povre. And they grudged agaynste her.

Tyndale is flat and only half accurate. 'What neded this waste of oyntment?' is a lumpen sentence compared with 'Why was this waste of the oyntment made?' Tyndale's version does not embrace the strange ambiguity of making something by wasting it which the Jacobean sentence conveys with economy, accuracy and its own form of resonant elegance. The King James Version steps beyond the question of liberalism versus gracefulness. It has plumbed and searched for the essence of the meaning and in that way is an exercise in passionate exactness. It doesn't choose between the clear and the rich but makes its elucidation into a kind of richness. It is a sleight of hand, but this is the central paradox of the translation: the richness of the words somehow represents a substance that goes beyond mere words and that is its triumph.

ELEVEN

The grace of
the fashion of it

> So likewise you, except ye vtter by the tongue words easie to be
> vnderstood, how shall it be knowen what is spoken? for ye shall
> speak into the aire.
>
> 1 Corinthians 14:9

he king and Bancroft had decided, at the very
beginning, that there should be 'a generall meet-
inge, which is to be of the chiefe persons of each
company, at ye ende of ye worke'. This was to be
the great forum for unification, the binding and melding together of all fifty or so Translators' efforts. By the end of 1608,
arrangements were being made for the various manuscripts to
be collected and gathered. The letter written on 5 December
that year by William Eyre, fellow of Emmanuel, to James
Ussher in Ireland mentioned to him that 'Two of everie company are chosen to revise & conferr the whole at London'. The
making of the King James Bible was now moving towards its
culmination.

But the gathering and collating went slowly, taking over a
year before the twelve divines could gather in Stationers' Hall
in London to make the final decisions. It may in part have been
a problem to do with money and payment. Except for those
rewarded by a bishop with a living in a rural parish, none of the

Translators had been paid until now and one or two of them were complaining.

The Cambridge divines translating the Apocrypha (generally acknowledged to be the least satisfactory part of the work) had been led by Andrew Downes, professor of Greek at the university. He was a man 'of an extraordinary tallness, with a long face and a ruddy complexion and a very quick eye', who treated his students kindly, but could also turn irascible, stalking out of church one day in Cambridge when the congregation jeered at him for the inadequacy of his sermon. 'He left, saying no one should see his face in the place again.'

By early 1609, having done his work on the Apocrypha, he was becoming increasingly ill-tempered and refused to come to London until he was 'either fetched or threatned with a pursivant', a government official with the powers to distrain and execute warrants. Even here, at this intimate level, there is no escaping the coercive presence of the Jacobean state. Downes pushed his case, complained to the Privy Council that he had worked harder than most and that he needed greater inducement than had already been provided. In May 1609, the king sent him £50.

But money was tight. By the end of the decade, royal finances were nowhere near capable of paying for the project. In 1608, Cecil had taken over as Lord Treasurer and was now attempting some kind of rationalisation of royal funding, but with James unable to resist the repeated gratification of making marvellous gifts to his friends, Cecil was pouring money into a leaking bucket. He sold quantities of land, reassessed rents, gathered the money granted by parliament in 1606 after the Gunpowder Plot which was still coming in, imposed tariffs on everything except basic food and ships' stores. By 1610 Cecil had managed to bring almost £1.2 million into the Treasury. In the same time, James doled out nearly £800,000 of that, the equivalent of building, panelling, equipping, gilding, decorating, upholstering, landscaping and in every way beautifying twenty Hatfields. The

man was a money hose. And the claims of a few indigent Translators were not going to make much headway at court.

There was, though, a commercial solution. Since 1577, the
right to publish Bibles in English had been sold by the Crown
as a monopoly to the Barker family, London printers, first Christopher, and then his son Robert. The Barkers had the right to
publish and sell both the Bishops' and the Geneva Bible but
because no one liked the Bishops' Bible, editions were few. They
made their money from a run of Geneva editions, the pocket
Bibles of Elizabethan England, in a string of different formats.

The financing of the publication of the King James Bible
remains obscure and only forty years later is there any record
of what Barker paid. A 1651 pamphlet claimed that he 'paid for
the amended or corrected Translation of the Bible £3,500: by
reason whereof the translated copy did of right belong to him
and his assignes'. Is this what Barker paid the king, squeezed out
of him by Cecil on the hunt for any source of cash he could
find? It is not clear and the Whitehall fire of 1619 destroyed any
documents dealing with the government end of the negotiations.

Perhaps through Barker's deal with Cecil, some money became available for the Translators, or at least those twelve who
were now going to form part of the final shaping committee.
Barker often sublet or subleased rights to individual editions of
the Bible, or at least shared the risk on them, with other printers
and publishers who were members of the Company of Stationers.
That may have happened this time too because it was through
the company that each man on the revising committee was paid
thirty shillings a week – the equivalent of the relatively high
annual salary of £75 – for the nine months or so it took to do
the work, a total of about £675. The rest of the £3,500 presumably went into the leaking royal bucket.

The general committee was to consider the translations produced by each of the six companies and make of them a single volume. There is no record of the membership of this review committee but something else, quite miraculously, has survived and it brings one more intimately into the heart of the translation process than any other document. Nearly all the notes and records of the Translators' discussions have disappeared: destroyed, thrown away, considered irrelevant, reused for grocery bills or in the bindings of other books. But one document has survived, yet again unrecognised and unacknowledged for centuries, rediscovered only in the late 1950s, lurking unseen in the library of Corpus Christi College in Oxford. Again, it took a pair of American scholars – Gustavus Paine and the same Ward Allen who analysed the Bodleian copy of the Bishops' Bible – to see these papers for what they were. They are remarkable. Here, for a brief moment, the making of the King James Bible, at its most crucial phase, can be seen occurring in front of your eyes. Jotted down in quickly assembled notes is the whole scene: the scholars arguing, consulting, losing their tempers, bringing in learned evidence from church fathers and classical authors, testing variants on each other, seeing what previous translators had done, insisting on the right rhythm, looking for the unique King James amalgam of the rich–plain word, the clarity within a majestic phrase, the court–Puritan perfection. It is as if the ghosts have walked on stage.

The document – it runs to thirty-nine pages – is a copy made by a late-seventeenth-century antiquarian, William Fulman, of some notes made by one of the Cambridge Translators, John Bois, who had worked on the Apocrypha with Samuel Ward, the Puritan diarist, and under the directorship of Andrew Downes, the Regius Professor of Greek. Bois had been Downes's pupil. It so happens that this John Bois, one of the near-anonymous of the world, was the subject of a memoir by his close friend, another clergyman and almost exact contemporary,

Anthony Walker. As a result, Bois is the only one of the King James workhorses who steps out of the shadows. Walker's short account of his friend's life, which survives in a British Library manuscript and was printed in an eighteenth-century collection of curiosities, brims over with affection and admiration but it is also much more than that: evidence of the depth and complexity of religious and scholarly experience which each of those Translators would have brought to the task. In this short biography, one can sense how much the King James Bible is a flower that grows from the deep mulch of sixteenth-century England.

In many ways, Bois's life is a familiar story, the story of Reformation England. His father William had been the clever son of a Yorkshire clothier and after school, in the late 1540s or early 1550s, had been sent to Trinity College, Cambridge. Here he took holy orders, fell under the influence of Martin Bucer, the fat, peace-loving, warm-hearted and compromise-minded leader of the Reformation in Strasbourg, who by then had been expelled from his city and was professor of divinity at Cambridge. Bois senior had a moment of revelation at Bucer's feet. With the sheer human reasonableness of this man as his model, the papacy and all its power structures seemed suddenly unnecessary and William Bois 'pull'd his neck from under his holinesses yoke'. He became a Protestant and at some time after 1553, as the Catholic regime of Queen Mary reimposed a loyalty to Rome, fled to the countryside.

He escaped to Hadleigh in Suffolk, a few miles west of Ipswich, a port city, full of the most vibrant mercantile connections to the ideas and presses of Protestant Europe. Hadleigh was, for those few Marian years, the headquarters of a concealed English Protestantism, a tiny, secretive, English, rural Geneva, full of refugees from the terror. As John Foxe described it in his *Book of Martyrs*, Hadleigh then 'seemed rather an university of the learned, than a town of cloth-making or labouring people'. William Bois concealed the fact that he was a clergyman, took a farm at Nettlestead just outside Hadleigh and married Mirabel Pooly, a Suffolk gentlewoman, when they were both in their mid-twenties. They had several children, but all except John died young.

Walker had in his possession a Book of Common Prayer that had belonged to Mirabel Bois, on the flyleaf of which John Bois himself had written:

> This was my mother's booke; my good mother's book. Hir name was first Mirable Poolye; and then afterwards Mirable Bois; being so called by the name of her husband, my father, William Bois . . . She had read the Bible over twelve times, and the Book of Martyrs twice; besides other bookes, not a few.

In the overwhelmingly male process of the translation, in which women appear only as the nagging wife, the mother of too many children, extravagant distractions from the seriousness of the male world, only Mirabel Bois rises into something like an independent existence.

John was born on 4 January 1561. His parents, confronted with the death of one child after another, were 'exceedingly careful' with him and his education. His father, who exceptionally rarely in Elizabethan England knew both Hebrew and Greek, taught John so well that he had read the whole Bible through, surely at his mother's knee, by the time he was five. A year later he was writing in Hebrew himself. This was in his spare time. The little boy walked every day the four miles into Hadleigh where he received further instruction at the grammar school and walked back in the evening. It is another sign of the intimate, interlaced nature of early modern England that his greatest friend when a boy at school was another Translator, John Overall, later Dean of St Paul's and Bishop of Norwich. They remained friends all their lives.

Bois's brilliance took him to St John's in Cambridge when he was only fourteen, where he was 'counted very early summer fruit'. Andrew Downes's eyes sparkled at the arrival of such a boy. Bois already knew more Greek than any other scholar in the college. And Downes clearly loved and nurtured him.

It was a high-pressured, intellectual upbringing and it produced the kind of person one might expect. Bois was a man of the book, often, at least in the summer time, going to the university library at four in the morning and staying till eight at night; and of a voracious intellectual appetite. He decided at one point to become an expert in medicine, bought a whole library of medical books, but then – a flicker of a joke from this serious man – found that 'whatsoever disease he read of, he was troubled with the same himself'.

He continued the life of the don with exemplary commitment and strictness, every week reading a Greek lecture to a group of fellows in his own rooms, usually at four o'clock in the morning, the men sitting round by candlelight. His fame spread beyond the university. The Earl of Shrewsbury nominated him one of his chaplains and in 1596 the rector of Boxworth in the flat rich land between Cambridge and Huntingdon, a Mr Holt, died with a curious provision in his will. He asked his friends 'if it might be by them procured [that] Mr Bois of S. John's might become his successor [as vicar of Boxworth], by the marriage of his daughter'.

In September, the extraordinary meeting envisaged by Mr Holt took place. John Bois, now thirty-five, as unflirtatious and unseductive a bachelor as could be imagined, his life bound up in the arcana of the Greek manuscripts in the university library, his experience one of intellectual debate in the candlelit dawns of his college rooms, rode out to Boxworth to inspect Miss Holt, the parsonage to which she held the key, and the seismic change in life she represented. And Miss Holt, brought up in the village, an agricultural life, her father recently dead, sees, coming up the dusty autumn lane from Cambridge, this cleric, with his tendency to hypochondria, short-sighted, innocent, pale-skinned, so *alien*. What can the poor girl have thought?

Anthony Walker is blandness itself: 'he went ouer to see her, and soon after (they taking liking each of other) he was presented to the parsonage'. The emotional aspect of the marriage gets squeezed into the brackets; the substantive part, the claiming of the property, stands out in the open air.

Bois moved his huge library to Boxworth parsonage. He proudly told his friends that every word preserved of any Greek author was to be found on his shelves. It was, he told Walker, 'his darling'. Miss Holt – her christian name is never recorded – was left to get on with the management of their lives almost unaided. Bois was still wedded to his university existence, riding there almost every day to hear Downes and Edward Lively, the nominal director of the Chaderton company, lecture on his beloved texts. En route, Bois allowed his horse to find his own way there, never looking to steer him, but making notes in a little pocket paper-book of the questions 'wherein he might require satisfaction of his learned friends in Cambridge'. On his way back in the evening, he used 'to chewe the cud, and lay up his new encrease of knowledge in his safe cabinet, his memory'. The man was not of this world.

Almost inevitably, things went wrong. Bois was not interested in money. He didn't share any of the burdens of the family finances.

> He minding nothing but his book; and his wife through want of age and experience, not being able sufficiently to manage other things aright, he was, ere he was aware, fallen into debt. The weight whereof (though it were not great) when he began to feel, he, forthwith, parted with his darling (I mean, his library).

The hurried sale meant that he received the worst possible price for the books. No record survives of what they were, but by chance the library of one of Bois's co-Translators on the Apocrypha, William Branthwaite, has been preserved in its entirety. It fills one bay of the library in Gonville and Caius

College in Cambridge, of which Branthwaite was master. Bois's shelves would have looked pretty much the same. Branthwaite had a thousand books (William Sancroft, the later, richer divine, had 5,000) and, as a modern historian of the college has written: 'as the eye roams up from the folios below to the tiny octavos among the ceiling joists, one seems to follow a course in the history of learning, from the medieval Bible and its glossators to the continental protestant divines of the late 16th century'. Foxe's *Book of Martyrs* sits alongside Roman Catholic histories of the church, St Bernard and Thomas Aquinas next to a huge range of Puritan commentary, as well as Greek and Hebrew texts: the world of the Translators is there.

Not much imagination is needed to envisage the terrible scene in the Boxworth parsonage, the anger and resentment on both sides, the books being loaded into a cart to be taken back to the Cambridge booksellers, the dusty nothing left in the vacated shelves, the atmosphere in the house of failure and betrayal. Walker says that Bois thought of leaving his wife and going abroad but that 'religion and conscience soon gave such thoughts a check'. Undoubtedly their poverty continued. They took in lodgers, including the sons of gentlemen to whom Bois would teach the rudiments. But the tension is palpable four hundred years later. Bois was a most particular man, full of a kind of exact and suppressed energy. He used to walk the twenty miles or so from Cambridge to his mother's house at West Stow for dinner, and back again in the evening. He loved swimming and was intensely self-preservative, only ever eating two meals: dinner at midday, supper in the evening. Nothing ever passed his lips between the two, unless – the hypochondriac rising to the surface – 'upon trouble of wind, some small quantitie of *aqua-vitae* [a brandy-like spirit] and sugar'. After lunch, he carefully picked at and rubbed his teeth so that he 'carryed to his grave almost an Hebrew alphabet of [them]'. He used to walk after meals and would fast once or twice a week. He always studied standing up, never stood in the window to read and never went to bed with cold feet. As a result, he arrived at old age unwrinkled, with clear sight, perfect hearing, a fresh skin and his body sound 'excepting a rupture, which he had for many years'.

There is something off-putting about Anthony Walker's portrait of his friend. Its enormous self-regard; its lack of love for his poor unintellectual wife (and the unspoken comparison with his adored Bible-reading mother, glowing in his memory as a figure from the heroic age of English martyrdoms); its preciousness; its arrogance – Walker says his 'humility made him think not many below himself'; its self-congratulation: 'neither did he want courage to reprove or advise, even the best and greatest of his friends and acquaintance, when he thought they stood in need of admonition'; its pickiness, that preservation of his teeth at a time when the English, awash with sugar from their new slave-worked plantations in the Caribbean, were embarking on their long career of oral decay. This is perhaps someone you might admire; it is not a man you would love.

There was goodness in him, though. He regularly sent money to the prisoners in Ely gaol and gave £3 every Christmas to the poor of his parish. In church he spoke with great simplicity, knowing that to preach a complicated sermon to a rural parish was to drive a young and tender flock too hard, 'a course more like to slay than feed their souls'. He could tell funny and delightful stories after supper. And he loved his children, four sons and three daughters. He prayed with them every day, kneeling with them on the bare bricks of the Boxworth parsonage floor. If they misbehaved, he didn't reprove them but instead denied them the blessing 'when, at usual times of morning and evening, they did in ordinary manner, request it. Not that he forbore to pray [for them] but he was pleased to forbear the vocal pronunciation thereof, sometimes for one, sometimes for two days.' All but two of them died before him, one as an infant, others in their teens, one at thirty. Two of them, his son Robert and his daughter

Mirabel, died within a month of each other, of smallpox, in the early summer of 1623. That May, Bois wrote in his notebook: '*Nulla unquam nox mihi acerbior fuit, quam illa, in qua Mirabella mea moriebatur.*' (Never has there been a more bitter night for me than that in which my Mirabel died.)

When Bois was chosen as one of the Cambridge Apocrypha company, it might have come as some relief. He went to live in St John's, returning to his family and parish in Boxworth only at weekends. Some of the Cambridge dons complained that they did not need 'any help from the country' but Bois, with his finicky precision, the awe-inspiring hours he devoted to his work, his monk-like removal from the world, was as great a scholar as England could provide. For four years he worked on the Bible, finishing his part early, and was then taken on as an assistant by another of the Translators (whose name is not recorded) who had been negligent and was not going to complete his portion on time.

This curious man, somehow shrunken by the minuteness of his scholarship, became the amanuensis for the meeting of the final committee. His notes contain some hints of who was there. They are scattered with references to 'A.D.', his mentor, the old, irascible and greedy Andrew Downes. In addition, there are references to a C., a B., a D. Harmar and D.H., D: Hutch. and Hutch. D. Harmar is the only one who can be identified for sure. He was John Harmar, one of the Abbot–Savile group, and the warden of Winchester College. The others are uncertain. There was a Ralph Hutchinson, President of St John's College, Oxford, who was a member of William Barlow's company translating the Epistles, but he had died in 1606, well before the revising committee began to meet, probably in 1610. It must be another Hutchinson, maybe the William Hutchinson who had gone with Lancelot Andrewes to interview the Separatist Henry Barrow in his prison cell so many years before? That will never be known. As for the 'C.' and the 'B.', there are too many candidates to make any guess reasonable. Among the Translators were a Dr Clark, a Mr Burleigh and a Mr Binge, all equally obscure; as well as William Bedwell, William Barlow, Laurence Chaderton, Dr Branthwaite and Bois himself. Again, there is no telling.

What is certain is that the meetings were voluble and at times fierce. It was John Bois's glory hour. 'Whilest they were conversant in this last businesse, he, & only he, tooke notes of their proceedings, which he diligently kept till his dying day.' The entire procedure, apart from Bois's note-taking – secretary to the secretaries, the ultimate recorder – was oral. The twelve of them sat with the sweet smell of the Stationers' Hall's new joinery in their nostrils, and according to a note made much later by John Selden, the radical jurist and parliamentarian,

> that part of the Bible was given to him who was most excellent in such a tongue (as the Apocrypha to Andrew Downes), and then they met together, and one read the translation, the rest holding in their hands some Bible, either of the learned tongues, or French, Spanish, Italian, etc. If they found any fault, they spoke up; if not, he read on.

This is exactly the picture that Bois's notes convey. The twelve of them are sitting around the room listening. Where everyone in the meeting accepted a reading, there is no note. Where someone objected, there is discussion, suggestion, variation. The noteless silences are as articulate as the interruptions, verse after verse going by with only the nodding of heads. But underlying that obvious point is something more important. This is the kingdom of the spoken. The ear is the governing organ of this prose; if it sounds right, it is right. The spoken word is the heard word, and what governs acceptability of a particular verse is not only accuracy but euphony. The new Bible, so extraordinarily carefully prepared, was intended to replace above all the Bishops' or Church Bible, whose main function was to be read aloud in church on Sundays. The Geneva Bible, the Bible of the private Calvinist experience, printed in far smaller type,

on far smaller pages, with encyclopaedic notes, maps of the Holy
Land and of the route there from Egypt, plans of the temple in
Jerusalem, diagrams of the Ark of the Covenant, computations
of the age of the world, was perhaps at first intended to continue
alongside the new Bible. No interdiction on its printing was
issued until 1616. English Christianity was to persist, in other
words, as the 'medley-religion' it had been since the Reformation. In private, Geneva-style interrogation and explication
of the text; in public, in church, the baroque music of the King
James manner, large, full-bodied, consciously beautiful. The
listening divines in the Stationers' Hall were, in one sense, the
new book's first audience, not its readers but its hearers, partici-
pating in, and shaping, the ceremony of the word.

As Bois's notes make clear, the meetings were brisk and far
from dry. They got through some thirty revisions a day.
Intriguingly, for the core discussion of the most formative text
in the English language, the notes are in Latin. Was the conversation in the general meeting also in Latin, the lingua franca of
international scholarship, in which these men's lives had been
steeped for decades? The atmosphere of Bois's notes at least
seems to hint at that. There are long disquisitions in Latin
peppered with Greek words and phrases. Short and pointed
remarks are made in Latin, focusing on the particular sub-text
and implications of words in the Greek testament. Latin and
Greek were the medium for Renaissance scholarship, for precision of thought. English was simply the target, the destination,
not the language in which questions of precise meaning were
naturally addressed. The English sentences were being prepared
for others, the non-educated, who had no access to the essence
of the text which these scholars, like Bois, had been drinking in
for decades. The English, in other words, was itself subservient
to the original Greek.

That linguistic hierarchy is also one of the sources of the
King James style. This English is there to serve the original not

to replace it. It speaks in its master's voice and is not the English you would have heard on the street, then or ever. It took up its life in a new and distinct dimension of linguistic space, somewhere between English and Greek (or, for the Old Testament, between English and Hebrew). These scholars were not pulling the language of the scriptures into the English they knew and used at home. The words of the King James Bible are just as much English pushed towards the condition of a foreign language as a foreign language translated into English. It was, in other words, more important to make English godly than to make the words of God into the sort of prose that any Englishmen would have written, and that secretarial relationship to the original languages of the scriptures shaped the translation.

Of course, individual English words and phrases are held up and examined on the point of a knife. Where, in Romans 3:9, the Greek has the word 'προεχομεθα', proechometha, meaning 'are we better?', the Translators toy with something a little more inflected: 'Are we safe, and out of danger? are we preferred? are we Gods darlings?' before settling on the simple version: 'are we better?' For God's attitude to those who request something, the final printed version says that he gives 'and upbraideth not'. Someone at the meeting suggested 'without twitting, or hitting in the teeth', which were rejected, presumably on grounds of decorum: God would not twit or hit in the teeth. For the beauty of a flower before it is withered by the sun they try 'the goodlynesse, sightlynesse of the appearance' before settling on 'the grace of the fashion of it'. They reject 'a wavering-minded man' for 'a double-minded man'. And so on: endless careful picking of the nuance of sound and meaning, the finely balanced, the audibly intelligible, more often than not choosing a form of words that embraces and bridges an ambiguity.

There are two moments involving Andrew Downes which are particularly revealing about the priorities at work. The first came when they were discussing Paul's Epistle to the Hebrews.

The apostle is reminding the Jews to behave well, to treat strangers courteously, 'for thereby some haue entertained Angels vnawares', when he suddenly interjects a verse (13:8) which in the printed version of the King James Bible says simply:

Iesus Christ, the same yesterday, and to day, and for euer.

Amidst all the exhortation towards good behaviour, those words appear to land from another dimension. When the Translators came to this passage, Andrew Downes suggested that the verse should read:

Iesus Christ, yesterday, and to day the same, and for ever.

His reason was not to do with meaning, but to do with sound, and the particular nature of the sound which his rearrangement would provide. 'If the words are arranged in this way, the statement will be more majestic,' he said. It is the only moment at which that all-important word appears in the discussions, and Downes was right: his version is more majestic than the one finally settled on; but his remark is important in showing that majesty was a quality being consciously sought in the Stationers' Hall. These men are interested not only in clarity and fidelity but in a grandeur of statement which colours the translation as a whole. (The finished book would include a genealogy of Jesus, drawn up by the map-maker John Speed, showing his descent from David – God was kingly just as the king was godly.)

A more passionate moment arose in their discussions over the first letter to the Corinthians 10:11. Here Paul is describing the sinful habits of the Jews in the past and the way in which God punished them. He then writes (as the verse appeared in the printed version of the King James Bible): 'Now all these things happened vnto them for ensamples: and they are written for our admonition.' This was a famous crux because the word that appears here as 'ensamples' – meaning 'illustrative instances' – translates the Greek word 'τυποι', typoi, which can be taken instead to mean 'type' or 'archetype'. A fundamental difference in worldview hinges on that difference: were the Jews archetypes of sinfulness, representing everything that had been wicked on earth? Or had they merely gone wrong sometimes, their behaviour to be seen simply as examples of what not to do? Were the Jews in other words simply fallible like us or essentially wicked, not like us at all?

Augustine had read 'τυποι' as 'archetypes' and condemned the Jews on the basis of this phrase to a collective and eternal damnation. The Roman Catholic English New Testament produced in Rheims in the 1590s had written 'figure', which tended down the same route as Augustine, implying that those who lived before Christ were in a different category to those who lived after. Andrew Downes agreed with them. The word used in the King James Bible, he insisted, must also damn the Jews. 'That the thought may be complete,' Bois noted, 'A.D. sharply and violently exerted himself beyond measure for the interpretation of Augustine, that is, that τυποι were understood as concerning the types and figures of the people of old.' But the committee resisted. Bois notes: 'The scope of the passage does not seem to admit this interpretation.' Nevertheless, true to form, the Bible as published hedges its bets, printing 'ensamples' in the main text, '*Or, Types*' in the margin beside it. The great irenicon held that both interpretations might be true.

In the end, Andrew Downes's jealousy of his brilliant pupil became too much. Through the translation, both of them had met Sir Henry Savile, and both had impressed him with their scholarship. He asked them to come to Eton to help with the preparation of the great edition of Chrysostom. (In Stationers' Hall, they had beside them those volumes of the eight-volume set that had already been printed.) But Bois outshone his old master and, disastrously, Savile asked him to check the notes which Downes had made on Chrysostom. Anthony Walker rubs his hands at the story:

At the end of the work, Sir Henry was pleased to manifest a little more approbation of [Bois's] notes than of Mr Downes's; who (mistaking the object of his anger, or it may be, giving place to envy, when he despaired of revenge) was so displeased with him, that he never was reconciled 'till his death.

Bois, with his eye on the main chance, and thinking of the dull, repetitive poverty at home, clung closely to Savile. The smooth, diplomatic knight had said something charming to him once ('He knew no reason why they should not live together') and Bois interpreted that as meaning Savile would make him one of the well-fed and beautifully housed fellows at Eton. It may also have been Bois who told a famous joke to Lady Savile. She claimed never to have heard of Chrysostom and was bored and annoyed by her husband's devotion to his enormous pile of Greek manuscripts. Coming up to him one day in the Eton library, she said, 'Sir Henry, I would I were a book too, and then you would a little more respect me.' Savile said nothing, but 'one standing by' – perhaps Bois – replied, '"Madam, you must then be an almanack, that he might change every year." Whereat she was not a little displeased.' It is the kind of gauche, donnish, unworldly joke Bois might have made.

For all his promises, Savile slipped out of this noose too. Bois was never made a fellow of Eton. And so Lancelot Andrewes, a better and a less self-serving man, did the right thing and in 1615 made Bois a prebendary of Ely Cathedral, where Andrewes was the bishop. Andrewes did it with grace, telling Bois that he had given him this promotion and this security freely, 'without any one moving him thereto'.

Bois eventually retired from Boxworth and spent the end of his life in the calm backwater of Ely. In January 1643, 'when death began to look him in the face, he met him, not as an enemy, with fear; but as a long expected friend and old acquaintance'. All the same, he suffered a long and painful illness – it might have been cancer – unwilling to be visited, feeling happier alone, as he must have spent most of his life. The day before he died, he asked to be moved into the room where his wife had died the previous May, an act of companionship at the last. There John Bois died in great distress, unable in the end to bear the pain any longer, 'groaning forth these words, "O my torment! my torment! my torment!"' He had never been heard to say anything of the kind before and those around him watched in horror.

He was never famous, even at the time, because, as Walker said, Savile took all the credit for the Chrysostom and the five years Bois had spent on the translation 'makes no noyse, because it carries no name'. He wasn't a particularly good man, nor particularly likeable, nor a man of any scale. John Bois was no William Tyndale, Lancelot Andrewes or Henry Savile. But as Miles Smith, Bishop of Gloucester, who famously walked out of a sermon in Chipping Campden to go to the pub, wrote in his Preface to the King James Bible, 'A man may be counted a vertuous man, though hee haue made many slips in his life ... also a comely man and louely, though hee haue some warts vpon his hand, yea, not onely freakles vpon his face, but also skarres.' That might be said of them all.

TWELVE

Hath God forgotten to be gracious? hath he in anger shut vp his tender mercies?

And I will make of thee a great nation, and I wil blesse thee, and make thy name great; and thou shalt bee a blessing:

And I will blesse them that blesse thee, and curse him, that curseth thee: and in thee shall all families of the earth be blessed.

Genesis 12:2–3

y the spring of 1611, a final text had emerged, ready for the printer. After the revising committee had done with it, to the annoyance of the Cambridge Puritans, Richard Bancroft is said to have altered a few words, emphasising the role of bishops in the early church. Summaries at the beginning of each chapter and running heads at the top of each page were added by Miles Smith, the brilliant and pacific Bishop of Gloucester, and by Thomas Bilson, the archetype of the Jacobean courtier–politician–bishop, more often at court than in his Winchester diocese, endlessly scheming for place and advantage, one of the churchmen with direct access to James's ear.

It may well have been Bilson who wrote the Epistle Dedicatory to the King, placed at the front of the translation, following the grandiloquent baroque frontispiece for which the Fleming Cornelius Boel, a member of young Prince Henry's household, and a client of Robert Cecil's, was paid £10. Boel's frontispiece is rigorously scriptural, with no hint of earthly powers (unlike the Bibles of Henry VII and Elizabeth, which often contained portraits of the monarch) and makes only a passing reference to the king. This is straightforwardly 'The Holy Bible Conteyning the Old Testament and the New, Newly Translated out of the Originall tongues: and with the former Translations diligently compared and reuised by his Maiesties Speciall Commandment. Appointed to be read in Churches.' But the Epistle Dedicatory that follows has no such compunction. The glories of the Jacobean state are emblazoned here in unequivocal pomp and glory. The title of the Bilson's Epistle is set in type far larger than anything in the text of the Bible itself, James is given far more prominence than anything to do with God, and his virtues are proclaimed like a gilded banner fluttering over the words of the translation. This is a book about kingdom, power and glory:

TO THE MOST
HIGH AND MIGHTIE
Prince, Iames by the grace of God
King of Great Britaine, France and Ireland
Defender of the Faith, &c.

Nor, in addressing this God-like figure, does Bilson stint: 'Great and manifold were the blessings (most dread Soueraigne) which Almighty GOD, the Father of all Mercies, bestowed vpon vs the people of England, when first he sent your Maiesties Royall person to rule and raigne ouer us.' James is the Sun that shines over us; his presence disperses all murk and mistiness. England itself is 'our Sion', James and God are virtually indistinguishable and the translation itself holds a divinely sanctioned place between the enemies on either side. It was a challenge, on one hand, to those 'Popish persons at home or abroad', whose only desire was to keep the people 'in ignorance and darknesse' – conveniently ignoring the great Catholic translation of the Bible made at the English college in Douai, from which these

Translators had lifted many plangent phrases; and on the other a summons to those 'self-conceited brethren, who runne their own ways, and giue liking unto nothing but what is framed by themselues, and hammered on their Anuile'. Here, in a few words, are the essential points of the Jacobean political programme. England is to be a model of irenic moderation. The majesty of God is to be elided with the majesty of King James; the light of the word is to be brought to those who are living in darkness; the subversive egotism of the harsher Puritans is to be rejected and revealed for the sterility it is. Bilson rises to his wildly overblown blessing:

> The Lord of heauen and earth blesse your Maiestie with many and happy dayes, that as his heauenly hand hath enriched your Highnesse with many singular and extraordinary graces; so you may be the wonder of the world in this later age, for happinesse and true felicitie, to the honour of that Great GOD, and the good of his Church.

Miles Smith – and it is his greatest monument – then wrote the long and beautiful Preface to the translation. It is rarely printed with the Bible nowadays, but, if there is a slight smell of corruption about Bilson's Epistle, Smith's words exude all that is best about Jacobean England, the hopes for this translation and the beliefs in the power and value of the work which was now so nearly complete. Like Bilson's letter, it is a defence of what they have done against the cavils of the Roman Catholics, and a paean to James as its progenitor. It insists on the virtues and necessity of translation, and snipes at the Catholics for their love of obscurity and darkness. It celebrates the virtues of accuracy but scoffs, happily enough, at the over-scrupulosity of the Puritans who insist on the same word being translated in the same way every time.

Its atmosphere is generous and majestic and never more sweepingly vigorous – the influence of the pulpit is everywhere

here – when describing the part that scripture might play in a man's life. The word of God, Smith wrote:

> is not onely an armour, but also a whole armorie of weapons, both offensiue, and defensiue; whereby we may saue our selues and put the enemy to flight. It is not an herbe, but a tree, or rather a whole paradise of trees of life, which bring foorth fruit every moneth, and the fruit thereof is for meate, and the leaues for medicine. It is not a pot of Manna, or a cruse of oyle, which were for memorie only, or for a meales meate or two, but as it were a showre of heauenly bread sufficient for a whole host, be it neuer so great; and as it were a whole cellar full of oyle vessels; whereby all our necessities may be prouided for, and our debts discharged. In a word, it is ... a fountaine of most pure water springing vp vnto euerlasting life. And what maruaile? The originall thereof being from heauen, not from earth; the authour being God, not man; the enditer, the holy spirit, not the wit of the Apostles or Prophets; the Pen-men such as were sanctified from the wombe, and endewed with a principall portion of Gods spirit; the matter, veritie, pietie, puritie, vprightnesse; the forme, Gods word, Gods testimonie, Gods oracles, the word of trueth, the word of saluation, &c. the effects, light of vnderstanding, stablenesse of perswasion, repentance from dead workes, newnesse of life, holinesse, peace, ioy in the holy Ghost.

Was anything ever written about a sacred text that was so fresh, so full of a delight in what these words might bring you? For all the lugubrious seriousness and monomaniac anger and violence that can hang around seventeenth-century religion, Bishop Smith, here writing at the very end of the long translation process in which he had been engaged throughout, remains buoyant with enthusiasm and with a quality that can only be called grace. He had his portrait painted the following year and it hangs in Christ Church College, Oxford. He was sixty-four years old and despite all the paraphernalia of the episcopal garb around him, there is in his eyes, perfectly detectably, the qualities that shaped this marvellous Preface: brightness, a real sweetness of nature, integrity, a Christian spirit which goes beyond the political. The optimism of which his Preface is so full marks the highpoint of all hopes in England for a unified culture. In the following decade, the political atmosphere would deteriorate. Royal relations with parliament collapsed in 1614 as the MPs refused to grant any more cash to fund the ludicrous extravagances; sexual and financial scandals engulfed the court; the interest James had once had in embracing Puritan opinion finally evaporated; the ceremonialist trend in church thinking began to dominate; in Europe, sectarian divisions degenerated into the viciousness of the Thirty Years' War, and although James tried to act the European peace-broker between Protestant and Catholic camps, the tide was against him and the subtle cross-cultural amalgam he had wished to create began to fall apart. The Bible which bears his name is a monument to hope, produced, ironically, at precisely the point in English history when that hope – for national integration under a beneficent king – was just beginning to look hopeless.

Integration is both the purpose and method of the King James Bible. And one sign of that attempt at integration is the degree to which the text the Translators had produced was an amalgam of the sequence of translations that had come before it. Take, as one small example of something that could be replicated over the entire volume of the work, Paul's second Epistle to the Corinthians 1:11. You would read it and think little of it: a typically complex reflection by the apostle, written for the young congregation in Greece, on the richly shared nature of church life, on its life as a web of mutual help and support:

> You are also helping together by prayer for vs, that for the gift bestowed vpon vs by the meanes of many persons, thankes may bee giuen by many on our behalfe.

These words are a tapestry of many different decisions taken over many decades, from Tyndale's first 1526 translation, to its adaptation for Thomas Cromwell's official Great Bible in 1539, the 1557 New Testament produced in Calvinist Geneva, the 1560 complete Geneva Bible and finally the 1568 Bishops' Bible, on the basis of which the Translators had done their work:

> You are also helping [Bishops' Bible] together [Geneva 1557] by [Bishops'] prayer for vs [Tyndale], that [Tyndale] for the [Geneva 1560] gift [Great] bestowed vpon vs [Geneva 1557] by the meanes of many [Tyndale] persons [Great], thankes may bee giuen [Tyndale] by [Geneva 1557] many on our behalfe [Tyndale].

This one tiny example of the minutely detailed nature of what the translators had done demonstrates their astonishing achievement. There is, on the whole, no telling that this text has been assembled like a mosaic floor, every tessera gauged and weighed, held up, examined, placed, replaced, rejected, reabsorbed, a winnowing of exactness from a century of scholarship. It is often said that the 1611 Translators contributed almost nothing to the versions which William Tyndale had produced in the 1520s and 1530s. Champions of Tyndale's name maintain that he is the great and unjustly forgotten hero of the English Bible. The powerful government enterprise of the seventeenth century, taking almost everything from the earlier work, they say, has done its best to obliterate the memory of the man we should all revere as the king of English translators, the man who gave us so many of the most treasured passages in the Bible.

Tyndale's, for example, is the Last Supper:

> And he toke breed, and gave thankes, and brake itt, and gave it unto them, sayinge: Thys is my body which is geven for you, Thys do in remembraunce of me. Lykewyse alsoo, when they had supped, he toke the cuppe, sayinge: This is the cuppe, the newe testament, in my bloud, which shall for you be shedde.

The 1611 Translators took that over, as so much else from Tyndale, very nearly wholesale, altering only the very last phrase, changing 'which shall for you be shedde' to the more accurate, the more poignant and the more memorable, 'which is shed for you', a change, as ever, which is minuscule but formative.

There is an important point here. Tyndale enthusiasts have calculated that 94 per cent of the New Testament in the King James Bible is exactly as Tyndale left it. Therefore, the argument goes, the Jacobean Translators were in some ways little better than plagiarists, promoting as their own work a translation that belonged essentially to another man, a Protestant martyr, who died a horrible death, attacked repeatedly and mercilessly by Thomas More, and who nevertheless reshaped the English language, who framed the phrases we all know: 'Love suffereth long and is courteous, Love envieth not'; 'When I was a child, I spake as a child, I imagined as a child'; 'eat, drink and be merry'; 'salt of the earth'; the 'powers that be'; 'as bald as a coot'; 'Our father which art in heaven', and so on.

But this is scarcely enough. Word-counting is no route towards understanding a translation, its intention or its effects, and wherever a less pedantic comparison is made between Tyndale's words and those of the Jacobean Translators, something else, far more significant, and in a way far more obvious, becomes apparent. Each is a reflection of its historical moment: Tyndale required and produced a simple and plain man's translation to be slapped in the face of the medieval church and its power-protective elite. He was, in that way, a straight Lutheran, looking for immediacy and clarity in scripture which could shake off the thick and heavy layers of medieval scholasticism and centuries of accumulated ecclesiastical dust. The Jacobean Translators had a different commission: to evolve a scriptural rhetoric which could be both as plain and dignified as Tyndale's and as rich and resonant as any book in the language.

What they did could not have been done without Tyndale,

but their task reached beyond his. And the heart of this richness and resonance is in the musicality of the Jacobean Translators' work. Tyndale was working alone, in extraordinary isolation. His only audience was himself. And surely as a result there is a slightly bumpy, stripped straightforwardness about his manner and his rhythm.

> Thys ys my commaundement, that ye love togedder as I have loved you. Gretter love then this hath no man, then that a man bestowe his lyfe for his frendes.

The Jacobean translation process was richly and densely social. Endless conversation and consultation flowed across the final judging committee, testing the translation not by sight but by ear. This Bible was appointed to be read in churches (and thus had no illustrations for study at home) and so its meaning had to be carried on a heard rhythm, it had to appeal to what T. S. Eliot later called 'the auditory imagination', that 'feeling for syllable and rhythm, penetrating far below the conscious levels of thought and feeling, invigorating every word'. Under these pressures, Tyndale's words become, very slightly but very significantly, musically enriched:

> This is my Commaundement, that ye loue one another, as I haue loued you.
>
> Greater loue hath no man then this, that a man lay downe his life for his friends.

The meanings of the two translations are not essentially different, but the Jacobean words are clarified where Tyndale's are clotted; they are memorable where Tyndale stumbles over his grammar; the Jacobean choice of word is more authoritative, 'one another' better than 'togedder', 'lay down' better than 'bestowe'; and the Jacobean sentences sound like the voice of a divine wisdom and certainty, establishing a marvellous law, where Tyndale conveys perhaps another Jesus: human, uncertain, seeking to articulate his revolutionary gospel.

Far from burying Tyndale, the 1611 Translators honoured him. They were quite explicit about their debt to the past. The king's own instructions had referred them to the sequence of sixteenth-century versions and Miles Smith's Preface is concerned to reiterate the point. The earlier translators 'deserue to be had of vs and of posteritie in euerlasting remembrance'. All they wanted was to improve the work that had gone before, so

> that whatsoeuer is sound alreadie ... the same will shine as gold more brightly, being rubbed and polished; also, if anything be halting, or superfluous, or not so agreeable to the originall, the same may be corrected, and the trueth set in place. And what can the King command to be done that will bring him more true honour than this?

The idea, in fact, was not to make a new translation, Smith maintained, but to make 'out of many good ones, one principal good one'. And that was their triumph: a polished collation, a refinement of a century's translating, a book that became both clear and rich.

Of course, what they delivered to Robert Barker was not entirely good. The Hebrew and particularly the Greek texts they were working from were not the most accurate, even by the standards of their own time. Theodore Beza, Calvin's successor as the head of the church in Geneva, had prepared an edition of the New Testament some forty years earlier based on a more ancient and less corrupt manuscript. The English scholars were still a little adrift on tenses in Hebrew, while *koine*, the form of rubbed down and difficult Greek in which the New Testament is written, so unlike the Greek of Plato and Aristotle, still held mysteries for them, which only later translations would correct. And there are some parts of the King James Bible, particularly in the dense and difficult passages of Paul's Epistles, that are now, and to some extent were then, virtually unintelligible. A famous example is 2 Corinthians 6:11–13:

O yee Corinthians, our mouth is open vnto you, our heart is enlarged.

Yee are not straitened in vs, but yee are straitened in your owne bowels.

Nowe for a recompense in the same, (I speake as vnto my children) be ye also inlarged.

Even though Tyndale's effort was even more opaque, this is clearly a translation done by people who didn't really understand what they were translating, and in those circumstances rhythmic language and interesting vocabulary can do very little to save the situation. As modern translations make clear, Paul is asking the Corinthians, as a father might ask his children, to be more open with him, since he feels he has been open with them himself, but no one would have divined that simple meaning from the muddle which (at least in this instance) the Jacobean Translators served up.

Some form of text was handed over to Robert Barker, 'Printer to the King's Most Excellent Maiestie', perhaps an annotated version of the Bishops' Bible, perhaps a manuscript. What was said to be the 'manuscript copy of the Bible' was sold twice in the seventeenth century, once to Cambridge University Press, once to a firm of London printers, but has now disappeared. According to one romantic theory, it was burnt in the Great Fire of London.

Barker's printshop began to apply its own level of chaos to the production process. It seems to have been a sort of anarchy. Either two editions were produced one after another; or both at the same time and sheets from each edition were bound together in single volumes. As a result no copy of the 1611 Bible is like any other. And they were riddled with mistakes. The Translators had intended that any word inserted to improve the sense should be printed in a different face. In fact, that principle became confused early on and if a word is in italics in the printed Bible, there is often no telling if it is in the original Greek or Hebrew or not. Marginal references to other relevant parts of the Bible are highly inaccurate, particularly in the Psalms, where references are made to the numbering system used in the Vulgate, not the numbering system in this Bible itself.

Calmly elegant Bibles in Roman typefaces had been in production in France and Switzerland for decades. This Bible, looking back to an imagined antiquity before the modern age, was given a heavy, antique feel with its dense blackletter typeface, a 'Gothic', non-Roman typeface, and a certain airlessness on the page. It may be that because the Geneva Bibles were printed in open and accessible Roman type, and the Bishops' Bible, which this was intended to replace, had itself been in blackletter, that Barker made this retrograde decision. Although editions of the King James Bible were appearing in Roman type within a few years, blackletter editions continued to be printed and sold, well into the first years of the eighteenth century. Even at its birth, this was sold as the Bible of Old England.

And it was littered with misprints, 'hoopes' for 'hookes', 'she' for 'he', three whole lines simply repeated in Exodus, and alarmingly 'Judas' for 'Jesus' in one of the Gospels. None of these was quite so catastrophic as a misprint that would appear in a 1631 edition, the so-called Wicked Bible, which failed to put the word 'not' in Exodus 20:14, giving the reading 'Thou shalt commit adultery', but the degree of muddle is scarcely what a modern scholarly text would tolerate. When, finally, in the nineteenth century, Dr F. Scrivener, a scholar working to modern standards, attempted to collate all the editions of the King James Bible then in circulation, he found more than 24,000 variations between them. The curious fact is that no one such thing as 'The King James Bible' – agreed, consistent and whole – has ever existed.

The book crept out into the public arena. Being only a revision of earlier translations, and not a new work, there was no need for it to be entered in the Stationers' Register, which recorded only new publications and so, in addition to this most famous book having no agreed text, it also has no publication date. Nor is it known how many were printed of the first big folio edition for use in churches. When the first state Bible, the so-called Great Bible, was issued in 1540, 20,000 copies were run off, more than enough to provide one for every parish church in England, costing 10 shillings each, 12 shillings bound. For the King James Bible, though, there is no record of either print-run or price.

Everything that could have been done for it had been done. Something approaching three hundred and fifty scholar years had been devoted to its excellence; the Crown and state church had given it their imprimatur; a laudatory preface and dedication, by permission, to the king, had been included. Any publisher would have hoped for the most enormous success.

They didn't get it. Some critics thought its dependence on a kind of English which seemed sixty or seventy years out of date (although its English was in fact a form no one had ever spoken) made it ridiculous and bogus. Hugh Broughton, a cantankerous and aggressive Puritan Hebrew scholar, who had wanted to be part of the great committee, sending papers and suggestions to Bancroft, but barred because of his incivility, lambasted the translation for its errors and its slavish following of the old Bishops' Bible. In the opening words of his Preface, Miles Smith had predicted such a reaction. 'Zeale to promote the common good', he had begun – and there is no phrase which encapsulates more precisely the ideals of the project – 'findeth but cold intertainment in the world.' Broughton castigated the Translators. Their understanding of Hebrew was inadequate; where they had stumbled on something worthwhile, they had usually relegated it to the margins. These worldly divines, he

said, were interested only in promotion in the church and crawling to royal authority. Blasphemy, most damnable corruptions,
intolerable deceit and vile imposture were terms scarcely bad
enough to describe the depths of their degeneracy. 'The late
Bible', he wrote,

> was sent to me to censure: which bred in me a sadness that
> will grieve me while I breathe, it is ill done. Tell His Majesty
> that I had rather be rent in pieces with wild horses, than any
> such translation by my consent should be urged upon poor
> churches . . . The new edition crosseth me. I require it to be
> burnt.

Not that Broughton was in any way bitter; these accusations
were, he said, not 'the dictates of passion, but the just resentment
of a zealous mind'.

The Geneva Bible continued to hold its position in English
affections, at least partly because it was so useful for its notes
and appendices, a guidebook to the world of the divine. It continued to flood off the presses: a folio and a quarto in 1611,
another folio in 1612, three quartos in 1614, two more in 1615
and a folio in 1616. Then, in 1616, the king put a halt to it, or
at least attempted to: no more editions of the Geneva Bible were
to be printed. The King James Bible (henceforth known as the
Authorised Version, although no document authorising its use
by the king, Council or anyone else survived the 1619 Whitehall
fire) was to become, by order, the only English Bible. But the
appetite for the Geneva text could not be so easily denied. Presses
in Amsterdam and Dort started to roll, producing Geneva Bibles
for the English market well into the 1630s. All too significantly,
Robert Barker, printer to the king, a chaotic man who would
end up in debtors' prison, bought up the Dutch Geneva editions,
added a title page with the fraudulent date 1599 clearly stamped
on it, and flogged them to a ready market. The King James Bible
languished on the side, a royal project, whose language it seemed
was not the language of the people.

Even more strangely, given the sanctity with which the text of the King James Bible has been regarded in later ages, the very people who might have championed it continued to use the Geneva Bible. Lancelot Andrewes nearly always took his sermon texts from the Geneva. Even William Laud, the most anti-Calvinist bishop in the church, quoted from the Geneva. Most extraordinarily of all, Miles Smith, in the Preface to the new translation, quotes from the very Geneva Bible which it was, in part, intended to replace. And in the Separatist congregations in Amsterdam, Leiden and eventually on the *Mayflower*, it was of course the Geneva Bible they took with them.

Geneva Bibles continued to be printed until 1644, and only after the Restoration in 1660 did the King James Bible, hallowed now as something that had its origins before the great rupture of the Civil War, redolent of monarchy and antiquity, come to take its place as the Bible itself, the national text and the symbol of England as God's country. In America, a slightly different process occurred, but with the same effect. Calvinist Christianity is inherently fissive. Its emphasis on the primacy of a vengeful God constantly throws into doubt the validity of worldly government, and its repeated emphasis on the difference between the elect, who would be saved, and the rest, who would be damned, is no basis on which to found a nation. These radically disruptive ideas are the repeated threnody of the Geneva Bible, the food and fuel on which the whole phenomenon of Separatism and the emergence of the Pilgrim Fathers was based.

As the American settlements widened and deepened, and their political processes matured, the need for a separatist gospel ebbed. The relationship of Puritan church and Puritan state in early America soon became, strangely enough, as close as any relationship between the Jacobean Crown and the Church of England. In early Massachusetts, heresy, witchcraft, profanity, blasphemy, idolatry and breaking the Sabbath were all civil offences, to be dealt with by civil courts. The new Americans may have dispensed with bishops, surplices and the Book of Common Prayer, but they had not replaced them with a Utopia of religious freedom. Seventeenth-century America was a country of strictly enforced state religion and as such needed a Bible much more attuned to the necessities of nation-building than anything the Separatists' Geneva Bible could offer. It is one of the strangest of historical paradoxes that the King James Bible, whose whole purpose had been nation-building in the service of a ceremonial and episcopal state church, should become the guiding text of Puritan America. But the translation's lifeblood had been inclusiveness, it was drenched with the splendour of a divinely sanctioned authority, and by the end of the seventeenth century it had come to be treasured by Americans as much as by the British as one of their national texts.

As such, the great Jacobean Bible, for all its faults, wrinkles and inaccuracies, has persisted. How can one, in the end, approach this mystery? What is it, uniquely, that the King James Bible gave the English? What need did it satisfy? Only comparison with some other attempts at translating scripture can give an idea of what the fifty-odd Jacobean men managed to achieve. Compare for example a passage from the Psalm 8(3–5) as the committee men produced it, and the same lines translated by Milton. In 1611, these were their words:

> When I consider thy heauens, the worke of thy fingers, the moone and the starres which thou hast ordained;
>> What is man, that thou art mindfull of him? and the sonne of man that thou visitest him?
>> For thou hast made him a little lower then the Angels; and hast crowned him with glory and honour.

The marvels of this passage consist above all in one quality, or at least in one combination of qualities: an absolute simplicity of vocabulary set in a rhythm of the utmost stateliness and majesty. The words are necessarily slowed to a muffled drumbeat of a pace. There is no hurrying this, no running away with it, as a Shakespeare speech can sometimes hurry, a rushed cataract of words tripping over itself even as it emerges. The characteristic sound of the King James Bible is not like that but, like the ideal of majesty itself, is indescribably vast and yet perfectly accessible, reaching up to the sublime and down to the immediate and the concrete, without any apparent effort. The rhetoric of this translation has, in fact, precisely the qualities which this psalm attributes to God: a majesty that is mindful of man.

When Milton addressed this Psalm 8 in the 1640s he wrote this:

> When I behold thy heavens, thy Fingers art,
>   The Moon and Starrs which thou so bright has set
> In the pure firmament, then saith my heart,
>   O what is man that thou remembrest yet,
>
> And think'st upon him; or of man begot
>   That him thou visit'st and of him art found:
> Scarce to be less then Gods, thou mad'st his lot,
>   With honour and with state thou hast him crown'd.

Although Milton is having to accommodate rhyme and the iambic pentameter, something has gone wrong here. The simplicity has been lost in a search for a more evolved and more sophisticated form. And with the loss of simplicity has come not only a loss in clarity, immediacy and obviousness, but, mysteriously, a loss in dignity, scale and grandeur. That precious Jacobean alloy, the fusion of light and richness, has gone.

Jump to the eighteenth century, and the decay in religious language has become even clearer. By the 1760s, the peculiar nature of Jacobean Bible English had started to irritate some Enlightenment tastes. In 1768 a Dr Edward Harwood, a Bristol Presbyterian, published a version of the New Testament which aimed, he said, 'to clothe the idea of the Apostles with propriety and perspicuity', replacing the 'bald and barbarous language of the old vulgar version with the elegance of modern English'. Even at the time he was something of a laughing stock, 'shunned by the multitude like an infected person' who 'could hardly walk the streets of Bristol without being insulted'. But what Harwood got wrong is another way of measuring the Jacobean achievement.

Take, for example, the Nunc Dimittis, the words of Simeon on seeing the child Jesus, which in the King James Bible had run as follows:

> Lord now lettest thou thy seruant depart in peace, according to thy word.
> For mine eyes haue seene thy saluation,
> Which thou hast prepared before the face of all people;
> A light to lighten the Gentiles, and the glory of thy people Israel.

Harwood wrote: 'O God, thy promise to me is amply fulfilled. I now quit the post of human life with satisfaction and joy, since thou hast indulged mine eyes with so divine a spectacle as the great Messiah.'

The Jacobean version has the great imperturbability, the air of irreproachable authority, which is the essence of sacred ritual. The Translators made a ceremony of the word. But the passage is also astonishingly vivid, turning those words into a tangible experience. They never lose sight of the physical and the bodily dimensions of existence – service, departure, eyes, sight, face, light, illumination – and adopt them as markers of and symbols for the divine. Poor Harwood's version has never left his library, has never known darkness and light, has none of the music and none of the utter memorability of the miraculous Jacobean translation. It should come as no surprise that Dr Harwood is never more at a loss than at moments of greatest spiritual intensity. At the Transfiguration, when the divinity of Jesus is revealed to the apostles, his clothes and face glowing and shining in front of them, Peter stood amazed, scarcely able to speak. Tyndale had translated his stumbling words as the slightly odd, 'Master here is good beinge for us', which was perhaps a mistake, perhaps an attempt to convey Peter's confusion. The King James Translators had him say simply, 'Lord, it is good for vs to be here.' Harwood, reaching high for propriety and perspicuity, managed to turn the apostle into a frock-coated, bewigged and slightly obsequious 1760s estate agent, exclaiming 'Oh, sir! what a delectable residence we might establish here!'

The nineteenth century veered the other way. By 1870, it had become obvious not only that the manuscripts on which the King James Bible had been based were no longer the best available, but that the Jacobean Translators had made many mistakes in translation. The first major revision of the English scriptures was set in train but Victorian England was so enamoured of Jacobean word forms and the rhythms of the King James version, that the translators were urged to make their new translation as much like a Jacobean text as they could. The King James Bible had been, at least in the mainstream, unchallenged for 270 years, eight or nine generations. Its language, archaic even in 1611, derived from a form of English current in the mid-sixteenth century, had come to seem like the language spoken by God. As a result the Revised Version, finally published in 1885, although introducing some very odd translatorese by following the Greek word order ('Thy will be done, as in heaven, so on earth') also introduced a string of Jacobethanisms which had not been in the 1611 text: howbeit, peradventure, holden, aforetime, sojourn and behooved all appeared in the new Bible, nineteenth-century changes posing as the real oak-panelled thing, as if a team of London solicitors suddenly appeared for work in ruffs and doublets.

The twentieth century took yet another turn. During World War II, military chaplains in the British army had been unable to make their soldiers understand the words of the Bible, or so it was claimed, and in 1946 the idea of another new translation was raised. Committees, sub-committees, translating panels, literary advisers, doctrinal experts: all were drafted in. Representatives from the Protestant churches, conformist and Non-conformist, were included. They even met in the Jerusalem Chamber in Westminster Abbey, where Lancelot Andrewes and his company had met, hoping perhaps to draw inspiration from the walls (even if, as perhaps they did not realise, those walls had been lined with mid-Victorian repro-Tudor linenfold panelling). Roman Catholics were allowed in to observe and the process took its time. Their version of the New Testament appeared in 1962, the complete New English Bible in 1970. The product, as T. S. Eliot wrote at the time, 'astonishes in its combination of the vulgar, the trivial and the pedantic'.

The committee had got itself lost. Dr C. H. Dodd, the general director of translation, ex-professor of Divinity at Cambridge, had asked for a 'timeless' prose, in which archaism and 'hallowed associations' were to be avoided, and 'a sense of reality' sought. But aiming for this plain accessibility, the New English Bible ended up as nothing much to anyone. Wanting timelessness, they achieved the language of the memo. Avoiding archaism, they embraced the banal. Looking for reality, they lost all feeling for the extraordinary and overpowering strangeness of the Bible, its governing sense of the metaphysical somehow squeezed, dragged and stretched, like Christ himself, into the world of men. They had somehow forgotten that ordinariness is not the Bible's subject.

Take the moment, for example, after Christ's crucifixion and resurrection, when he appears to the apostles on the shores of the Sea of Galilee. The men have been fishing all night but have caught nothing. This is how it was translated in the seventeenth century, drawing very heavily here, as so often, on William Tyndale:

> But when the morning was now come, Iesus stood on the shore: but the disciples knewe not that it was Iesus.
>
> Then Iesus saith vnto them, Children, have ye any meat? They answered him, No.
>
> And he said vnto them, Cast the net on the right side of the ship, and yee shall finde. They cast therefore, and now they were not able to draw it, for the multitude of fishes.
>
> Therfore that Disciple whome Iesus loued, saith vnto Peter, It is the Lord. Now when Simon Peter heard that it was the Lord, he girt his fishers coate vnto him, (for hee was naked) & did cast himselfe into the sea.

Every rhetorical decision is right here. The first sentence – afloat on 'now' – brings an effortless immediacy; we are with the apostles in the boat, with the dawn and the exhaustion of a futile night around us. 'Iesus stood on the shore': no explanation, a miraculous appearance from nowhere, simply there. 'Iesus saith vnto them, Children, have ye any meat?' He talks to them, no shouting, no calling out, a conversational tone even though they are a hundred yards or more away on the waters of the lake. And as he is their father, they are his children. He says to them, 'The right side of the ship', a casual use of language, its authority consisting in its ease, but then a subtle technicality 'yee shall finde' – the huntsman's and fisherman's word for 'coming on prey'. The apostles then catch and draw up 'a multitude of fishes': a murmured pun thrown forward to the time when these men would be fishers of men, a multitude of people drawn into their nets. The final verse, written in a language as ruggedly straightforward as the fishermen would have used themselves, brings to a point the intense reality of this unreal scene. This is a form of writing which is consistently alert to its many purposes. It translates an alien moment through intelligible description. It makes that moment quiveringly alive, folding up the space of sixteen or twenty-one centuries. It is ever conscious of the miraculous nature of what is happening.

Turn to the twentieth-century attempt at this passage and it becomes clear enough what has been lost. Every right decision by the Renaissance Translators is abandoned, every wrong fork taken.

> Morning came and there stood Jesus on the beach, but the disciples did not know that it was Jesus. He called out to them 'Friends, have you caught anything?' They answered 'No'. He said, 'Shoot the net to starboard, and you will make a catch.' They did so, and found they could not haul the net aboard, there were so many fish in it. Then the disciple whom Jesus loved said to Peter, 'It is the Lord!' When Simon Peter heard that, he wrapped his coat about him (for he had stripped) and plunged into the sea.

This is dead; there is no immediacy to it, nothing vibrant. The tone of surprise is too overt and so the shock is diminished. It is a description of an inert normality, mundane, tensionless and mystery-free. The atmosphere is of a 1930s bathing party.

Again and again, the seventeenth-century phrases seem richer, deeper, truer, more alive, more capable of carrying complex and multiple meanings, than anything the twentieth century could manage. It happens in linguistic history that languages lose aspects of themselves, whole wings of their existence withering, falling off, disappearing into the past. Has it now happened to English? Does English no longer have a faculty of religious language?

Of course, alongside this history of dissatisfaction with the inherited text, and of constant attempts to renew it in the light of current fashion, the King James Bible persisted, the touchstone, the national book, the formative mental structure for all English-speaking people. For generation after generation, it gave the English, and the English in America, a template against which to measure their own utterances. It was in many households the only book and became itself a spur to literacy. It is surely no coincidence that its creation coincides with the first great surge in literacy levels in England.

The King James Bible, gradually replacing the Geneva Bible, was in the vanguard of that movement and it gave the English, more than any other book, a sense of the possibilities of language, an extraordinary range of richness, more approachable than Shakespeare, more populist than Milton, a common text against which life itself could be read. This is more about rhetoric, a certain way of speaking or writing, than about the dogma or the many conflicting theologies which the Bible can be found to contain. The sense of the many threads by which the real physical world is bound to a magnificence which goes beyond the physical; the simple word held in a musical rhythm; a poetic rather than a philosophical approach to reality, an openness to the reality of dreams and visions: all of these treasured qualities of Englishness can be seen to stem from the habits of mind which the Jacobean Translators bequeathed to their country. It emerges powerfully of course in the seventeenth century, in Milton, Thomas Browne, John Bunyan, dives a little underground perhaps in the eighteenth century, and re-emerges with renewed power in the nineteenth century. Coleridge's poetry is couched for line after line in the rhythms of the King James Bible. The Romantics' hunger for the archaic, which in English consciousness seems scarcely distinguishable from the poetic, is at one with the Jacobean search for the ancient and the primitive, a deeply retrospective habit of mind which searches for meaning in the past. The old, for the English, is holy and beautiful, largely because the language of the King James Bible has conveyed that to them.

Take the opening lines of Wordsworth's sonnet 'On Westminster Bridge', smoothed a little compared with Jacobean vigour but nevertheless an encapsulation of the sensibility which the King James Bible enshrines:

Earth has not anything to show more fair:
    Dull would he be of soul who could pass by
A sight so touching in its majesty.

The idea that 'majesty' might be 'touching' is precisely what the Jacobean Translators embraced, both as a conscious political programme and, as this book has attempted to argue, in the rhetoric of the Bible they created.

As the essence of an inclusive polity, few ideas have been more powerful and in America that rhetoric of 'a touching majesty' has formed the backbone of the great milestone speeches in the country's history. Lincoln's Gettysburg address, repeated in New York on the first anniversary of 11 September 2001, would have been impossible without the King James Bible. The great speeches of twentieth-century America, including J. F. Kennedy's inaugural address and the series of speeches made by Martin Luther King in the eighteen months leading up to his death, are descendants in a direct line from the words and the evaluating minds, and ears, of the divines who gathered in the wainscoted rooms in Westminster, Cambridge, Oxford and the City of London 400 years ago.

The churches and biblical scholarship have, by and large, abandoned the frame of mind which created this translation. The social structures which gave rise to it – rigid hierarchies; a love of majesty; subservience; an association of power with glory – have all gone. The belief in the historical and authentic truth of the scriptures, particularly the Gospels, has been largely abandoned, even by the religious. The ferocious intolerances of the pre-liberal world have been left behind – it is inconceivable now that a Henry Barrow would be executed, or a Henry Garnet, or that the Scrooby Separatists would have been forced to leave home and country – and perhaps as a result of that change, perhaps as a symptom, religion, or at least the conventional religion of ordinary people, has been drained of its passion. There is no modern language that can encompass the realities which the Jacobeans accepted as normal. Modern religious rhetoric is dilute and ineffectual, and where it isn't, it seems mad and aberrational. It is an appalling fact that the manner of speech which approaches most nearly to the language of these Jacobean divines comes from the mouths of murderous fundamentalists. When asked by a reporter in October 2001 if he was responsible for the anthrax attacks then occurring in the United States, Osama bin Laden answered: 'These diseases are a punishment from God and a response to oppressed mothers' prayers in Lebanon, Iraq, Palestine and everywhere.' That is the kind of remark which would not have raised an eyebrow in Jacobean England. This is not to suggest that the Translators of the King James Bible would have approved of religious terrorism. They certainly wouldn't; their reactions to 5 November prove that. Even so, there is something that connects the God-shaped mentality of Jacobean England more intimately with the world of modern Muslim fundamentalists than with our own softened, liberal tolerance. These men, and their Bible, exist on the other side of a gulf, which can be labelled liberal, secular, democratic modernity. We do not live in the same world.

It is impossible now to experience in an English church the enveloping amalgam of tradition, intelligence, beauty, clarity of purpose, intensity of conviction and plangent, heart-gripping godliness which is the experience of page after page of the King James Bible. Nothing in our culture can match its breadth, depth and universality, unless, curiously enough, it is something that was written at exactly the same time and in almost exactly the same place: the great tragedies of Shakespeare.

That is no chance effect. Shakespeare's great tragedies and the King James Bible are each other's mirror-twin. Both emerge from the ambitions and terrors of the Jacobean world. They are, from their radically diverging cores, the great what-ifs of the age. *King Lear* pursues the implications of a singular and disastrous decision to divide a kingdom; the King James Bible embraces the full breadth of absorbed and inherited wisdom in order to unite one; *Lear* contemplates, more fearlessly than any text had ever done or has ever done, the falling away of all meaning; the King James Bible enshrines what it understands as the guarantee of all meaning; the rhetoric of *King Lear* breaks and shivers into multi-faceted shards of songs, madness, grandeur, argument, pathos; the King James Bible masks its immensely various sources under one certain, all-over musical sonority; everything in *Lear* falls apart, everything in the King James Bible pulls together; one is a nightmare of dissolution, the other a dream of wholeness.

Lear himself, when exposed to the consequences of his actions, comes to long for the very things which the rhetoric of the King James Translators aimed to enshrine: the necessity of social bonds, reliance on old customs, the place of performance and ceremony as the core of social being. His nakedness is both pure and deprived, both the perfect, stripped, humbled condition which the Puritans longed for, and the utterly diminished condition of an unclothed king. What he needs in that state are the comforts of tradition and inheritance. They are what the text of the King James Bible has on offer. Both play and translation, in that way, might be seen as profoundly conservative texts, both promulgating 'the old way of doing things' against the modern, 'novelist' requirement for clarity and pure light. But in fact both are strung between those polarities: honesty and tradition, purity and ceremony, nakedness and the comforts of a shared and familiar life. *Lear* looks the King James version in the mirror because these are clearly the concerns of the Translators too: to hold themselves consciously poised between the claims of accessibility and beauty, plainness and richness, simplicity and majesty, the people and the king.

I am no atheist but I am no churchgoer, perhaps because these things are no longer voiced in church. These great questions are not the medium of modern religion. But they are there in the King James Bible, a text which embraces the polarities modern religion seems to steer past. I am drawn equally to the richness of ceremony, to the cave-like darknesses you find in the Orthodox Church, its candles and crumbling gilt glimmering in the darkness, its age-blackened icons, the unforgettable sight in a monastery on Mount Athos of a lit chandelier, hanging from the dome high above us, all its candles ablaze, sixty or eighty of them, being swung by the priest in a huge and heavy gilded arc, a vast and dynamic embodiment of glimmering light, orbiting above our heads.

And at the same time, I am deeply drawn to the holiness of the plain and the stripped, a clarified strictness, of a plain light, of the austerity of those hermitages in the Egyptian desert and on tiny islands along the Atlantic fringes of Europe, where removal from power does not deprive you of glory but gives you access to it.

There is no need, though, to choose between these things, and that avoidance of choice is, in the end, the heart of the King James Bible. It does not choose. It absorbs and includes. It is in that sense catholic, as Jacobean Englishmen consistently called their church: not Roman but catholic, embracing all.

Unlike the churches themselves, the words of this Bible remain alive, a way of speaking and a form of the language which is still a vehicle of meaning in circumstances when little else can be. Not long ago, I was talking to a man I have known for years, a fisherman all his life, about his son who drowned in the sea about ten years ago. I knew the son very slightly. Everybody loved him. He was drowned because he couldn't kick off his big sea boots or struggle out of his waterproof smock after another fishing boat had collided with his – he was setting nets – when no one, or so they said, had been in the wheelhouse of the other boat to keep a look out. The boy was thrown into the sea and was drowned there. The other boat was unaware that anything had happened. He was twenty-four. There was a boy in the boat with him who just saw his hand going down and could not reach it.

His father told me to read Psalm 77. I didn't know it. It is a poem of the most utter desolation – or debilitation really – of the deepest doubt and sorrow, more straightly expressed, in its terrible, repetitive questioning, than anything else in the language.

> Will the lord cast off for euer? and will he be fauourable no more?
>> Is his mercy cleane gone for euer? doth *his* promise faile for evermore?
>> Hath God forgotten to be gracious? hath he in anger shut vp his tender mercies?
>> And I sayd, this is my infirmitie . . .

The father did not talk much about it, but I went to see the boy's gravestone. It's in the burying ground at Luskentyre, on the west coast of Harris in the Outer Hebrides, where the Atlantic rolls in, week after week, month after month, in vast, American-scale combers. The wind blows the sand from the beach over the graveyard so that even in midsummer it seems to have a light dusting of snow. There's an engraving of the boat on the stone, and a verse from the psalm:

> Thy way *is* in the sea, and thy path in the great waters: and thy footsteps are not known.

That is not consolation, nor the muffling of experience by religion: it is the heightening and realising of experience through language, a statement of the cruelty of things and the unknowable purpose of the universe. A lament written in the seventh or eighth century BC, translated 400 years ago, by Laurence Chaderton's company in Cambridge, communicating itself now in a way which is quite unaffected, neither literary nor academic, not historical, nor reconstructionist, but transmitting a nearly incredible immediacy from one end of human civilisation to another. That is the everlasting miracle of this book. As Miles Smith wrote in the Preface:

> Translation it is that openeth the window, to let in the light, that breaketh the shell, that we may eat the kernel; that putteth aside the curtain, that we may look into the most Holy place; that removeth the cover of the well, that we may come by the water.

APPENDICES

The most High and Mighty Monarch IAMES by the grace of God king
of Great Brittaine, France, and Ireland. Borne the 19 of Iune. 1566.

The most excellent Princesse ANNE Queene of Great Brittaine,
France. and Ireland. Borne the 12. of October. 1574.

THE SIXTEENTH-CENTURY BIBLE

In the early summer of 1604, Richard Bancroft, Bishop of London and soon to be Archbishop of Canterbury, drew up his instructions to the Translators. They were to base their revisions, he told them, on the Bishops' Bible but they were to consult, he said, '**Tindall's, Matthews, Coverdales, Whitchurch's, Geneva**'. He was listing the great landmarks in the evolution of the sixteenth-century English Bible, part of the astonishing wave of Bible translation that swept across Reformation Europe.

There is no connection between the advent of printing and the coming of Protestantism. Early sixteenth-century Europe was awash with printed versions of traditional Catholic prayers and orders of service. The old church and the new technology were the closest of allies. The very trigger of the Reformation, the indulgences sold by the Catholic Church to ease the path into heaven and fill the church's coffers, were by the late fifteenth century printed documents. Nevertheless, the mere existence of a busy and dynamic publishing industry certainly helped the spread of Protestantism. The first printed Bible had been a Latin Vulgate (the great medieval Bible translated from the Greek and Hebrew by St Jerome in the late fourth century) produced by Johann Gutenberg in Mainz in 1454–56, an exquisite folio book, very expensive, modelled precisely on the finest medieval manuscripts, some printed on paper but many on vellum. But when in 1522 Luther, the first genius of mass communications, published his German New Testament, 3,000 copies were immediately printed for sale at a fraction of the cost of a manuscript. One German printer reckoned, forty years later, that he had sold at least 100,000 Lutheran Bibles.

The backlash was already there: the first burning of Protestant books in 1521, the first burning of a Protestant printer in 1527. Meanwhile, the translated word of God spread across Europe. The Czechs had enjoyed the Bible in the vernacular since the fourteenth century and the first printed Czech Bible appeared in 1488. The rest of Europe soon joined in the Lutheran wave. In 1524 the New Testament appeared in Swyzerdeutsch, followed in 1526 by the first complete Bible in Dutch, and in 1530 in French (although a translation of the Vulgate, not from the original tongues). In the same year a New Testament was published '*tradotto in lingua toscana*'. An Icelandic New Testament appeared in 1540, the first complete Swedish Bible in 1541, a Finnish New Testament in 1548 and a complete Danish Bible in 1550. The first Bible in Spanish was published only in 1569, printed in Basle and later distributed from Frankfurt. Spain itself remained implacably hostile to the vernacular. Further east, a Slovene New Testament was published in 1557–60, a Croat New Testament in 1563, a Polish Bible (Catholic, from the Vulgate) in 1561, a Hungarian Bible in 1590.

This astonishing Europe-wide movement is the context in which the sixteenth-century history of English Bible-translation must be set. Parts of the Bible had been translated into Anglo-Saxon and Middle English, but not until the end of the fourteenth century had there been a complete text. From about 1382, the followers of John Wycliffe, a blunt Yorkshireman and Master of Balliol College, Oxford, produced a large number of manuscript English Bibles, often clumsily and over-literally translated, but many of which survive. Although they were outlawed by the church in 1407–09, they remained in secret circulation even into the sixteenth century, some beautifully illuminated, clearly considered as treasured objects.

The English Lutheran **William Tyndale** fled to the continent when his projected translation of the Bible looked as if it would offend the authorities. In 1525 he began printing his fluent and idiomatic translation of the New Testament in Catholic Cologne before the work was disrupted by the city magistrates. The complete book was only finished the following year on presses in Worms. The octavo sheets were smuggled into England in bales of cloth and sold at 9d a set. Three copies of this precious book survive, only one of them complete.

Tyndale pressed on with the Old Testament. In 1531, his translation of the Book of Jonah was published, and in 1534, the same year as Martin Luther's complete German Bible appeared, Tyndale's New

Testament was reprinted with corrections and revisions, this time in Antwerp.

Meanwhile, under the encouragement of the bishops of the English Church, another translation had been made by **Miles Coverdale**, an ex-assistant of Tyndale's, working for a printer perhaps in Antwerp, perhaps in Cologne and perhaps in Zurich. (The whole milieu of the early translations is a mixture of the covert and the commercial.) It was fulsomely dedicated to Henry VIII and Coverdale's translations of the psalms remain those in use in the Church of England, never replaced by the slight alterations made to them in the King James Bible.

In 1536 William Tyndale was martyred in Flanders, garotted and then burnt, betrayed by an English spy who was perhaps in the pay of Sir Thomas More, his old enemy. Tyndale died before he could complete his translation of the Old Testament. His work was continued by another of his Antwerp friends, John Rogers, who under the pseudonym of Thomas Matthew published the so-called **Matthew's Bible** in 1537. The king licensed 1,500 copies of it and Matthew's became the first Bible in English that could be legally sold in England. It is largely a conflation of Tyndale and Coverdale. Rogers was later burnt at Smithfield by Queen Mary.

The next year, in 1538, Henry VIII ordered a Bible to be placed in every church in England, half the cost to be carried by the parishes themselves. For this purpose, yet another revision, the 1539 Great Bible, was produced by 'dyverse excellent learned men', bearing the name of **Edward Whitchurch**, its printer, on the title page. It is a revision of Matthew's Bible, directed by Miles Coverdale himself.

In 1560, English Calvinist exiles in Geneva published the **Geneva Bible**. A beautiful piece of Renaissance printing, the first English Bible in Roman type, full of illustrations, appendices, maps and tables, almost a forerunner of the family encyclopaedia in feeling, it was the work of at least three translators, many of whose phrases were adopted by the King James Translators. Its highly contentious notes, many of which threw doubts on the validity of unconstrained royal power, made it the favourite of Puritans and suspect in the English royal establishment. It was the version of the Bible which the pilgrims took with them to America.

Partly in response to it, in 1568, the English Church commissioned a new Bible from a committee of about seventeen translators, most of whom were bishops, chaired by Matthew Parker, the Archbishop of Canterbury. Their rather ponderous style, and the absence of Geneva's helpful notes and hints on how to interpret the scriptures, never made the **Bishops' Bible** very popular, although it was the one from which lessons were read every Sunday in Elizabethan England.

The English Catholics abroad in Rheims produced their own translation of the New Testament in 1582 and in 1609–10, having moved to Douai, of the Old Testament. The King James Translators certainly knew and used the Rheims–Douai Bible although Richard Bancroft made no mention of it in his instructions to them.

THE SIX COMPANIES OF TRANSLATORS

The names of fifty of the Translators are recorded. Some are little more than a name; of others a great deal is known. As this list attempts to show, they were bound together in a complex web of shared experience at both school and university and in a set of mutually reliant networks of clientship and patronage, by which leading members of the church promoted their favourites into well-rewarded positions of influence. A crucial step was to become 'a prebendary', a member of a cathedral chapter who receives a yearly 'prebend' or share of the income from the cathedral estates. It was the principal means of providing an income for rising stars in the church, for whom the well-worn route went from fellow of a college at Oxford or Cambridge to master of the college, prebendary at a cathedral, dean at a cathedral and finally to a bishopric, beginning usually with somewhere poor, like Rochester or St David's, ending somewhere well-endowed, such as Winchester, Lincoln or London. Many of the Translators pursued some or all of these steps. The translating of the Bible was only one episode on what really mattered: the career path.

The First Westminster Company
Genesis, Exodus, Leviticus, Numbers, Deuteronomy, Joshua, Judges, Ruth, I Samuel, II Samuel, I Kings, II Kings

LANCELOT ANDREWES (Director)
1555–1626 born London; Merchant Taylors' school (with Thomas Harrison); Pembroke Hall, Cambridge; 1589 Master of Pembroke (with brother Roger Andrewes a fellow); chaplain to and client of Archbishop Whitgift; royal chaplain to both Elizabeth and James; client of the Cecils; prebendary at St Paul's; 1601 Dean of Westminster (with

Saravia and Barlow as prebendaries); 1605 Bishop of Chichester; 1609 Bishop of Ely; 1609 Privy Councillor; 1618 Bishop of Winchester; 1619 Dean of Chapel Royal.

JOHN OVERALL

1559–1619 born Hadleigh, Essex; Hadleigh Grammar School (with John Bois); Trinity College, Cambridge; 1596 Regius Professor of Divinity at Cambridge; 1598 Master of Catharine Hall; 1601 Dean of St Paul's (with Lancelot Andrewes a prebendary); 1614 Bishop of Coventry and Lichfield; 1618 Bishop of Norwich; friend of Andrewes; loathed by Abbot; member of court of High Commission.

HADRIAN À SARAVIA

1531–1613 born Hesdin, Artois; half-Flemish, half-Spanish, both parents Protestants; 1582 professor of Divinity at Leyden; 1588 to England; propagandist on behalf of episcopacy; 1595 prebendary of Gloucester; 1601 prebendary of Westminster (with Lancelot Andrewes as dean); client of the Cecils.

RICHARD CLARKE

?–1634; fellow of Christ's College, Cambridge; vicar of Minster and Monkton in Thanet.

JOHN LAYFIELD

?–1617; fellow of Trinity College, Cambridge; 1598 chaplain to Earl of Cumberland on Puerto Rico voyage; 1601 rector of St Clement Dane's, London.

ROBERT TIGHE

?–1620 born Deeping, Lincolnshire; Archdeacon of Middlesex; parson of All Hallows, Barking; left his son an estate worth £1,000 a year.

GEOFFREY KING

?Fellow of King's College, Cambridge; Regius Professor of Hebrew; friend of Hugh Broughton; severe anti-Catholic.

RICHARD THOMSON

?–1613 born in Holland of English parents; 'a debosh'd drunken English Dutcheman'; translator of Martial's epigrams; Andrewes when Bishop of Ely presented him to Snailwell Rectory, Cambridgeshire.

WILLIAM BEDWELL

1561–1632 Arabic scholar and mathematician; Rector of St Ethelburgh's, Bishopsgate; Lancelot Andrewes, as Bishop of Ely, made him vicar of Tottenham High Cross.

FRANCIS BURLEIGH

?–1590; Andrewes appointed him vicar of Bishop's Stortford.

The First Cambridge Company

I Chronicles, II Chronicles, Ezra, Nehemiah, Esther, Job, Psalms, Proverbs, Ecclesiastes, Song of Songs

EDWARD LIVELY (Director)

?1545–1605; Trinity College, Cambridge; 1575 Regius Professor of Hebrew; 1597 author of 'A true Chronologie of the Persian Monarchie'; 1602 prebendary at Peterborough thanks to Whitgift; 1604 rector of Purleigh, Essex, thanks to Richard Bancroft; becomes client of William Barlow; too many children; died young.

JOHN RICHARDSON

?–1625 born Linton, Cambridgeshire; Clare Hall Cambridge; 1585 fellow of Emmanuel College, Cambridge, under Laurence Chaderton; 1607 Regius Professor of Divinity; 1609 Master of Peterhouse; Master of Trinity College, Cambridge; increasingly ceremonialist and fat.

LAURENCE CHADERTON

1537–1640 born Lancashire; disinherited on becoming Protestant at Cambridge; inspirational figure; 1568 fellow of Christ's College, Cambridge; part of radical Puritan movement in 1580s; 1584–1622 first Master of Emmanuel College.

ROGER ANDREWES

Londoner; brother and client of Lancelot Andrewes; fellow of Pembroke Hall, Cambridge; 1606–07 prebendary, archdeacon and chancellor at Chichester; prebendary at Ely; 1618 Master of Jesus College, Cambridge. Widely loathed.

THOMAS HARRISON

1555–1631 born London; Merchant Taylors' school (with Lancelot Andrewes); part of radical Puritan movement with Chaderton in 1580s; Vice-Master of Trinity College, Cambridge.

ROBERT SPAULDING
Fellow of St John's College, Cambridge; 1605 Regius Professor of
Hebrew (after Lively's death).

ANDREW BING
1574–1652; fellow of Peterhouse; 1608 Regius Professor of Hebrew
(after Spaulding).

FRANCIS DILLINGHAM
Born Dean, Bedfordshire; fellow of Christ's College, Cambridge;
Puritan admirer of Chaderton's; parson of Dean and of Wilden,
Bedfordshire.

The First Oxford Company
Isaiah, Jeremiah, Lamentations, Ezekiel, Daniel, Hosea, Joel, Amos,
Obadiah, Jonah, Micah, Nahum, Habakkuk, Zephaniah, Haggai,
Malachi

JOHN HARDING (Director)
1591 Regius Professor of Hebrew; President Magdalen College,
Oxford; Rector of Halsey, Oxfordshire.

JOHN REYNOLDS or RAINOLDS
1549–1607 born Devon; 1566 fellow and (1598) president of Corpus
Christi; 1592 criticised by Elizabeth: 'she schooled Dr John Rainolds
for his obstinate preciseness, willing him to follow her laws and not
run before them'; 1593 Dean of Lincoln; anti-theatre; anti-bishop;
'a prodigy in reading, a living library and a walking museum'.

THOMAS HOLLAND
1539–1612 born Ludlow, Shropshire; Balliol College, Oxford; 1585
chaplain to Earl of Leicester in Netherlands; 1589 Regius Professor
of Divinity; 1592 rector of Exeter College; fierce Puritan; ended
sermons with words 'I commend you to the love of God and to
the hatred of all popery and superstition'; friend of Richard Kilby
and of Reynolds; enemy of Laud's whom he rebuked in 1604 for
contending that 'there could be no true churches without diocesan
episcopacy'.

RICHARD KILBY
1560–1620 born Radcliffe, Leicestershire; Lincoln College, Oxford;
1590 rector of Lincoln College with Richard Brett as fellow; 1610
Regius Professor of Divinity; a severe and frowning man; presided

over chaotic period in Lincoln's history when number of fellows reduced to three.

MILES SMITH

1554–1624 born Hereford; Corpus Christi and Brasenose; on revision committee, author of the Preface; strict Calvinist, hated Laud; author of 'Certain plaine, brief, and comfortable notes on Genesis'; 1612 Bishop of Gloucester; 'covetous of nothing but books'; kept no books in his library he had not read.

RICHARD BRETT

1567–1637 born into Somerset gentry family; Hart Hall, Oxford; 1595 vicar of Quainton; fellow of Lincoln under Richard Kilby; scholar in Latin, Greek, Chaldee, Arabic, Hebrew and Aethiopic tongues.

RICHARD FAIRCLOUGH (or FEATLEY)

1578–1645 born Charlton, Oxfordshire; 1602 fellow of Corpus Christi, Oxford; chaplain to George Abbot and his client; vicar of Lambeth, All Hallows, Bread Street, and of Acton; 1642 almost martyred by parliamentarians; a small man.

The Second Cambridge Company
The Apocrypha

JOHN DUPORT (Director)

?–1617; 1583 rector of Fulham; 1585 precentor of St Paul's; 1590 Master of Jesus College; 1609 prebendary of Ely (thanks to Andrewes).

JOHN BOYS or BOIS

1561–1644 born Suffolk; St John's College, Cambridge; 1584 Greek lecturer at Cambridge; assisted Savile with edition of Chrysostom; 1615 prebendary of Ely (thanks to Andrewes); rector of Boxworth.

WILLIAM BRANTHWAITE

?–1620; 1582 Clare Hall, Cambridge; 1584 founding fellow of Emmanuel College under Chaderton; 1607 Master of Gonville and Caius (the safe government candidate, put in to replace a man suspected of Catholicism).

ANDREW DOWNES
?1549–1628; St John's College; 1585 Regius Professor of Greek; irascible, lazy and jealous of John Bois, his ex-pupil who outshone him; helped Savile with his edition of Chrysostom at Eton.

JEREMIAH RADCLIFFE
?–1612; fellow of Trinity College, Cambridge; 1588 vicar of Evesham; 1590 rector of Orwell; 1597 Vice-Master of Trinity College.

ROBERT WARD
Fellow of King's College; prebendary of Chichester Cathedral, thanks to Andrewes.

SAMUEL WARD
?–1643 born Durham; Puritan diarist; Christ's College, Cambridge; 1595 fellow of Emmanuel under Chaderton; 1610 Master of Sidney Sussex College, Cambridge; 1611 king's chaplain; 1615 Archdeacon of Taunton; 1615 prebendary of Wells (thanks to James Mountague); 1618 prebendary of York: 1623 Lady Margaret Professor of Divinity at Cambridge.

The Second Oxford Company
The Gospels, Acts of the Apostles, Revelation

THOMAS RAVIS (Director)
1560–1609 born Surrey; Westminster School; 1582 Christ Church, Oxford; 1591 rector of All Hallows, Barking; 1592 canon of Westminster; 1596 Dean of Christ Church; 1605 Bishop of Gloucester; 1607 Bishop of London; pursues Nonconformists with a vengeance.

GEORGE ABBOT
1562–1633 born Guildford; a severe and grave figure, stiffly principled, habitually gloomy; 1582 Balliol College, Oxford; 1592 private chaplain to Thomas Sackville, later Earl of Dorset; 1597 Master of University College, Oxford; 1600 Dean of Winchester (a post he bought for £600); 1608 helped re-establish bishops in Scotland; 1609 Bishop of Coventry and Lichfield; 1610 Bishop of London; 1612 Archbishop of Canterbury; 1619 shot and killed a gamekeeper by mistake.

RICHARD EEDES

1555–1604; Westminster School; Christ Church College, Oxford; 1584 prebendary at Salisbury; 1590 prebendary at Hereford; queen's chaplain; 1596 Dean of Worcester; as a young man a poet composing plays, mostly tragedies; 'held in great admiration at court, not only for his preaching, but his most excellent and polite discourse'. Died before he could contribute to the translation.

GILES TOMSON

1553–1612 born London; University College, Oxford; fellow of All Souls; queen's chaplain; rector of Pembridge, Herefordshire; 1602 Dean of Windsor; 1611 Bishop of Gloucester; praised by Lord Burghley for his habit of 'cutting short his compliments and proving himself brief, learned and discreet'.

SIR HENRY SAVILE

1549–1622 born Bradley, Yorkshire; Brasenose College, Oxford; 1565 fellow of Merton; tutor in Greek to Queen Elizabeth; 1585 Warden of Merton; 1596 Provost of Eton – 'Thus this skilful gardener had, at the same time, a nursery of young plants, and an orchard of grown trees, both flourishing under his careful inspection'; 1604 knighted; publisher of Chrysostom edition 1610–13; founded Savile professorships of geometry and astronomy at Oxford; 'a magazine of learning', tall and handsome, neglected his wife for his books.

JOHN PERYN or PERNE

?–1615; 1575 fellow of St John's College, Oxford; Regius Professor of Greek; 1605 resigned post to work on King James Bible; vicar of Wafting in Sussex (thanks to Andrewes when Bishop of Chichester).

RALPH RAVENS

?–1615; vicar of Easton Magna in Essex.

JOHN HARMAR

?–1613 born Newbury, Berkshire; Winchester College; 1574 fellow of New College; 1585 Regius Professor of Greek; 1596 warden of Winchester College; client of the Earl of Leicester, travelling with him to Paris where he debated with the doctors of the Sorbonne; translated Theodore Beza's French sermons into English; strict Calvinist.

LEONARD HUTTEN

?1557–1632 Westminster School; Christ Church College, Oxford
(both school and university with Ravis, this company's director, and
Eedes, whom he probably replaced); 1601 vicar of Floore; 1609 prebendary of St Paul's (thanks to Ravis, now Bishop of London).

JOHN AGLIONBY

1566–1609 born Cumberland; Queen's College, Oxford; perhaps
appointed to translation instead of Eedes; royal chaplain; principal
of St Edmund Hall, Oxford.

JAMES MOUNTAGUE or MONTAGU

?1568–1618; Christ's College, Cambridge; 1595 first Master of Puri-
tan Sidney Sussex College, Cambridge; 1603 Dean of Lichfield; 1604
Dean of Worcester; 1608 Bishop of Bath and Wells; 1616 Bishop of
Winchester; 1616 edited and translated works of James I.

The Second Westminster Company
The New Testament Epistles

WILLIAM BARLOW (Director)

?–1613 born Barlow, Lancashire; Trinity Hall, Cambridge; client of
Whitgift; 1603 prebendary of Westminster (with Lancelot Andrewes
as Dean) and Dean of Chester; 1605 Bishop of Rochester; 1608
Bishop of Lincoln; court propagandist and operator.

JOHN SPENCER

1559–1614, born Suffolk; Corpus Christi College, Oxford (with
John Reynolds); great friend and amanuensis of Richard Hooker;
1589 vicar of Alveley, Essex; 1592 vicar of Broxborn; 1599 vicar of
St Sepulchre's, beyond Newgate, London; 1607 president of Corpus
Christi College after Reynolds's death; 1612 prebendary in St Paul's.

ROGER FENTON

1567–1617 born Lancashire; fellow of Pembroke Hall, Cambridge
and client of Lancelot Andrewes; 1606 vicar of Chigwell, Essex; 1609
prebendary at St Paul's in succession and thanks to Andrewes; vicar
of St Stephen's Walbrook; a weak and sickly man.

RALPH HUTCHINSON
?1553–1606; Merchant Taylors' school (with Lancelot Andrewes); 1590 president of St John's College, Oxford.

WILLIAM DAKINS
1567–1606; Westminster School; Trinity College, Cambridge; 1603 Vicar of Trumpington; 1604 professor of Divinity at Gresham College, London, as payment for his work on the translation, and thanks to Cecil.

MICHAEL RABBET
Rector of St Vedast, Foster Lane, London.

THOMAS SANDERSON
Perhaps a student at Balliol College, Oxford; 1606 perhaps Archdeacon of Rochester.

CHRONOLOGY

England 1603–1611

1603

March 24: Queen Elizabeth dies

James accedes to throne of England and begins to promote union of England and Scotland

Catholic Bye and Main Plots to turn England Catholic effectively neutralised by Cecil

Lord Chamberlain's Men become King's Men

Outbreak of plague in England

1604

March: James's first parliament

August: Spanish envoys sign peace with England in Somerset House. The peace is sworn on a copy of the Vulgate, St Jerome's Latin Bible

James writes *Counterblast against Tobacco*

Othello, Merry Wives of Windsor and *Measure for Measure*

The King James Bible and its Translators

1603

April: Millenary petition presented to James requesting reform of church

William Barlow becomes prebendary at Westminster

1604

Hampton Court Conference on future of church

King and Bancroft draw up Rules for Translators

Translators appointed

Bancroft issues new canons for the church and becomes Archbishop of Canterbury

Work begins on the initial phases of translation

Henry Savile knighted (for £1,000 fee)

James Mountague becomes Dean of Worcester

William Dakins becomes Professor of Divinity at Gresham College, London

John Overall's wife elopes

1605

Masque of Blackness by Inigo Jones
and Ben Jonson
November: Gunpowder Plot
Merchant of Venice, *King Lear*,
Volpone, *Westward Ho!*
Francis Bacon's *Advancement of
Learning*

1605

Edward Lively dies
Lancelot Andrewes becomes Bishop
of Chichester
Andrewes, Barlow and Ravis preach
against Gunpowder Plot
Thomas Ravis becomes Bishop of
Gloucester
William Barlow becomes Bishop of
Rochester

1606

Gunpowder Plotters mutilated and
executed at St Paul's
Jesuit Henry Garnet hanged, drawn
and quartered
Parliament reassembles; anti-papist
legislation; £435,000 voted to the
king
Death of Princess Sophia; William
Barlow buries her
Christian IV of Denmark and
retinue make hay in London

1606

Ralph Hutchinson dies

1607

120 colonists leave for Virginia
James swops Theobalds with Robert
Cecil for Hatfield
Separatists in Lincolnshire come
under pressure
Robert Carr catches the king's eye
Thames freezes over

1607

William Dakins dies
John Reynolds dies; John Spenser
becomes President of Corpus
Christi
William Barlow becomes Bishop of
Lincoln
Thomas Ravis becomes Bishop of
London

1608

Brewster and Scrooby Separatists
flee to Amsterdam
Robert Cecil becomes Lord
Treasurer

1608

Lancelot Andrewes involved in controversy with Cardinal Bellarmine
James Mountague becomes Bishop
of Bath and Wells
Samuel Ward becomes his chaplain
The king demands that the new
translation is completed 'as soone
as may be'

1609

James brokers truce between Spain and the United Provinces as part of his programme for universal peace

Robert Cecil sets up Britain's Burse on the Strand

1609

Andrewes becomes Bishop of Ely and Privy Councillor

George Abbot becomes Bishop of Lichfield and Coventry

Thomas Ravis dies

Roger Fenton becomes prebendary at St Paul's in succession and thanks to Andrewes

Andrew Downes paid £50 by the king to persuade him to attend the Revision Committee

1610

Henry IV of France stabbed to death; James turns white at the news

February: Parliament reassembles. Parliament makes grant of £200,000 to king but Cecil's attempt to set royal finances on reliable basis (the Great Contract) breaks down

Shakespeare *Sonnets* published

The Tempest played at Whitehall

Royal debts mount

1610

Revision Committee meets in Stationers' Hall in London

Samuel Ward becomes Master of Sidney Sussex

George Abbot becomes Bishop of London

Henry Savile begins publication of Chrysostom edition

Richard Bancroft establishes open access library at Lambeth

1611

Chapman's translation of Homer published

Raleigh in the Tower writes the *History of the World*

William Bedwell gives communion to Henry Hudson before he embarks on exploratory voyage to Cathay via North-West Passage

1611

King James Bible published

Giles Tomson becomes Bishop of Gloucester

SELECT BIBLIOGRAPHY

Abbot, George, *Sermons* (London, 1600)

——, *A briefe Description of the whole worlde* (London, 1605)

Acheson, R. J., *Radical Puritans in England 1550–1660*, (London, 1990)

Akrigg, G. P. V., *Jacobean Pageant* (London, 1962)

——, (ed.), *Letters of King James VI and I* (London, 1983)

Allen, Ward S., *Translating for King James: Notes Made by a Translator of King James's Bible* (London, 1970)

——, *Translating the New Testament Epistles 1604–1611* (Ann Arbor, 1977)

Allen, Ward S. and Jacobs, Edward, *The Coming of the King James Gospels – A Collation of the Translators' Work-in-Progress* (Arkansas, 1995)

Alter, Robert and Kermode, Frank (eds) *The Literary Guide to the Bible* (London, 1987)

Andrewes, Lancelot, *XCVI Sermons* (London, 1629)

——, *Preces Privatae* (London, 1648)

Anon, *A collection of Certaine Sclaunderous Articles Gyven out by the Bisshops* (Dort, 1590)

Ashley, Maurice, *England in the Seventeenth Century* (Harmondsworth, 1961)

Ashton, Robert (ed.), *James I by his Contemporaries* (London, 1969)

Aubrey, John, *Brief Lives* (London, 2000)

Babbage, S. B., *Puritanism and Richard Bancroft* (London, 1962)

Barlow, William *The Sermon preached at Paules Crosse, the tenth day of November, being the next Sunday after the Discouerie of this late Horrible Treason* (1606)

——, *The Summe and Substance of the Hampton Court Conference* (London, 1604)

Beard, Thomas, *The Theatre of God's Iudgments* (London, 1597)

Bedwell, William, *Mohammedis Imposturae* (London, 1615)

——, *Mesolabium Architectonicum* (London, 1631)

Bendall, S. A., Brooke, Christopher and Collinson, Patrick, *A History of Emmanuel College Cambridge* (Woodbridge, 1999)

Benjamin, Walter, *Illuminations*, trans. by Harry Zorn (London, 1970)

Birch, Thomas, *The Court and Times of James the First* (London, 1849)

Bobrick, Benson, *The Making of the English Bible* (London, 2001)

Bownde, Nicholas, *The Doctrine of the Sabbath* (London, 1595)

——, *Medicines for the Plagve* (London, 1604)

Brooke, C. N. L., *A History of Gonville & Caius College, Cambridge* (Woodbridge, 1985)

Bruce, John (ed.) *Correspondence of King James VI of Scotland with Sir Robert Cecil and others in England . . .* (London, 1861)

Burke, Peter, *Popular Culture in Early Modern Europe* (Aldershot, 1994)

Cameron, Euan, *The European Reformation* (Oxford, 1991)

Campbell, Mildred, *The English Yeoman under Elizabeth and the Early Stuarts* (New Haven, CT, 1942)

Campbell, O. J., and Quinn E. G., *A Shakespeare Encyclopaedia* (London, 1966)

Carey, John, *John Donne: Life, Mind and Art* (London, 1981)

Carson, D. A., *The King James Version Debate: A Plea for Realism* (Grand Rapids, OH, 1979)

Cecil, Lord David, *Hatfield House* (Hatfield, 1973)

Clapham, Henoch, *Epistle Discoursing upon the Present Pestilence* (London, 1603)

Collinson, Patrick, *The Religion of Protestants: The Church in English Society, 1559–1625* (Oxford, 1982)

——, *Godly People: Essays in English Protestantism and Puritanism* (London, 1984)

——, *The Birthpangs of Protestant England: Religious and Cultural Change in the Sixteenth and Seventeenth Centuries* (London, 1988)

Cranmer, Thomas, *Book of Common Prayer* (London, 1552)

Croft, Pauline (ed.), *Patronage, Culture and Power: The Early Cecils 1558–1612* (New Haven, CT, 2002)

Curtis, M. H., *Oxford and Cambridge in Transition 1558–1642* (Oxford, 1959)

Daiches, David, *The King James Version of the English Bible: An Account of the Development and Sources of the English Bible of 1611 with Special Reference to the Hebrew Tradition* (Chicago, 1941)

Daniell, David, *William Tyndale: A Biography* (New Haven, CT, 1994)

de Hamel, Christopher, *The Book: A History of the Bible* (London, 2001)

Duffy, Eamon, *The Stripping of the Altars: Traditional Religion in England c 1400–1500* (New Haven, CT, 1992)

Fincham, K., *Prelate as Pastor: The Episcopate of James I* (Oxford, 1990)

—— (ed.), *The Early Stuart Church, 1603–1642* (London, 1993)

Fletcher, A., and Roberts, P. (eds), *Religion, Culture and Society in Early Modern Britain* (Cambridge, 1994)

Foxe, John, *Acts and Monuments of the English Church* (London, 1563)

Fraser, Antonia, *The Gunpowder Plot–Terror and Faith in 1605* (London, 1996)

Fuller, Thomas, *The Church History of Britain*, (London, 1868)

Gardiner, S. R., *History of England from the Accession of James I to the Outbreak of the Civil War, 1603–1642* (London, 1883–84)

Goodare, Julian and Lynch, Michael (eds), *The Reign of James VI* (Phantassie, 2000)

Greenslade, S. L. (ed.), *The Cambridge History of the Bible – the West from the Reformation to the Present Day* (Cambridge, 1966)

Griffiths, Paul and Jenner, Mark S. R. (eds), *Londinopolis: Essays in the Cultural and Social History of Early Modern London* (Manchester, 2000)

Halliwell, J. O. (ed.), *College Life in the Time of James the First, The Autobiography and Correspondence of Sir Symonds d'Ewes*, Bart. (London, 1845)

Haynes, Alan, *Robert Cecil, 1st Earl of Salisbury, 1563–1612: Servant of Two Sovereigns* (London, 1989)

Highfield, J. R. L, 'An Autograph Manuscript Commonplace Book of Sir Henry Savile', *Bodleian Library Record*, Vol. vii, no. 2, 78–83 (July 1963)

Hill, Christopher, *The Century of Revolution 1603–1714* (London, 1961)

——, *Society and Puritanism in Pre-Revolutionary England* (London, 1964)

——, *The English Bible and the 17th Century Revolution* (Harmondsworth, 1993)

Hill, C. P., *Who's Who in Stuart Britain* (London, 1988)

Hirst, Derek, *Authority and Conflict: England 1603–1658* (London, 1986)

Jonson, Ben, *Masque of Blacknesse* (London, 1605)

Kamen, Henry, *The Rise of Toleration* (London, 1963)

Kee, H. C. et al. (eds) *The Cambridge Companion to the Bible* (Cambridge, 1997)

Kenyon, J. P., *The Stuart Constitution 1603–1688, Documents and Commentary* (Cambridge, 1986)

Kirk-Smith, H., *William Brewster: The Father of New England: His Life and Times 1567–1644* (Boston, 1992)

Knappen, M. M. (ed.), *Two Elizabethan Puritan Diaries* (Richard Rogers and Samuel Ward) (Chicago, 1933)

Layfield, John, 'The Voyage to Puerto Ricco', in *Hakluytus Posthumus or Purchas His Pilgrimes*, Vol. xvi (Glasgow, 1906)

Lake, Peter, *Anglicans and Puritans? Presbyterianism and English Conformist Thought from Whitgift to Hooker* (London, 1988)

Larkin, James F. and Hughes, Paul L., *Stuart Royal Proclamations* (Oxford, 1973)

Laslett, Peter, *The World We Have Lost Further Explored* (London, 1983)

Lockyer, Roger, *James VI and I* (London, 1998)

Lossky, Nicholas, *Lancelot Andrews the Preacher (1555–1626): The Origins of the Mystical Theology of the Church of England* (Oxford, 1991)

McClure, Alexander, *The Translators Revived: A Biographical Memoir of the Authors of the English Version of the Holy Bible* (Mobile, 1858)

McEachern, C. and Shuger, D., *Religion and Culture in Renaissance England* (Cambridge, 1997)

McGrath, Alister, *In the Beginning: The Story of the King James Bible and How It Changed a Nation, a Language and a Culture* (New York, 2001)

Martin, G. H. and Highfield, J. R. L., *A History of Merton College* (Oxford, 1997)

Morrill, J. S. (ed.), *The Oxford Illustrated History of Tudor and Stuart Britain* (Oxford, 1997)

Moynhahan, Brian, *If God Spare My Life* (London, 2002)

Muir, Kenneth (ed.), *King Lear* (London, 1952)

Nichols, John, *Progresses etc . . . of King James the First* (London, 1828)

Norton, David, 'John Bois's Notes on the Revision of the King James Bible New Testament: A New Manuscript', *The Library*, 6th series, Vol. 18, no. 4 (December 1996)

Opfell, Olga S. *The King James Bible Translators* (Jefferson, 1982)

Ormsby, G. (ed.), *Corespondence of John Cosin* (London, 1869–70)

Parker, Richard, *A Scholasticall Discourse against Symbolizing with AntiChrist in Ceremonies: especially in the Signe of the Crosse* (London, 1607)

Partridge, A. C., *English Biblical Translation* (London, 1973)

Peck, Linda L. (ed.), *The Mental World of the Jacobean Court* (Cambridge, 1991)

Pollard, A. W. (ed.), *Records of the English Bible* (Oxford, 1911)

Pullein, Thomas, *Ieremiah's Teares* (London, 1608)

Quintrell, B. W., 'The Royal Hunt and the Puritans 1604–5', *Journal of Ecclesiastical History*, Vol. 31, no. 1 (January 1980)

Raines, F. R. (ed.), *Journal of Nicholas Assheton* (1848)

Raven, C. E., *English Naturalists from Neckham to Ray* (Cambridge, 1947)

Robinson, Douglas, *Western Translation Theory from Herodotus to Nietzsche*, 2nd edn (Manchester, 2002)

Rogerson, John (ed.), *The Oxford Illustrated History of the Bible* (Oxford, 2001)

Rowse, A. L., *Court and Country* (Oxford, 1964)

Schochet, Gordon J., *Patriarchalism in Political Thought: The Authoritarian Family and Political Speculation and Attitudes especially in Seventeenth-Century England* (Oxford, 1975)

Scrivener, F. H. A., *The Authorised Edition of the English Bible, 1611, its Subsequent Reprints and Modern Representatives* (Cambridge, 1884)

Sharpe, Kevin, *Remapping Early Modern England: The Culture of Seventeenth-Century Politics* (Cambridge, 2000)

Sharpe, K. and Lake, P. (eds), *Culture and Politics in Early Stuart England* (London, 1994)

Shriver, F., 'Hampton Court Re-visited: James I and the Puritans', *Journal of Eccclesiastical History*, Vol. 33 (1982)

Slack, Paul, *The Impact of Plague in Tudor and Stuart England* (London, 1985)

Somerville, J. P., *King James VI and I: Political Writings* (Cambridge, 1994)

Starkey, David, *The English Court from the Wars of the Roses to the Civil War* (London, 1987)

Steiner, George, *After Babel: Aspects of Language and Translation*, 3rd edn (Oxford, 1998)

Stephen, Leslie and Lee, Sidney, *The Dictionary of National Biography* (Oxford, 1917–1922)

Stone, Lawrence, *The Family, Sex and Marriage in England 1500–1800* (London, 1977)

Stow, John, *A Survey of London* (London, 1598)

Strang, Barbara, *A History of English* (London, 1970)

Strong, Roy, *Henry Prince of Wales and England's Lost Renaissance* (London, 1986)

Summerson, John, *Architecture in Britain 1530–1830*, 9th edn (London, 1993)

Thomas, Keith, *Man and the Natural World, Changing Attitudes in England 1500–1800* (London, 1983)

——, *Religion and the Decline of Magic* (Harmondsworth, 1985)

Thomson, Elizabeth (ed.), *The Chamberlain Letters* (New York, 1965)

Tomlinson, H. (ed.), *Before the English Civil War: Essays on Early Stuart Politics and Government* (London, 1983)

Trevor-Roper, Hugh, *Laud* (Cambridge, 1954)

Tyacke, Nicholas, *Anti-Calvinists: The Rise of English Arminianism c. 1590–1640* (Oxford, 1987)

——, *Aspects of English Protestantism 1530–1700* (Manchester, 2001)

—— (ed.), *England's Long Reformation, 1500–1800* (London, 1997)

Underdown, David, *Fire from Heaven: Life in an English Town in the Seventeenth Century* (London, 1992)

Wabuda, Susan and Litzenberger, Caroline (eds), *Belief and Practice in Reformation England: A Tribute to Patrick Collinson from His Students* (Aldershot, 1998)

Welsby, Paul A., *Lancelot Andrewes 1555–1626* (London, 1958)

Wilson, Thomas, *The arte of rhetorique* (London, 1553)

Womersley, D., 'Sir Henry Savile's Translation of Tacitus', *Review of English Studies*, Vol. xlii, no. 167 (August 1991)

Wootton, David (ed.), *Divine Right and Democracy: An Anthology of Political Writing in Stuart England* (Harmondsworth, 1986)

Wrightson, Keith, *English Society, 1580–1680* (London, 1982)

Youings, Joyce, *Sixteenth-Century England* (Harmondsworth, 1984)

INDEX

Note: The King James Bible has, in places, been abbreviated to KJB.

P.S.

Ideas,
interviews
& features...

Portrait

Adam Nicolson talks to Sam Leith

'YOU KNOW HOW you fantasize about living at different times?' says Adam Nicolson. 'I would choose the first decade of the seventeenth century – as just so alive and so full, so full of the multiple. As I wrote the book I completely fell in love with the time. My book is not about God, or in fact the Book. It's about the moment, and why the moment made this.'

I was Adam's editor on his *Daily Telegraph* column for a little under a year, though we never met. In our meandering Monday morning phone calls to discuss ideas, I became accustomed to a roomy, lateral, civilized mind, in which there'd be floating a gumbo of tenuously related concepts or items in the news that had caught Adam's attention. By deadline, the gumbo would invariably have boiled down to something interesting. His attraction to diversity and negotiation – to the colour and contradictions of the Jacobean court – are entirely in keeping.

The man who meets me at Stonegate station resembles, unusually, his photo-byline. He's tall, humorous, hesitant, shaggy of demeanour, muddy of trouser and shoe. He has spent the morning fixing a puncture on his wife's car, and is resigned rather than splenetic when, as we turn into his driveway, we pass that very vehicle, abandoned, with a flat on a different tyre entirely. They're clipping the hedgerows and sharp bits, apparently, will tend to fall out. 'They cut them with those strimmer things,' he says.

'It's a symptom of the wrongness of the modern world.'

Adam's home is a Sussex farmhouse, Perch Hill, where his wife, Sarah Raven, runs a gardening business. There's a sense of well-ordered bohemianism. On the wall of their large, bright kitchen hangs a framed poster of the Sylvia Plath poem 'Mushrooms' – a gift to Sarah in tribute to her 'obsession' with edible fungi, and framed with dates significant to them as a couple. At one end of the room a row of pumpkin lanterns testifies to a recent Halloween. At the other, around the phone, dozens of names and numbers are scribbled directly onto the wall in biro. His daughters drift in and out worrying about homework and making toasted sandwiches, and a lunchtime ragu of pork and rosemary simmers on the hob. A ginger cat and a pair of well-fed labradors make themselves known.

Adam has both writing and bohemianism in his family. His grandparents were 'Harold Nicolson: diplomat, novelist, cultural biographer, politician, blah blah – gay', and 'Vita Sackville-West: poet, biographer, novelist and gardener – gay'. He says he overheard his prospective mother-in-law warning Sarah, when they got engaged: 'Are you absolutely sure, darling? You do realize his entire family consists of drunks and homosexuals?' Actually, publishers and writers seem to have the numerical advantage, by a whisker, and Adam says ▶

3

◀ 'I always knew I wanted to be a writer'.

By the kitchen door are two photographs, identically posed at the corner of the same garden bench. One shows, in ascending order of age, Adam's son, a young, floppy-haired Adam, and, nearest to the camera, his father Nigel. Above it is another, looking to be two decades or so older: Adam aged maybe six, then a young Nigel, then Adam's grandfather, Harold Nicolson. It was taken, he startles me by saying, on the day his grandmother died.

French windows lead to a gravelled herb garden with a beautiful view over the Sussex countryside, and down to the sties where he keeps his two pigs. He and Sarah used to run Perch Hill as a farm themselves, but contracted out the day-to-day running when they tired of it. Adam has the envious gift of being able to live his life as if he were on holiday – of following whims and idiosyncrasies and, by writing about them, turning them into a living.

That fed his approach to his book. 'I did this book the only way I could have done it, because I couldn't adopt a sort of Olympian, all-knowing air. It's like a travel book, I think sometimes. It's like me turning up in seventeenth-century England going, "Crikey, they're weird, aren't they?" I think that's what it's like. The word "I" only appears once, but it is actually written as if there's an "I" in there: as if this moment is writing about that moment.' To handle the autograph manuscripts of the documents that gave rise to the book, he says, was the

About the author

high point of his eighteen months of scholarship: 'that is very deeply exciting'.

Since then, he has changed tack for the present. 'It was so grievous an experience sitting at my desk reading other people's books about seventeenth-century England for a year and a half, that I decided to get a boat and sail round the west coast of the British Isles. So that's what I've been doing this year.' Adam is one of few people who can boast of having inherited an archipelago on his twenty-first birthday ('three small islands in the Hebrides ... there's a tiny house a quarter the size of this room on one of them, but incredible birds, and half a million puffins'). He stopped in for ten days there in the summer, eating only what he could catch. 'Sixteen lobsters in forty-eight hours,' he says. 'I'm never going to eat lobster again.' ∎

Life
Drawing

What is your idea of perfect happiness?
New bread, unsalty butter, spring morning,
Pyrenean beechwood, swimming in a
stream, sunshine, snow on the mountains,
Sarah, the children, the dogs, completeness,
cider and an afternoon sleep.

What is your greatest fear?
Drowning.

Which living person do you most admire?
Mandela.

What objects do you always carry with you?
None.

*What single thing would improve the quality
of your life?*
The guaranteed happiness of my children.

*What is the most important lesson life has
taught you?*
The balance of love and will.

*Which writer has had the greatest influence
on your work?*
Auden.

Do you have a favourite book?
The Odyssey.

Where do you go for inspiration?
Cambridge University Library and
abebooks.com.

Which book do you wish you had written?
Ulverton by Adam Thorpe.

What are you writing at the moment?
A book about Trafalgar and heroism.

Top Ten
Favourite Reads

1. **The Odyssey**
   Homer

2. **King Lear**
   William Shakespeare

3. **The King James Bible**

4. **The English Auden:
   Poems 1927–1939**
   W. H. Auden

5. **The Desert Fathers**
   Helen Waddell

6. **Anna Karenina**
   Leo Tolstoy

7. **The Woodlanders**
   Thomas Hardy

8. **The People of the Sea**
   David Thomson

9. **Nigger of the Narcissus**
   Joseph Conrad

10. **Poems**
    Anna Akhmatova

A Critical Eye

ADAM NICOLSON'S WRITING has received consistent acclaim on both sides of the Atlantic. *When God Spoke English* is no exception. The *New Yorker* wrote 'It is a popular book as popular books used to be, a breeze rather than a scholarly sweat, but humanely erudite, elegantly written, passionately felt … Nicolson's excitement is contagious', while *Newsweek* said 'Nicolson shows us in captivating detail how the diverse translators of the King James Bible captured compelling debates that remain relevant to this day.' The *Independent* picked up on the relevance to the politics and culture of the contemporary world, saying '*When God Spoke English* … pays that Bible eloquent tribute, not least in its passionate homage to the power of language as, and in, history. His own words give us not only the rich history but a moving commemoration of the Bible that has so much shaped our utterances and lives.' In *The Spectator*, Philip Hensher wrote 'Adam Nicolson's book is unobtrusively learned, rich in curious and purposeful detail, an ideal balance between fervent enthusiasm and elegantly witty detachment. The story of the translation's origins and production is a subject which, one always felt, would be nice to hear from a really sparkling and sharp guide. This volume strikes me as exactly that, a brilliantly entertaining, passionate, funny and instructive telling of an important and gripping story.' ■

Literature by
Committee

A CAMEL, AS the old commonplace has it, is a horse designed by a committee. New Labour, as the new commonplace has it, is a government designed by a focus group. Committees, these days, get a bad press.

Yet the theme that runs most insistently and most startlingly through Adam Nicolson's account of the making of the King James Bible runs exactly counter to that received wisdom. He shows us something of luminous and enduring literary quality being produced collaboratively – and, what is more, produced expressly under the auspices of political authority. There is evidence to show that, far from simply setting the project off, the King took a close interest throughout the process.

Why is this so strange? As Nicolson suggests, the modern reader is accustomed to an image of literary excellence still infused with ideas that took hold in the Romantic period: of the lone genius and of the 'egotistical sublime'. Authority and author-ity, in the post-Romantic age, are seen as inimical. Author-ity, in the sense of authorship, is understood as being essentially subversive: the making of art as an act of individual resistance to Power. Authority – as exercised by kings and governments – works to suppress it. This is the image of the writer as rebel, as outcast, as, in Shelley's phrase, one of the 'unacknowledged legislators of the world'.

Theory and practice in recent years ▶

Literature by Committee *(continued)*

◀ seem to bear out the orthodoxy. State art is bad art – from brutal Fascist architecture, via crude busts of Mesopotamian despots, to those old Soviet images of headscarved working women, toting broomsticks in their beefy forearms as if they were weapons of revolution.

Yet the oral precursors of modern literature are necessarily collaborative – if not directly, then in an evolutionary manner, with set phrases and tropes transmitted and transformed through successive storytellers. We personalized, notoriously, the image of Homer as a blind bearded sage, nodding away to himself. In fact there's little evidence that the *Odyssey* and the *Iliad* are the work of a single, still less the same, hand.

Since the Enlightenment, we've been happy – narratives of lone geniuses wallowing in their baths or being conked on the head by falling apples notwithstanding – with the notion of science (empirical, testable) being a collaborative endeavour. That gave us, at the margins, the composition of things like the great encyclopedias – started in the eighteenth century with the 35-volume *Encyclopédie* supervised by Diderot.

But the Romantics aggressively counterposed art to science. To the post-Romantic mind, the King James Bible's method of composition, if not its outcome, looks much more like science than art. The fact remains: the single work that most influences our literature was the work of colleges of churchmen – some comically starchy, some nakedly political – revising and comparing and combining a number of prior texts under the eyes of the King.

It was, by chance, the contemplation of a huge, collaborative, arguably creative, state-driven project in our own time that first led Adam Nicolson to the making of the King James version. He was writing a book about the making of the Millennium Dome. A colleague mentioned to him that it might be interesting, by point of comparison, to look at a similarly ambitious, yet wildly more successful, parallel four centuries before.

And the great white elephant on the Greenwich peninsula was in some ways a parallel. It, too, was intended as an irenicon of sorts – a literalization of New Labour's 'big tent' cultural politics. It was also intended as a legacy – the 'first line' of Labour's next manifesto, as the Prime Minister rashly promised. The King James translators aimed for a high style that, even in its own age, sounded archaic – an appeal to the authority of the past; the New Millennium Experience Company appealed instead to futurity. It promised to dazzle visitors with hi-tech edutainment – from an encounter with a pubic louse the size of a Volkswagen beetle to the chance to see 'Surfball – the sport of the future'. Perhaps the architects of the Dome should have thought harder about content.

'In the beginning God created the heaven and the earth,' wrote the translators of the King James Bible. 'And the earth was without form, and void; and darkness was upon the face of the deep. And the Spirit ▶

Literature by Committee (continued)

◄ of God moved upon the face of the waters.' The cadences of these words are still lodged deep in the Western mind.

At the time of writing we're still waiting, with ebbing hope, to play Surfball. ∎

Have you read?

Wetland Life in the Somerset Levels
(with Patrick Sutherland)
This book captures the existences of the men and women for whom this part of England forms the background and substance of their lives. As the wetlands come under threat from both the forces of modern farming and the contradictory, complex demands of conservation, this is a lasting poetic record of what may well be a passing way of life.

Restoration: The Rebuilding of Windsor Castle
An account of the restoration of Windsor Castle, which had been devastated by fire, revealing the decisions made – from dealing with the fire, to the finance of restoring, to the decisions on whether to restore or change.

Smell of Summer Grass
Somewhere between an imaginary rural idyll packed with breathtaking scenery and charming rustics, and the hard end of real farming life, Adam Nicolson found Perch Hill, a run-down farm in the Sussex Weald. Driven there by the pressures of metropolitan life, he and his family moved to the failed farm and set about trying to put it to rights. This is the story of three years spent building a personal Arcadia, full of insight into rural life and society.

Sea Room
Have you ever wondered what it would be like to own your own group of islands? ▶

Have you read? *(continued)*

◄ Adam Nicolson inherited the Shiants, off the coast of Lewis, when he was twenty-one. This is the story of his experiences there, the violence and danger of the surrounding seas; the songs and poems that cluster around the islands; the accounts of attempted murder, witchcraft, and catastrophe; and the treasured place the Shiants still hold in the Hebridean mind. ■

If You Loved This,
You'll Like…

The Cradle King: A Life of James VI and I
Alan Stewart

....

Scotland's Last Royal Wedding:
The Marriage of James VI and Anne
of Denmark
David Stevenson

....

Reformation
Diarmaid MacCulloch

....

The Gunpowder Plot:
Terror and Faith in 1605
Antonia Fraser

....

Fire from Heaven: Life in an English Town
in the Seventeenth Century
David Underdown

....

Man and the Natural World:
Changing Attitudes in England 1500–1800
Keith Thomas